Legal Assistant's Letter Book

Sonia von Matt Stoddard

Estrin Publishing

Prentice Hall
Englewood Cliffs, New Jersey 07632

Library of Congress Cataloging-in-Publication Data

Von Matt Stoddard, Sonia.
    The legal assistant's letter book / Sonia von Matt Stoddard.
        p.   cm.
    Includes index.
    ISBN 0-13-533084-X
        1. Legal correspondence—United States.   2. Forms (Law)—United
    States.   3. Legal assistants—United States—Handbooks, manuals,
    etc.   I. Title.
    KF320.L48V66   1996
    808'.06634—dc20   95–3025
                                          CIP

*To my family and especially my husband Scott,
who provided constant encouragement, plenty of feedback,
understanding and tolerance throughout*

Acquisitions editor: Elizabeth Sugg
Editorial/production supervision: Inkwell Publishing Services
Cover design: Marianne Frasco
Buyer: Ilene Sanford

 © 1996 by Prentice-Hall, Inc.
A Simon & Schuster Company
Englewood Cliffs, New Jersey 07632

Printed in the United States of America

10 9 8 7 6 5 4 3 2 1

ISBN 0-13-533084-X

PRENTICE-HALL INTERNATIONAL (UK) UNITED, *London*
PRENTICE-HALL OF AUSTRALIA PTY. LIMITED, *Sydney*
PRENTICE-HALL OF CANADA INC., *Toronto*
PRENTICE-HALL HISPANOAMERICANA, S.A., *Mexico*
PRENTICE-HALL OF INDIA PRIVATE LIMITED, *New Delhi*
SIMON & SCHUSTER ASIA PTE. LTD., *Singapore*
EDITORA PRENTICE-HALL DO BRASIL, LTDA., *Rio de Janeiro*

Contents

Foreword   *ix*
Acknowledgments   *x*
How to Use This Book   *xi*
Introduction   *xiii*

CHAPTER ONE. ELEMENTS OF EFFECTIVE CORRESPONDENCE   1

1.1 / Importance of Good Communication   *1*
1.2 / Goals in Writing Effective Correspondence   *2*
1.3 / Before You Begin Writing   *2*
1.4 / Organizing Your Writing   *3*
1.5 / Stating the Facts   *4*
1.6 / Choosing an Appropriate Tone   *5*
1.7 / Replying to Correspondence   *5*

CHAPTER TWO. THE BASICS OF LANGUAGE AND GRAMMAR   8

2.1 / Business Language vs. Legal Language   *8*
2.2 / Legal Citations   *10*
2.3 / Grammar   *10*
2.4 / Punctuation   *12*
2.5 / Proofreading for Mistakes   *12*
        Table 2.1. Proofreading Marks: Use and Meaning   14

CHAPTER THREE. ETHICS AND THE ROLE OF THE PARALEGAL   15

3.1 / Importance of Maintaining Confidentiality   *15*
3.2 / Curing Conflicts by Using "Ethical Walls"   *16*
        Form 3.1.   Ethical Wall Memorandum   17
3.3 / Always Identify Yourself as a Paralegal   *18*
3.4 / Follow Firm Policies about Signatures   *18*
        Form 3.2.   Ethical Wall Notice   19
3.5 / Signatures by Legal Secretaries   *20*
3.6 / Confidentiality When Sending Facsimiles   *20*
        Form 3.3.   Fax Transmittal Cover Sheet   22

CHAPTER FOUR. LETTER STRUCTURE AND FORMATS   24

4.1 / Purposes of Correspondence   *25*
4.2 / Basic Parts of a Letter   *26*
4.3 / Sender's Address   *26*
4.4 / Date of the Letter   *27*
4.5 / Recipient's Address   *28*
4.6 / Use of the Re: Line   *29*
4.7 / Salutation   *29*
4.8 / Body of the Letter   *30*

4.9 / Closing Phrase   *31*
4.10 / Firm Name in the Signature Block   *31*
4.11 / Signer's Name   *32*
4.12 / Signer's Title   *32*
4.13 / Identifying Initials   *32*
4.14 / Enclosures or Attachments   *33*
4.15 / "Carbon" Copies   *33*
4.16 / Computer File Locator Information   *34*
4.17 / Subsequent Page Identification   *34*
    Form 4.1.   Basic Parts of a Letter   35
4.18 / Types of Letter Formats   *36*
4.19 / Popular Block Format   *36*
4.20 / Modified Block Format   *37*
4.21 / Full Block Format   *37*
    Form 4.2.   The Popular Block Letter   38
    Form 4.3.   The Modified Block Letter   39
    Form 4.4.   The Full Block Letter   40

CHAPTER FIVE. MEMOS AND REPORTS   42

5.1 / How Memos Are Used   *42*
5.2 / Formal and Informal Memos   *43*
5.3 / Effective Presentation of Memo Content   *43*
    Form 5.1.   Basic Interoffice Memo Structure   44
5.4 / Reports to Supervising Attorneys and Managers   *45*
5.5 / Requests for Information, Status Reports, and Cover Memos   *46*
5.6 / Using Memos to Convey Complex Information   *46*
    Form 5.2.   Forms Supply Request Memo   47
    Form 5.3.   Reminder Memo for Case Status Reports   48
    Form 5.4.   Effective Use of Humor in Requesting Information   49
    Form 5.5.   Short Form Assignments Status Report   50
    Form 5.6.   Detailed Assignments Status Report   51
    Form 5.7.   Report of Witness Location Efforts   53
    Form 5.8.   Cover Memo with Accompanying Reports   54
    Form 5.9.   Report Analyzing Possible Document Coding Project   56

CHAPTER SIX. ADMINISTRATIVE LETTERS   58

6.1 / Importance of Administrative Duties   *58*
6.2 / Finding Vendors   *59*
6.3 / Vendor Requests for Proposal (RFP)   *60*
    Form 6.1.   Request for Proposal to Vendor   61
6.4 / Complaint Letters   *62*
    Form 6.2.   Complaint Letter   63
6.5 / Letters Denying Payment   *65*
6.6 / Letters Requesting Payment   *65*
    Form 6.3.   Denial of Payment   66
6.7 / Letters of Appreciation   *67*
6.8 / Letters to Professional Colleagues   *67*
    Form 6.4.   Request for Payment from Opposing Counsel   68
    Form 6.5.   Short Letter of Appreciation to Vendor   69
    Form 6.6.   Letter of Appreciation to Vendor   70
    Form 6.7.   Response to a Survey Request   72
    Form 6.8.   Notice and Invitation to Association Meeting   73

CHAPTER SEVEN. RECRUITING AND EMPLOYMENT   74

7.1 / Overview of Employment-Related Correspondence   *75*
7.2 / Rejection Letters to Prospective Employees   *75*
    Form 7.1.   Long Form Rejection Letter   77

          Form 7.2.   Short Form Rejection Letter for Advertised Position   78
          Form 7.3.   Short Form Response to an Unsolicited Inquiry   79
          Form 7.4.   Letter Returning Materials Provided During Interview   80
          Form 7.5.   Letter Indicating Interest Without Commitment   81
          Form 7.6.   Short Letter Inviting Future Discussion   82

7.3 / Accepting a Candidate for Employment   *83*
7.4 / When You Are in the Job Market   83
       Form 7.7.   Letter Requesting Reference Information   84
          Form 7.8.   Letter Expressing Interest in a Candidate   85
          Form 7.9.   Memo Announcing Hiring of Temporary Employee   86
          Form 7.10. Memo Announcing Arrival of New Employee to All Staff   87

7.5 / Notes of Appreciation and Policy Memos to Staff   88
          Form 7.11. Letter Expressing Interest in Employment   89
          Form 7.12. Thank-You Letter After Interview   90
          Form 7.13. Change of Position/Address Notification   91
          Form 7.14. Memo Setting Forth New Policy   93
          Form 7.15. Memo Extending Congratulations for Good Performance Reviews   94
          Form 7.16. Short Form Letter of Recommendation   95
          Form 7.17. Detailed Letter of Recommendation   96
          Form 7.18. Confirmation of Employment Letter   98

CHAPTER EIGHT. LITIGATION   *99*

8.1 / The Paralegal Role   *101*
8.2 / Accepting a New Client   *101*
8.3 / Rejecting a Client   *103*
8.4 / Preparing for Discovery   *104*
8.5 / Searching for Documents   *105*
8.6 / Lack of Response to Discovery   *106*
8.7 / Confirming Extensions of Time to Respond   *107*
8.8 / Assisting the Client to Respond   *107*
8.9 / Depositions   *108*
8.10 / Working with Witnesses   *108*
8.11 / Preparing for Trial   *109*
8.12 / During the Trial   *110*
8.13 / Settlement   *110*
8.14 / Other Frequently Used Letters   *111*
          Form 8.1.   Acknowledging File and Documents to the Client   112
          Form 8.2.   Acknowledging Documents from Another Law Firm   113
          Form 8.3.   Acknowledging Documents Received for Review   114
          Form 8.4.   Acknowledgment with Outline of Fee Structure   115
          Form 8.5.   Rejection of a Potential Client   117
          Form 8.6.   Letter to Client Describing Demurrer   118
          Form 8.7.   Helping the Client to Organize Documents   119
          Form 8.8.   Memo to Attorney Before Trial   120
          Form 8.9.   Document Search   121
          Form 8.10. Failure to Respond to Discovery   122
          Form 8.11. Confirmation of Granting of Extension of Time to Respond   123
          Form 8.12. Confirmation of Extension of Time to Respond to Discovery   124
          Form 8.13. Obtaining Client Answers to Interrogatories   125
          Form 8.14. Short Form Transmittal of Discovery to Client   127
          Form 8.15. Transmittal of Discovery to Client with Instructions   128
          Form 8.16. Sending Notice of Deposition to Client   129
          Form 8.17. Scheduling a Predeposition Meeting with Client   130
          Form 8.18. Scheduling Depositions   131
          Form 8.19. Deposition Transcript Review   132
          Form 8.20. Deposition Transcript Review   133
          Form 8.21. Providing the Court with Deposition as Exhibit   134

Form 8.22. Letter to Witness   135
Form 8.23. Request to Postmaster for Forwarding Address   136
Form 8.24. Scheduling Expert Deposition   137
Form 8.25. Deposition of Opposing Party's Expert Witness   138
Form 8.26. Long Form Subpoena Letter to Witness with On-Call Agreement   139
Form 8.27. Short Form Subpoena Letter to Witness with On-Call Agreement   142
Form 8.28. Informing the Client of a Settlement Conference   143
Form 8.29. Informing the Client of the Trial Date   144
Form 8.30. Getting Client Contact Information Before Trial   145
Form 8.31. Letter to Client About Scheduled Mediation   146
Form 8.32. Arranging for Receipt of Daily Trial Transcripts   147
Form 8.33. Settlement Letter to Opposing Counsel   148
Form 8.34. Settlement Letter to Client with Release for Signature   149
Form 8.35. Release Letter for Client's Signature   150
Form 8.36. Short Transmittal Letter   151
Form 8.37. Transmittal Form Letter   152
Form 8.38. Letter to a Clerk of the Court   153
Form 8.39. Transmittal of Several Documents to Court Clerk   154
Form 8.40. Letter to Magistrate   155
Form 8.41. Instructions for Service of Summons and Complaint   156
Form 8.42. Instructions for Service of Subpoena   157
Form 8.43. Thank-You Letter to Witness After Trial   158

CHAPTER NINE. CORPORATE LAW   160

9.1 / The Paralegal Role   160
Form 9.1.   Reservation of Corporate Name   164
Form 9.2.   Setting Up the Corporation   165
Form 9.3.   Information to and Request from Client   166
Form 9.4.   Filing a UCC-1   167
Form 9.5.   Preincorporation Information Request to Client   168
Form 9.6.   Information Letter Following Formation of Corporation   169
Form 9.7.   Stock Transaction Information Letter   173
Form 9.8.   Restricted Stock Letter   174
Form 9.9.   Dissolution Acknowledgment and Information to Client   176
Form 9.10. Memorandum Re: Findings   177

CHAPTER TEN. LABOR LAW AND EMPLOYEE BENEFITS   179

10.1 / The Paralegal Role   179
Form 10.1. EEOC Information Letter   182
Form 10.2. EEOC Acknowledgment Letter   183
Form 10.3. Application for Benefit Plan   184
Form 10.4. Termination Letter   185
Form 10.5. Letter Agreement Re: Binding Arbitration   186
Form 10.6. Answer to Request for Information from Union   187
Form 10.7. Freedom of Information Act Request   188
Form 10.8. Employee Access to Medical Records   189
Form 10.9. Certification and Demonstrations Under Rev. Proc. 91-66.   190

CHAPTER ELEVEN. ENVIRONMENTAL LAW   195

11.1 / The Paralegal Role   195
Form 11.1. Confidentiality Agreement   197
Form 11.2. Transmittal of Assessment Statements   199
Form 11.3. FOIA (Freedom of Information Act) Request for a Specific Item   200
Form 11.4. Assignment of FOIA Request for Identification Number   201
Form 11.5. FOIA Request for Documents   202
Form 11.6. Typical FOIA Request to Federal Agency   203
Form 11.7. Typical FOIA Request to State Agency   204

Form 11.8.   Public Records Act Request for Specific Information   205
Form 11.9.   Public Records Act Request for Documents and Records   206

CHAPTER TWELVE. ESTATE PLANNING AND PROBATE   *207*

12.1 / The Paralegal Role   *207*
Form 12.1.   Hearing Advisement Letter   *210*
Form 12.2.   Signature Documents Transmittal   *211*
Form 12.3.   Information Letter to Client/Attorney   *213*
Form 12.4.   Outline of Information—Duties and Responsibilities   *215*
Form 12.5.   Transmittal of Will Draft to Client for Review   *226*
Form 12.6.   Publication Request to Newspaper   *227*

CHAPTER THIRTEEN. FAMILY LAW   *229*

13.1 / The Paralegal Role   *229*
Form 13.1.   Request for Copies of Court Documents   *232*
Form 13.2.   Sample Information Request Letter   *233*
Form 13.3.   Attorney-Client Agreement   *234*
Form 13.4.   Preliminary Disclosure and Asset/Debt Checklist   *237*
Form 13.5.   Claim of Community Property Interest in Employee Benefits   *239*
Form 13.6.   Claim of Interest to Employee Benefits   *242*
Form 13.7.   Outline of Dissolution Agreement   *244*
Form 13.8.   Notification of Attorney Unavailability   *246*
Form 13.9.   Notice of Continued Health Coverage Entitlements   *247*
Form 13.10. Transmittal of Final Dissolution   *249*

CHAPTER FOURTEEN. INSURANCE DEFENSE   *251*

14.1 / The Paralegal Role   *251*
Form 14.1.   Indemnification Demand/Notification of Lawsuit   *253*
Form 14.2.   Corresponding with the Client-Subrogation Matter   *254*
Form 14.3.   Corresponding with Opposing Party   *256*
Form 14.4.   Information Transmittal to Client   *257*
Form 14.5.   Letter Re: Discovery and Request for Execution of Verification   *258*
Form 14.6.   Request for Corporate Information   *259*

CHAPTER FIFTEEN. REAL ESTATE   *261*

15.1 / The Paralegal Role   *261*
Form 15.1.   Transmittal to Client for Review and Execution   *264*
Form 15.2.   Demand for Beneficiary Statements   *265*
Form 15.3.   Demand for Payoff of Subordinate Liens   *267*
Form 15.4.   Letter to Title Company to Modify Terms of Loan   *269*
Form 15.5.   Closing Documents; Instructions to Escrow   *270*
Form 15.6.   Letter of Advice Re: Eviction   *273*
Form 15.7.   Letter of Advice Re: Eviction   *274*

CHAPTER SIXTEEN. PERSONAL INJURY   *276*

16.1 / The Paralegal Role   *276*
Form 16.1.   Letter to Opposing Counsel Transmitting Medical Summary   *279*
Form 16.2.   Authorization for Release of Medical Information   *280*
Form 16.3.   Letter to Potential Client Declining Representation   *283*
Form 16.4.   Demand Letter to Opposing Counsel   *284*
Form 16.5.   Letter to Opposing Counsel Claiming Damages   *285*
Form 16.6.   Request to Client for Additional Information   *287*
Form 16.7.   Letter to Opposing Counsel Re: Expert Deposition   *288*
Form 16.8.   Letter Requesting Medical Charges and Records   *289*
Form 16.9.   Letter Requesting Copies of Medical Records   *290*
Form 16.10. Additional Medical Records Request   *291*

Form 16.11. Request for Records, History, and x-Rays   292
Form 16.12. Request for Billing Records   294
Form 16.13. Request for Records of Driver   295
Form 16.14. Letter to Obtain DMV Collision Reports   296

CHAPTER SEVENTEEN. COLLECTIONS AND CREDITORS' RIGHTS   298

17.1 / The Paralegal Role   298
Form 17.1.   Client Letter Re: Delinquent Account   301
Form 17.2.   Second Client Letter Re: Delinquent Account   302
Form 17.3.   Demand Letter   303
Form 17.4.   Settlement Letter, Informal   304
Form 17.5.   Settlement Letter, Formal   305
Form 17.6.   Letter Setting Forth Earnings Withholding Procedures   306
Form 17.7.   Instructions to Marshal for Levy of Personal Property   307
Form 17.8.   Letter Advising Equipment Availability and Sale   309
Form 17.9.   Letter to After Sale of Equipment   310
Form 17.10. Transmittal of Sister State Judgment   311
Form 17.11. Notice of Intent to Sell Repossessed Equipment   312

CHAPTER EIGHTEEN. INTELLECTUAL PROPERTY   314

18.1 / The Intellectual Property Practice   315
18.2 / Trademark Responsibilities   316
18.3 / Patent Responsibilities   316
18.4 / Copyright Responsibilities   316
Form 18.1.   Request for Permission to Reprint   317
Form 18.2.   Permission Granted to Reprint   319
Form 18.3.   Unauthorized Use of Copyrighted Material   320
Form 18.4.   Application to Customs Department to Record Copyright Registration   322
Form 18.5.   Request for Additional Certificate   324
Form 18.6.   Transmittal of Copyright Certificate and Registration   325
Form 18.7.   Notice of Copyright Registration Renewal   326
Form 18.8.   Request to Copyright Office for Special Handling of Copyright Application   327
Form 18.9.   Transmittal of Patent Information to Client   329
Form 18.10. Patent Application Transmittal   330
Form 18.11. Execution of Assignment   331
Form 18.12. Foreign Filing Listing   332
Form 18.13. Notice of Patent   333
Form 18.14. Transmittal of Patent   334
Form 18.15. Registration Notification and Information   335
Form 18.16. Registration Information   337
Form 18.17. Amendment for Alleged Use   338
Form 18.18. Information Re: Notice of Allowance   339
Form 18.19. "Intent to Use" Status to Client   340
Form 18.20. Transmittal of Filing Receipt   341
Form 18.21. Trademark Search Information Letter   342
Form 18.22. Transmittal of Application for Trademark   344
Form 18.23. Service Mark Application   345
Form 18.24. Request for Extension of Time to File a Statement of Use   346
Form 18.25. Request for Correction to Filing Receipt   347

Reference Books   349

Index   351

Foreword

When I first started in the practice of law, I was immediately confronted with the daunting job of writing a letter to a client. This letter, which needed to be concise and yet convey the necessary information, went through repeated rewrites and revisions and still proved unsatisfactory to the attorney who was supervising my work. Then I realized there needed to be a resource available that could be utilized to assist someone faced with such a task. This book is that resource.

The formats and content of this book will undoubtedly alleviate the agony suffered by both novice and experienced letter writers alike. This book provides the essentials of business communication. Equally important, however, is the interrelationship between communicating the correct thought, with the substantively correct content (in the legal sense). What one finds here is a discussion of both fundamentals, which are so necessary for the successful paraprofessional.

In today's challenging and dynamic business environment paralegals have become an integral part of the legal team. As clients demand greater cost effectiveness and efficiency in the delivery of legal services, lawyers are relying on legal assistants with ever-increasing frequency. Tasks that, even five years ago, were routinely performed by attorneys are now performed by paralegals. This progression of roles from attorney to paralegal has dramatically increased the requirement of legal assistants to expand their professionalism, business acumen, and general knowledge.

The *Legal Assistant's Letter Book* provides just such a guide for dedicated paralegals who desire to increase their knowledge of the day-to-day practice of law. Sonia's book, however, is not just a guide to law office or paralegal letter writing. Its usefulness transcends the boundaries of the office and can and should be used for effective written communication in all aspects of the reader's professional and personal life.

In the "information society" of the 1990s, the written word is the engine that drives the train.

Jeffrey A. Clark, Esq.
Clark & Kramer
Los Angeles

Acknowledgments

It is with gratitude that I acknowledge the valued contributions of my outstanding professional colleagues. Their assistance, collaborative efforts, and work deserve appreciation and special thanks: Brenda Jan Britton; Gila Brownstein; Lana J. Clark, CLA; Stephanie A. Danelson; Linda Dmytryk; Patricia A. Dris; Kerri W. Feeney, CLAS; Dana L. Graves, J.D.; Annette Mahoney; Cynthia Y. Minier, CLA; Marjorie L. Mizerak; Susan L. Oder; Judy L. Quan; Kathleen M. Reade; Dorene Ridgway; Angela Schneeman; Craig B. Simonsen; Scott Wilcox Stoddard; Rick Wallace; Katherine S. Wong; Mary C. Wright; and Mariellen Yark, Esq.

A special acknowledgment to Chere B. Estrin, who realized I needed a special project and took the risk that she was picking the right person for the job. And to Dana L. Graves, for answering the telephone almost every time I called for help. Your being there gave me strength.

The following reviewers must also be thanked for their thoughtful comments and suggestions: Elizabeth A. Gildersleeve (American Institute), Judy A. Long (Rio Hondo College), Robert D. Loomis (Spokane Community College), Anne M. Knappenberger (Howard, Rice, Nemerovski, Canady, Robertson, Falk, and Rabkin), and Kathleen Reed (University of Toledo Community and Technical College).

I also wish to acknowledge the following copyright holders for permission to use their works:

- Form 14.3: Letter to Party Re: Decline of Claim by Kathleen M. Reade, which is found in her book, *Plaintiff's Personal Injury Practice Handbook* (1994); letter reprinted with permission of Estrin Publishing and Clark Boardman Callaghan.

- David Lee Goodrich

- NALA

- Angela Schneeman

- Prentice-Hall

- Nancy Pulsifer

- Rick Wallace

How to Use This Book

Ideally, every book should be read from front to back. I was one of those readers who *always* skipped the foreword, the introduction, and the acknowledgments. I rarely bothered with the contents pages and skipped to the index. I looked up what I needed and generally ended my quest at that point.

I understand the temptation to skip everything except what is immediately needed, but I realize I probably cheated myself out of a lot of good information. I don't do this anymore and neither should you.

In the real world, it is not always possible or practical to read an entire book. In fact, I envision (and fear) the reader perusing the table of contents for the letter they need—then copying the letter right out of the book. But this book is meant to be an on-the-job, useful tool for practical applications.

Don't cheat yourself in the long run. If you need to, skip the text today. But set aside some time and read through it from start to finish. Even if you have written letters for years, the content in this book will prove invaluable to you.

I learned a lot while writing this book. I now pay more attention to the letter structure and what the reader's needs are. In fact, I remembered many rules I'd forgotten over the years. The letters I write now are much easier for the reader to understand. I am able to say more in less time than I used to.

The introductory chapter of this book outlines what the chapters contain. If you are searching for general information, this section will provide you with direction. The reference section offers you valuable resources that can be used to guide you on a daily basis and increase your communication skills. Even with software that checks your spelling and grammar, I still find the dictionary and thesaurus my most valuable resources.

I would like to bring to your attention the fact that the return address on the form letters is Los Angeles, California. Please don't feel that this is restrictive to you, except in checking your local rules for authority. The form letters contributed came from paralegals all across the United States and the formats (i.e., return addresses) used here were done for the sake of practicality. The goal of this publication is to provide you with actual letters that have worked for others in the individual practice areas.

Also, when going through the form letters in the practice sections, you may note that the titles of the individuals signing each letter vary. This was done intentionally, to give you an idea of how varied this particular item can become. The important thing to remember is that paralegals must always identify the fact that they are not attorneys, in as clear a fashion as possible.

Above all else, remember every single letter you write, no matter how short or unnecessary you may feel it is, is written contact with another individual (or company) that can never be deleted and erased. It is lasting evidence of your communication skills and a testimonial to your existence.

Introduction

> Writing is easy. All you have to
> do is cross out the wrong words.
> —MARK TWAIN

The written word is the most effective means of communication and record-keeping. Letters and memos have heightened importance because they take the place of personal contact. They also document a communication that may be crucial for the future.

Writing letters, memoranda, and reports is one of the most important tasks paralegals perform. Chances are a large portion of your total billable hours reflects time spent drafting and editing documents. Of course, legal assistants write documents on their own behalf, but they also prepare (or "draft") documents for signature by others.

Because attorneys are trained in the nuances of language (after all, that's how "the law" is expressed), they are very sensitive to both the proficient and the poor use of the written word. This means that you're writing for a *very* tough audience. Details must be accurate, the tone correct, and information conveyed in a way the reader can easily understand.

This handbook provides paralegals with a foundation for writing effective correspondence in the law firm or corporation. It contains the practical tools to help you write clearly, accurately, and concisely. Although the discussion highlights law firms, most of the guidelines can be applied to the law firms and the legal departments of other organizations.

The *Legal Assistant's Letter Book* is divided into three distinct parts. *Part I* focuses on writing well. You will find some grammar school reminders frequently forgotten over time. You will find different types of correspondence (letters, memos and reports), their various components and general guidance on good writing style. *Part II* provides specific sample letters needed for the administrative side of the paralegal's functions, dealing with vendors and job applicants. Finally in *Part III,* you'll find the heart of the book: the extensive collection of sample letters to be used in a number of different legal practice areas.

Chapter 1 outlines correspondence content and elements and the importance of good communication. The basic components of letter writing in a legal setting are discussed in *Chapter 2*, including a discussion on the basics of grammar and style. *Chapter 3* addresses ethics and the role of the paralegal. The parts and various formats of letters are discussed in *Chapter 4.*

Chapter 5 provides the basics for drafting various types of memoranda and reports. *Chapters 6* and *7* contain guidelines of preparing letters to vendors, and addresses correspondence involved in recruiting and administration.

Chapters 8 through *18* discuss specific practice areas:

- Litigation
- Corporate law
- Labor and employment
- Environmental law
- Estate planning and probate
- Family law
- Insurance defense
- Real estate
- Personal injury
- Creditors' rights
- Intellectual properties

These chapters include forms of sample letters frequently written by paralegals, either for their own signature or the attorney's. Many experienced legal professionals contributed letter samples they use every day, giving you real-world illustrations of letters (memos and reports) that "really work."

You must, however, *always* research your specific attorney, firm, or corporation, or even state practice guidelines. Also check to see if any city, county, district, province, or specific court requirements apply. You may find that rules vary greatly from courtroom to courtroom (even though they're located in the same city). One may require a formal pleading to continue a hearing, yet another may not. Another courtroom may require instead a precise letter, along with proof that all parties were provided with appropriate, complete information and notice.

No amount of care taken in compiling sample letter forms will substitute for the specific research that each client's situation merits. The aim, however, is that the information and forms that follow will assist you in doing the best job possible.

ELEMENTS OF EFFECTIVE CORRESPONDENCE

1.1 / Importance of Good Communication
1.2 / Goals in Writing Effective Correspondence
1.3 / Before You Begin Writing
1.4 / Organizing Your Writing
1.5 / Stating the Facts
1.6 / Choosing an Appropriate Tone
1.7 / Replying to Correspondence

1.1 / Importance of Good Communication

Communication truly *is* the key to success. And nowhere is this more important than in the legal environment. Lawyers work with words every day. Part of law school training involves becoming sensitive to the nuances of language, because the meaning of statutes and case law can turn on a single word or phrase. There is, after all, a world of difference between "may" and "shall."

As a result, legal assistants must be equally adept with their use of language both verbally and in written form. To avoid misunderstandings you must choose your words carefully. You must also structure your thoughts so they are presented logically and clearly. Particularly in letters requesting action, the response you require from the recipient must be obvious.

As a legal assistant your performance is judged by your ability to communicate accurately and effectively. Precision, especially in law, is a necessity. Since the written word may last forever, anything you misstate, misconstrue, or state unclearly may come back to haunt you.

This book focuses on written communications of all kinds—letters, memoranda, and reports. If you can effectively communicate facts, thoughts, and information in a clear and concise manner, you have accomplished one of the most important—and sometimes most difficult—of all paralegal responsibilities.

1.2 / Goals in Writing Effective Correspondence

Correspondence not only transmits information, it speaks for you when you're not around. Keep in mind the following goals when you sit down to prepare letters and memoranda:

- Know why you are writing before you begin. It seems like such an obvious point, but this may be the most important point of all. Always keep in mind the *purpose* of the correspondence.
- Write clearly and accurately. Make sure the reader will understand your intended meaning. The best way to write clearly is to write *simply*.
- Choose an appropriate tone based on the purpose of the communication and the intended recipient.
- Avoid writing threatening letters. Unless you are simply utilizing a standard letter form, leave this type of dangerous communication to the lawyers.
- Put yourself in the reader's situation by asking yourself what would *you* want the letter to say?
- Respond to correspondence as promptly as possible.

1.3 / Before You Begin Writing

Detailed organization of your thoughts and all relevant information and documentation are the preliminary steps to writing an effective letter. Before you begin to draft a letter it is imperative to

- outline your thoughts *on paper*; and
- make sure you have *all* the documentation you will be referring to *in front of you.*

In her article, "Five Quick Tips for Writing Effective Legal Correspondence," Dr. Bonnie Botel–Sheppard asks the most important question: "What does your reader need or want to know?"[1] She also points out that "[m]any writers don't use the reader's original concerns or questions as the primary focus of their correspondence and, therefore, their writing loses its effectiveness."[2]

Not having *all* the information at hand is one of the most common mistakes and wastes of time. More specifically, your outline must include the following:

- the person you are writing to,
- what you are writing about,
- what you want to accomplish by sending this letter,
- what information you would want if you were on the receiving end, and
- a list of all the facts, items, documents, and issues—each identified clearly.

Once you have gathered this information, organize:

- the order in which you will present your information,
- where you will use relevant documentation, and
- an introduction giving your reason for the correspondence and introducing the point you will expound upon.

1.4 / Organizing Your Writing

When writing any type of correspondence, you need to have a beginning or *introduction*, a middle or the *body*, and an end or *conclusion* to the letter.

- The introduction should *introduce* the topic or purpose of your letter. It must logically lead into the body of the letter.
- The body should then describe the action or reaction concerning your topic and directives. Elaborate on your purpose and include information that supports your contentions. Briefly and simply summarize the issue(s).
- The conclusion should include what you want the reader to do or what you will be doing next.

While you need a beginning, a middle, and an end, you do not necessarily have to write a letter in any prescribed order. Dr. Botel–Sheppard suggests:

(1)   Begin writing your letter where you feel comfortable—even at the middle or at the end of your correspondence. Add your opening after the letter has started flowing.

(2)   Think about what you're trying to say in your letter. You might have been in such a hurry to get something on paper that you

didn't get a chance to look at the big picture—express what you know about the topic.

(3)   When you complete your first draft of the letter, come back and revise your work after a brief rest. Even if you take one or two minutes to get a cup of coffee, you are now more able to return to your letter and revise it.[3]

Some days the work of putting words on paper will flow so fluidly you will question why you didn't choose writing as a career. Other times the juices just dry up and you find writing a simple transmittal letter presents difficulties.

1.5 / Stating the Facts

If facts and issues are your bread and butter, incorrect presentation of one or the other can be disastrous. The cardinal rule of all letters: state the issues, then the facts supporting them.

As we've discussed, present the information in your letter clearly and accurately. You cannot afford to unintentionally offer incorrect, confused, or clouded information. In other words, write *simply*.

- Avoid unnecessary words.
- Write shorter sentences.
- Break up long paragraphs.
- Use the active voice.
- Use bulleted lists to display information.

There may be occasions when you want correspondence to be somewhat vague. For example, you may want to solicit a response without tipping your hand as to the purpose of your inquiry. However, vague communication can backfire, so this technique should generally be avoided.

Double-check the accuracy of all facts stated in correspondence. Review the document to which you are replying or check the file for the background information that may be at issue in the correspondence. In addition, you should *always*

- confirm the correct spelling of the names and titles of all people mentioned,
- proofread for context,
- check for correct usage of punctuation, and
- spell check every document.

Pride of authorship must be swallowed at times. Regardless of whether or not you have gone to law school, you may be drafting a letter on behalf of someone else The attorney's word at the time of the assignment is law. You must follow the attorney's guidelines to create a successful product. Make it a rule not to include your opinion on the matter.

If you must present a conclusion, do so objectively, based on the facts as they exist. If you are writing for an attorney, listen carefully about the issues that are to be presented. Make sure you give the attorney all the facts you have and that they are understood. However, present only those issues you are instructed to present. If you are not told to include all the issues, don't do so, or your version will be flawed.

1.6 / Choosing an Appropriate Tone

Conveying an appropriate tone is a key element in effective communication. The tone you choose to incorporate depends on

- the purpose of the communication, and
- the intended recipient.

Much of the body of standard letters—the points covered and the sequence of the correspondence—will remain fairly constant from case to case. Of course if the details contained within a letter differ, a change in tone may also be appropriate.

Sometimes the tone should be tailored to the type of matter for which the correspondence is needed. For example, when drafting correspondence in a family law case you may frequently utilize a tone of consolation and understanding. But if the purpose of the communication is to request assistance, you can achieve the necessary result by adopting a rather obsequious tone, particularly when the recipient is not required to provide any help.

In contrast, and in keeping with the purpose of the communication, a somewhat threatening tone may be appropriate in collection letters or creditors' rights situations. But for the most part, avoid writing threatening letters.

You must be extremely careful when using threats, even implied ones, to influence the behavior of the recipient. There are laws governing exactly what type of language may and may not be used in such situations. Because the attorneys bear the ultimate responsibility, such correspondence should not be sent without the attorney's permission and review.

1.7 / Replying to Correspondence

Sometimes the purpose of correspondence is to answer the recipient's questions or concerns. Be sure to completely address the reader's issues. For example if you are the client, are you simply looking for consolation because of your loss? Do you want to know every detail about your case? Do you just want reassurance that the case is moving forward?

Just as important as why you are writing correspondence is how quickly you respond to the correspondence you receive. Respond as promptly as possible. It's generally a good idea to respond to all correspondence within a day. Of course, this is not always possible.

> In most offices, [the 24-hour] rule is not realistic, but answers should be prompt. If the answer will be a while in coming, the requester should be sent something promptly, with an indication of when the full answer can be expected. If there is further delay, another explanation should be sent with the new expected date for a response.[4]

If you cannot respond for a good reason, perhaps because you lack the appropriate documentation or because your client has not been consulted, say so. Don't get into the habit of delaying the inevitable.

If the person waiting for a reply feels ignored, hostility may develop. Ultimately, that recipient may conclude that you are stalling to prevent disclosure of facts that are not favorable to you.

You can develop a better professional relationship by maintaining an element of cordiality. A positive rapport can weigh in your favor in the transmittal of thoughts and theories and in the outcome of the final settlement.

Ideally you should read your mail each day with the intention of responding to it immediately. Set aside a regular time when you can lock your door and concentrate. Let the office staff know that you need uninterrupted time for this important task.

One of the largest time consumers in a law office is what can be termed "spectating" paper. You look at it with wonderful intentions then set it aside or put it into a "to-do" pile. Later in the day or week you look at it again and attempt to reprioritize, based on your current workload. Maybe you'll set it in another "to-do" pile and eventually it will surface again. You have just spent several blocks of time looking at the same document and you are no closer to taking action than you were the moment you opened the envelope. To combat this tendency, follow these suggestions:

- When you sit down with the mail, do so with the determination to respond.

- Make it every day's goal to get paper off your desk and onto someone else's.

- At the very least, write or dictate some notes immediately. Prepare a memo to the file on your initial impressions of the letter's intent and a list of possible responses. Later, you can fill in the blanks, redraft, and/or edit if necessary.

- Not every letter warrants a written response. Don't waste time writing formal letters to respond to trivial requests. You can pick up the telephone or pay a personal visit in response.

Remember that every letter you respond to will most likely require another response at a later date. If you need additional motivation, think of every immediate response as the feeding and nurturing of more potential work and income for your firm in the future.

If your time is severely limited and the required response is short, it is perfectly acceptable to write a message by hand directly onto the correspondence you have received. (Of course, return the letter using a new envelope!) For correspondence that you anticipate will require substantiation or documentation at a later date, make a photocopy of the annotated letter for the file. This way, you will have both a record of the correspondence received and your response.

End Notes

[1] Bonnie Botel–Sheppard, "Five Quick Tips for Writing Effective Legal Correspondence," *Legal Assistant Today*, p. 41 (Jan./Feb. 1991).

[2] Id.

[3] Id. at 42.

[4] Reed K. Bilz, "Letter Writing in the Law Office," *Legal Assistant Today*, p. 44 (Nov./Dec. 1989).

T*wo*

THE BASICS OF LANGUAGE AND GRAMMAR

2.1 / Business Language vs. Legal Language
2.2 / Legal Citations
2.3 / Grammar
2.4 / Punctuation
2.5 / Proofreading for Mistake
    Table 2-1. Proofreading Marks: Use & Meaning

2.1 / Business Language vs. Legal Language

Lawyers are trained to write with caution and have a reputation for using incomprehensible technical language. A reader who is not an attorney may not understand the contents of a letter. Professor Richard Wydick's now-classic *Law Review* article, *Plain English for Lawyers,* provides excellent guidance on how to avoid writing incomprehensible "legalese" and it is highly recommended.[1] (*See also* the "Appendix of Reference Books on Writing and Language Use" for information on how to obtain a reprint of this outstanding article.)

You must write for the benefit of the reader. I once worked for an attorney who always ended a demand for payment with the phrase, "kindly govern yourself accordingly." While this is a nice turn of phrase, at the time, most of the recipients of these letters had a limited knowledge of English. They probably understood that the letter came from an attorney, but I'm sure the meaning of that pompous phrase was entirely lost.

Legal language has always been formal and legal writing should maintain a *degree* of formality. However, you can write more effectively by avoiding words such as "affirmative," "facilitate," and "sufficient." Instead, use

8

"yes," "help," "make easy or easier," and "enough." When drafting correspondence, *always* keep the intended reader in mind:

- Is the intended recipient an attorney, a legal assistant, an engineer, an auto mechanic, a retail clerk, or a nurse?
- How much technical, legal knowledge does this individual possess?
- What are your language barriers, if any?
- What information does the recipient want?

To a large extent, you should write as you speak. If a client asks a question requiring a positive response, you would not say, "Affirmative, you will need to facilitate our office with sufficient information." You would say something like, "Yes, you can help by giving us the information we need." The latter response is much more effective.

When appropriate, use a conversational tone. Translate archaic language into contemporary, easy-to-understand phrases and sentences. Instead of using "the above-mentioned letter," just say "this letter." That way you appear gracious and friendly instead of cold and distant.

Another concern in legal correspondence deals with legal diplomacy. Because it is important to appear diplomatic in legal correspondence, legal writing tends to be quite passive. It is important to limit the use of the passive voice. When using the passive voice, the subject of a sentence is acted upon. Sometimes the passive voice is appropriate when what is done is more important than who is doing it.

Use the active voice. Active voice allows the subject in a sentence to act. Using the active voice breathes life into your writing. It is particularly effective when trying to persuade someone to do something. You be the judge of which sentence is stronger:

- The assignment was finished before the scheduled deadline. (Passive voice.)
- I finished the assignment before the scheduled deadline. (Active voice.)

Do not be afraid to let your personality show by using humor or by being curious. However, while informality is trendy, it is not always appropriate. Because situations will vary, you will have to use your best judgment to determine which direction to take.

You should never let your writing display anger or hostility. If your correspondence threatens legal action, limit your communication to the issue without letting personalities or pettiness intrude.

The best thing you can do is to simply get to the point. Say what you need to say appropriately. Unless you are asked for a detailed report, do not embellish, elaborate, or belabor any more than is absolutely necessary.

2.2 / Legal Citations

In your attempt to avoid writing incomprehensible legalese you still need to adhere to legal style. This is particularly true when it comes to citations within your correspondence. The authors of *The Legal Research Manual* define "citations" as follows:

> . . . a legal authority or reference work, such as a constitution, statute, court decision, administrative rule, or treatise. In order to find the legal authority or precedent you need, you must know how to read and understand citations. Thus, citations play an essential role in legal research. It isn't necessary to remember all the details, but to do legal research you will need to have a basic working familiarity with citation form.[2]

The model of legal citation form and structure is *The Bluebook: A Uniform System of Citation* (now in its fifteenth edition). Another legal citation guidebook that is gaining popularity is *The University of Chicago Manual of Legal Citation*. This text uses citation forms specified by *The Bluebook*.

2.3 / Grammar

Before you can sit down to prepare anything you have to understand some basics of grammar and style. The information supplied here is intended to be a very brief summary of key points that are sometimes overlooked under the pressures of day-to-day deadlines. (*See* the "Appendix of Reference Books on Writing and Language Use" for recommended reading materials that treat this subject with the depth it deserves.)

A well-written letter does not draw attention to itself. Remember these tips when preparing your correspondence:

- Use active voice more often than the passive. Passive forms make writing weak and vague. "The job was completed." Who completed what job? Instead write, "I finished cleaning the car."

- The use of personal pronouns like "I," "me," and "we" lessens the distance between you and the reader. "We went to the store" communicates more directly than "the store was visited."

- The tense of verbs must be consistent throughout the correspondence.

- The subject and verb must agree in number: plural subjects take plural verb forms and vice versa.

- Use descriptive language to explain, clarify, and simplify whenever possible.

- Use adjectives and adverbs properly. Remember, adjectives describe the subject, while adverbs describe the verb.

- Do not overuse adjectives and adverbs.

- Get rid of extra words that add little to your message.

Avoid speaking on one subject and then wandering off to another. Group like ideas with similar issues and facts. Refer to your outline if you have difficulty separating your thoughts. If necessary, literally break down your letter into separate sections that will become your paragraphs upon completion. Also remember the following:

- A sentence must consist of a subject and a verb.

- State one complete train of thought in a sentence. Don't try to mix fragments of different thoughts.

- Avoid run-on sentences.

- Avoid clichés or trite expressions.

- Don't generalize too much, but don't go overboard with explanations either. Use your judgment.

- Vary sentence length and structure.

- Avoid long sentences. Break down your individual thoughts as much as possible. Long sentences can be confusing since the reader will probably forget the beginning by the time he or she reaches the end.

- Vary the length and structure of your sentences within a paragraph to add interest and flow.

- Ideas should flow easily from one paragraph to another. Generally a new thought, idea, or angle merits a new paragraph.

- Use appropriate punctuation.

- Separate independent clauses with a period or semicolon, not a comma.

Do *not* capitalize words unless they are proper names or parts of proper names. It is unsettling to read a letter in which many items are unnecessarily capitalized. It is easier for the eye to follow lower-case characters.

When a number starts a sentence, spell it out: "Thirty-seven men died," not "37 men died." Within a sentence, rules generally fall into two categories. One approach is to spell out numbers one through nine and use numerals for 10, 11, and so on. Another approach is to spell out numbers one through ninety-nine and use numerals above that.

In two specific instances however, numerals communicate much more effectively. Use numerals when listing more than two numbers in a series ("2, 7, 56, and 434"), and when expressing time ("7:30 A.M.").

The key is to be consistent. You should adopt a set of rules and stick with it. Check with your firm to see if there are such rules in place. Generally the firm will decide these style questions.

You will also be able to find computer programs like Grammatik III that scans documents for grammatical and general writing errors. If you are not sure of your grammar or punctuation skills, and the available forms and source books are not satisfactory, ask someone in the office who has good skills to read it over for you.

2.4 / Punctuation

Your elementary school English classes may or may not bring back pleasant memories. However, the basics they covered really are the *basics* of structure. If you have a good grasp of these you will be surprised by the simplicity of legal letter writing. To recap, remember the following punctuation basics:

- A period (.) completes a sentence.

- A comma (,) separates phrases, clauses, or items in a series.

- A question mark (?) completes a question.

- An exclamation point (!) portrays emphasis or surprise.

- A hyphen (-) holds two things together. (For example, a well-organized office.)

- A dash (—) pushes things apart. It marks a sudden change in tone. Do not put a space before or after a dash.

- Quotation marks (" ") begin and end quoted material.

- Parentheses ( ) and brackets [ ] enclose tangential information.

- An ellipsis (. . .) shows omitted information.

- Colons (:) introduce an item or list.

- Semicolons (;) can separate clauses in a compound sentence.

2.5 / Proofreading for Mistakes

Proofread *carefully*. This may very well be the most important task in the letter–writing process. No matter how articulate and witty a letter is, if the reader comes across a single blunder, all may be lost. Even "just one" mistake is too many and the letter must be redone. Proofreading is especially important when drafting letters for attorneys:

Attorneys who sign documents will read them, of course, but do *not* expect them to read word for word, or look for misspelled words and other errors. Attorneys rely on you to provide documents for review in "final draft form." Do not present any document about which *you* are not completely happy.[3]

Particularly when the letter is long, or you have worked for some time on crafting it, you will sometimes overlook small errors. When you edit, remember to do the following:

- Make revisions in colored pen, preferably red. Black ink blends in with type too easily and the correction may be missed.

- Make check marks in the margins to flag lines where corrections have been made, especially if the corrections are minor.

- The most common error is in spelling. Double-check the spellings of names, companies, and unusual words.

Of course, word processing programs can cure this problem with a touch of a button. Most computer software packages used in law firms today utilize spell checking features. Specialized computer dictionaries containing medical and legal terminology can be added. Additionally, software for checking grammar and punctuation has become both more useful and generally available.

However, do *not* rely on software to detect every problem because most software packages cannot "read" for the context to determine how a word is used. If a particular word is listed in the dictionary it will not be questioned by the system. For instance, if the word "form" is typed by mistake instead of "from," the system will not detect an error because these are both correctly spelled words.

Whether or not your office is computerized, always check just-drafted documents carefully. Sometimes, it's best to ask someone else to proofread and correct typographical errors since it can be difficult to detect your own errors. Often, the very words that are misspelled are ones used the most often. You can get so used to what a document is supposed to say that errors are easily overlooked. Keep a good general dictionary, thesaurus, medical dictionary and *Black's Law Dictionary* handy at all times. Don't hesitate to look up any words which you are uncertain about (either spelling or meaning).[4]

If you have several complicated corrections, consider dictating the document again if that would take less time than crossing out, rewriting, reading, and retyping.

Effective proofreading requires familiarity with proofreading marks. Table 2.1 shows each symbol, its meaning, and an example of how to use it.

PROOFREADING MARKS

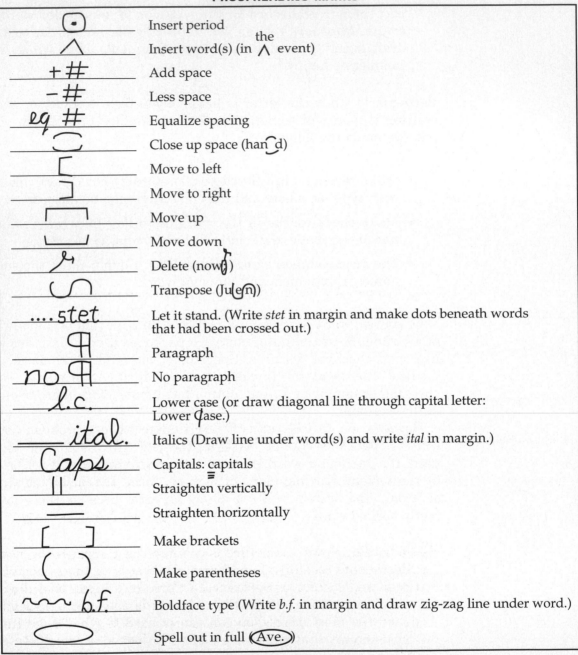

Table 2.1. Proofreading Marks: Use and Meaning

End Notes

[1] See Richard C. Wydick, *Plain English for Lawyers*, 66 Cal. L. Rev. 727 (1978).

[2] Christopher G. Wren & Jill Robinson Wren, *The Legal Research Manual: A Game Plan for Legal Research and Analysis* 20 (1986).

[3] Kathleen M. Reade, *Plaintiff's Personal Injury Handbook* §9.5 (1994).

[4] Id. § 9.4.

Three

ETHICS AND THE ROLE OF THE PARALEGAL

3.1 / Importance of Maintaining Confidentiality
3.2 / Curing Conflicts by Using "Ethical Walls"
    Form 3.1. Ethical Wall Memorandum
    Form 3.2. Ethical Wall Notice
3.3 / Always Identify Yourself as a Paralegal
3.4 / Follow Firm Policies about Signatures
3.5 / Signatures by Legal Secretaries
3.6 / Confidentiality When Sending Facsimiles
    Form 3.3. Fax Transmittal Cover Sheet

3.1 / Importance of Maintaining Confidentiality

As a paralegal, you have a responsibility to maintain secrecy regarding information and files in any legal matter. Of course, the American Bar Association's Model Rules of Professional Conduct governs the conduct of attorneys.[1] But, as set in the ABA's Model Guidelines for the Utilization of Legal Assistant Services, paralegals also must abide by the Model Rules.[2] In addition, the national paralegal associations have also prepared guidelines for ethical conduct. Both the National Association of Legal Assistants (NALA) and the National Federation of Paralegal Associations (NFPA) have promulgated codes which stress the importance of confidentiality to the client.[3]

The NALA maintains the "Code of Ethics and Professional Responsibility," which is made up of twelve canons. With regard to the issue of confidentiality requirements, NALA's Code of Ethics states:

Canon 7:   "A legal assistant must protect the confidences of a client, and it shall be unethical for a legal assistant to violate any statute now in effect or hereafter to be enacted controlling privileged communications."

Canon 12: "A legal assistant is governed by the American Bar Association Code of Professional Responsibility."[4]

In addition, NFPA's "Affirmation of Responsibility" provides: "A paralegal shall maintain the highest standards of ethical conduct" and "shall preserve client confidences and privileged communications."[5]

Exercise reasonable care to prevent outside parties from accessing information relating to a client, unless that client has specifically asked for disclosure. While it is understood that various firm employees are privy to specific details of a case, take care in judging which items you discuss with other members of the staff.

Also remember that elevator and hallway discussions are taboo. You never know who will hear or understand the content of a conversation, even when names, dates, or other identifiable pieces of information are not mentioned.

I once walked by a judgment debtor and his attorney in the hallway of a court building, when the debtor asked his attorney if he should volunteer any information about his out-of-state property. The whole exchange took less than ten seconds. When the debtor's name was called at the hearing, I was surprised (happily) to see this was the person I would examine that day. Although I did not hear the attorney's response to his client's question in the hallway, I am sure the client was cautioned *not* to volunteer the property-related information. He was under no obligation to do so if I did not ask him directly. Ten seconds in the hallway gave me a valuable advantage. Don't be the victim of unintentional disclosure.

As a paralegal you should be bound by the American Bar Association's guidelines as well as those of NALA and NFPA, and also by any regional codes or canons within your geographic area. If you are concerned that you may be crossing *any* boundaries:

· check with your supervising attorney or paralegal manager,
· call on a colleague, or
· contact your local or national professional organization.

Everyone should have at least one professional colleague with whom they can speak openly and honestly to discuss opinions and problematic situations. These colleagues may be people you never meet face to face, yet their professional acquaintance and advice may be invaluable. These colleagues also make good networking contacts for future opportunities.

3.2 / Curing Conflicts by Using "Ethical Walls"

There may even be instances when you or other members of the firm need to be isolated from a particular matter to avoid conflicts of interest. Most often this occurs to individuals who have been in the paralegal field for many years and have worked for several firms. A letter or memorandum to the firm informing them of the situation is necessary. The following format (Form 3.1) is a good one to follow.

MEMORANDUM

To: All Employees of DEMP&W

From: Michelle Mitchell

Date: [Date]

Re: [CASE TITLE, CASE NUMBER]

Please be advised that [NAME OF EMPLOYEE], the firm's [TITLE], formerly occupied an indirect consulting position with respect to [NAME OF ENTITY]. Because of that past indirect relationship, it is necessary to isolate [HIM/HER] from all matters involving our clients associated with [NAME OF ENTITY].

Consequently, [NAME OF EMPLOYEE] is to have no contact with anyone in the firm relating to, referring to, or in any way connected with our representation of any person or entity associated with [NAME OF ENTITY] or any matter undertaken on behalf of any such person or entity. All files reflecting any aspect of our representation of [NAME OF ENTITY] have been and will remain restricted, from [NAME OF EMPLOYEE]. No one will engage in any discussion regarding any aspect of our representation of such clients in the presence of or within earshot of [NAME OF EMPLOYEE]. No correspondence concerning such representation is to be left in plain sight or otherwise accessible to anyone other than those actively engaged in such representation.

The foregoing is to be regarded as inviolate and is to be strictly construed and enforced. Discretion to treat the foregoing in other than its most literal sense does not exist. These procedures are for the protection of our clients, the firm, and [NAME OF EMPLOYEE]. Any questions concerning this memorandum are to be directed to [NAME OF CONTACT IN FIRM].

Form 3.1. Ethical Wall Memorandum

The previous letter is addressed to the entire office. The formal language is entirely appropriate and will be understood by everyone involved. It is also legally correct.

However, you risk losing the reader—even a law office employee—by your stiff introduction. Remember to think about your reader. While personnel in the law office may understand the language, it does come across as a little distant.

A better approach would be to attach an attention-grabbing cover sheet to the letter. That way more people are likely to read it. Form 3.2, The Ethical Wall Notice, is this type of form.

3.3 / Always Identify Yourself as a Paralegal

According to the American Bar Association's definition of a paralegal or legal assistant,[6] attorneys bear all liability for the work product of the firm. This includes the work of legal assistants short of flagrant negligence. Ethical rules are very clear regarding the need to establish a paralegal's identity, even on correspondence that may not be considered important.[7]

In this respect, an attorney will typically sign letters without including the title "attorney." But always list your name *and* your title. Clearly communicate that you are not an attorney. Use whatever job title—paralegal or legal assistant—that has been established by your firm.[8]

It is vital that no misrepresentation or mistake be made. Keep in mind that return correspondence will almost certainly be addressed exactly as you have signed your name. If you omit your job title, the reader may assume you are an attorney and address the letter to you as such.

If you receive correspondence erroneously addressed to you as "Esq.," or if someone mistakenly calls you an attorney, you *must* set the record straight. You must always identify yourself as a paralegal when telephoning.[9] You may feel complimented if someone mistakes you for an attorney, but you will be courting possible criminal prosecution if it appears that you are practicing law without a license. Make sure you make mention of it with every contact no matter how insignificant that contact may seem.

3.4 / Follow Firm Policies about Signatures

Many times, the correspondence you draft will be on behalf of an attorney, for that person's signature. What happens when the attorney is not available to sign the letter when it needs to go out? The following is very good advice:

Anticipate the possibility that the lawyer may not be available to sign documents by establishing general rules ahead of time. Should you:

- use the lawyer's signature stamp?

- sign his name and put your initials beside it?

NOTICE OF ETHICAL WALL

Attached please find a letter which involves all staff members and security on [CASE NAME] involving [NAME OF EMPLOYEE]. Please make sure all information, documents, and conversations are kept confidential in this matter, more specifically set forth in the attached memorandum.

Thank you for your cooperation.

Form 3.2. Ethical Wall Notice

> · wait for him to return, however long it takes (and risk missing the deadline?, or
>
> · have the letter or document changed so that it can be signed by someone else who is so authorized?
>
> Lawyers have different opinions on the signature issue, and firms have different policies. Prepare for this problem so you can avoid the headache of ... not knowing what he expects you to do in his absence.[10]

Whether or not you write letters only for your own signature or that of the supervising attorney, the issue is a very important one and requires sound judgment. A colleague of mine works for a firm where the policy on signatures is so specific and all-inclusive that she cannot sign anything that goes out on the firm's letterhead.

On the other hand, my supervising attorney used to sign everything until he felt I could personally handle any response generated by correspondence. In that situation, I signed every piece of correspondence I produced unless it involved rendering an opinion or something completely outside a paralegal's ordinary scope of responsibilities. Authority to sign a letter will depend on the practice area as well as the policy of the firm or attorney. No matter how your firm handles these matters, always inform the attorney of your decision.

3.5 / Signatures by Legal Secretaries

In the same way an attorney is responsible for your work product, you are responsible for your secretary's work. It is your responsibility to carefully edit and scrutinize every document that leaves your desk. Make sure the secretaries with whom you work abide by the firm's standardized policies and produce a quality error-free work product.

The perfection (or imperfection) of every document you produce will reflect directly upon you and your employer. This is true whether you write letters for an attorney's signature or your own. Never allow typographical mistakes, misspelled names, or other easily rectified mistakes under *any* circumstances.

If your secretary signs letters for you or prepares form transmittals, the secretary must sign on your behalf. The secretary must include his or her name and title along with your name and title:

```
Sincerely, [CLOSING]



[SIGNATURE]
Cynthia Jones
Secretary to Angela Shapiro, Senior
Paralegal
```

3.6 / Confidentiality When Sending Facsimiles

Facsimile ("fax") machines are wonderful and useful tools, especially in the business world. References can be transmitted immediately, sometimes during a telephone conversation discussing documents and often directly to someone's desk top.

But confidentiality may be a problem when using fax machines. Keep in mind that fax machines are usually found in fairly public areas of firms. Even if the recipient's fax machine is on that person's desk, he or she may not be present the moment the fax arrives. *Never* send any confidential or personal material by fax, unless you know the recipient is standing by to receive your transmission.

When you transmit documents via facsimile, be sure to include a cover sheet with the documents you send. The cover sheet should list the following information:

- · name of the recipient,
- · the number of pages transmitted, and
- · a Notice of Confidentiality.

This latter item is of primary importance to law firms. Most firms use "Notice of Confidentiality" language similar to the following:

NOTICE OF CONFIDENTIALITY

This transmittal and any accompanying documents are intended for the use of only the individual or entity to whom they are addressed. These documents may contain information that is privileged, confidential, or otherwise exempt from disclosure by prevailing laws.

If you have received this communication in error, please notify the sender IMMEDIATELY by:
1) collect telephone call to the above number, and 2) making arrangements to return the misdirected documents to the above address. You will be reimbursed for postage. **Thank you for your prompt attention to this matter.**

Other information—the date and sender—will be transmitted automatically. Fax transmissions are required by FCC law to list the date and time of transmissions along with the phone number and other, optional identification information about the sender.

Some fax machines can also be programmed to send a cover sheet. Many computers are equipped to send faxes directly from your terminal using a modem, as mentioned before. If your computer does not have that capability, keep a blank copy of your firm's facsimile transmission cover sheet on your personal computer.

DeLost, Ernst, Miessner, Powell & Wilcox
Attorneys at Law
1257 Main Street, Suite 900
Los Angeles, CA 90066
(310) 555-6000

— FACSIMILE COVER SHEET —

To: _____

Fax No.: _____

From: _____

Total Number of Pages (Including This Page): _____

Date: _____

File Identification: _____

_____

If you do not receive all the pages as listed, please call [SENDER'S NAME OR CONTACT] immediately at [PHONE NUMBER].

COMMENTS: _____

_____

_____

( ) AN ORIGINAL IS BEING MAILED

( ) AN ORIGINAL IS BEING DELIVERED

( ) AN ORIGINAL IS AVAILABLE UPON REQUEST

( ) FACSIMILE TRANSMITTAL ONLY.

The information contained in this facsimile message may be attorney privileged and confidential information intended only for the use of the individual named above. If the reader of this message is not the intended recipient, or the employee or agent responsible to deliver it to the intended recipient, you are hereby notified that any dissemination, distribution, or copying of this communication is strictly prohibited. If you have received this communication in error, please immediately notify the sender by telephone and return the original message to above address via the U.S. Postal Service.

Form 3.3. Fax Transmittal Cover Sheet

End Notes

[1]Canon 1:   A lawyer should assist in maintaining the integrity and competence of the legal profession.

Canon 3:   A lawyer should assist in preventing the unauthorized practice of law.

Canon 4:   A lawyer should preserve the confidences and secrets of a client.

American Bar Association, *Model Rules of Professional Conduct* (1983).

[2]**Guideline 1:** A lawyer is responsible for all of the professional actions of a legal assistant performing legal assistant services at the lawyer's direction and should take reasonable measures to ensure that the legal assistant's conduct is consistent with the lawyer's obligations under the ABA Model Rules of Professional Conduct.

American Bar Association, *Model Guidelines for the Utilization of Legal Assistant Services* (1991). *See also* Therese A. Cannon, Ethics and Professional Responsibility for Legal Assistants, p. 19 (1992). The ABA's Guidelines are reprinted in Cannon at p. 329 (Appendix A).

[3]The National Association of Legal Assistants first adopted its "Code of Ethics and Professional Responsibility" in 1979 (revised in 1988), and the National Federation of Paralegal Associations adopted its "Affirmation of Responsibility" in 1977 (revised in 1981). You can find NALA's Code reprinted in its popular handbook, National Association of Legal Assistants, Inc., *Manual for Legal Assistants*, p. 376 (2nd ed., 1992). Both NALA's Code and NFPA's Affirmation are reprinted in Cannon at pp. 347 and 367 (Appendix C and Appendix D, respectfully).

[4]NALA Manual at pp. 376–377.

[5]David Lee Goodrich, *The Basics of Paralegal Studies*, pp. 127–128 (1991).

[6]According to the definition approved American Bar Association in 1986, a legal assistant is someone:

· qualified through education, training, and/or experience, who,

· under the supervision of an attorney,

· performs substantive legal work requiring knowledge of legal concepts and processes,

· which is customarily but not exclusively performed by an attorney, and which,

· for the most part, absent a paralegal, would be performed by an attorney.

ABA Standing Comm. on Legal Assistants, Model Guidelines for the Utilization of Legal Assistant Services (Adopted by the ABA House of Delegates, August 1991).

[7]ABA Model Rule 5.5; ABA Model Code DR 3-101. *See also* Therese A. Cannon, Ethics and Professional Responsibility for Legal Assistants, pp. 56–59 (1992):

One of the main functions of many legal assistants is acting as liaison to persons outside the law firm—clients, witnesses, opposing law firms, courts, and so forth. This contact may take the form of telephone conversations, correspondence, or less frequently, meetings in person. A key ethical aspect of the liaison role is ensuring that the person with whom the legal assistant is dealing is *fully aware that the legal assistant is not a lawyer.*

Id. at 56 (emphasis added).

[8]Although "paralegal" and "legal assistant" are the most common job titles, the use and meaning of these titles can vary. To make it absolutely clear that legal assistants are *not* attorneys, Alabama Bar Association uses the title "non-lawyer legal assistant." Further,

As legal assistants have become more specialized and firms have developed career paths for them, new titles have been created, such as senior legal assistant and litigation support specialist. As a general rule, any title that does not potentially mislead a third party into believing that the legal assistant is an attorney is permissible. One interesting twist on this rule is that in the state of Iowa, legal assistants may not sign correspondence using the title "certified legal assistant" even though they are certified by the National Association of Legal Assistants (NALA). This [state bar ethics] opinion has been challenged by NALA.

Id. at 58.

[9][A] legal assistant who is mistaken for an attorney may be called on to perform functions that are tantamount to [the] *unauthorized practice of law.* If a client believes a legal assistant is an attorney, the client may ask for legal advice. This places the legal assistant in the uncomfortable position of having to backtrack in the conversation to explain his or her status and how that status makes giving a legal opinion impossible or inappropriate.

Id. at 57 (emphasis added).

[10]Nancy Pulsifer, "Unwritten Rules: A Guide to Successfully Working with Attorneys," in *How to Survive in a Law Firm* , pp. 31–32 (1992).

LETTER STRUCTURE AND FORMATS

4.1 / Purposes of Correspondence

4.2 / Basic Parts of a Letter

4.3 / Sender's Address

4.4 / Date of the Letter

4.5 / Recipient's Address

4.6 / Use of the Re: Line

4.7 / Salutation

4.8 / Body of the Letter

4.9 / Closing Phrase

4.10 / Firm Name in the Signature Block

4.11 / Signer's Name

4.12 / Signer's Title

4.13 / Identifying Initials

4.14 / Enclosures or Attachments

4.15 / "Carbon" Copies

4.16 / Computer File Locator Information

4.17 / Subsequent Page Identification

    Form 4.1. Basic Parts of a Letter

4.18 / Types of Letter Formats

4.19 / Popular Block Format

4.20 / Modified Block Format

4.21 / Full Block Format

    Form 4.2. The Popular Block Letter

    Form 4.3. The Modified Block Letter

    Form 4.4. The Full Block Letter

4.1 / Purposes of Correspondence

As discussed in Chapter 1, you must first understand why you are writing before you begin drafting a letter. Following a simply and clearly defined purpose in correspondence will help readers understand your expectations and what you are attempting to communicate. As stated in the National Association of Legal Assistants' *Manual for Legal Assistants,* the purpose of legal correspondence follows the same general principles as business correspondence. Such correspondence should serve at least one of the following four functions:

- to obtain action,
- to provide information,
- to maintain goodwill, and
- to create a record.[1]

Correspondence intended to obtain action requires the recipient of the correspondence to either act or deal with the consequences of failing to do so. These letters should establish a time limit in the last paragraph by which an answer or response is needed.[2]

A letter providing information is generally more involved than other correspondence. It is usually written in response to a request for more information by a client, the opposition, or the court. In the conclusion of this letter, it is usually a good idea to include a sentence requesting further contact if the information provided is insufficient.

It is important to maintain goodwill through correspondence with clients, the court, your adversaries, and all court system employees. Many times, an opponent in a difficult and contentious piece of litigation will be a codefendant in some future action. You can bet the effects of discourtesy and rudeness will carry over into the next case. If an opponent acts offensively, correspondence reflecting a similar attitude serves no purpose and reflects a lack of professionalism.

Remember that trial and pretrial discovery activity is a complicated series of maneuvers. Legal assistants should help the relations between the attorney and others in the legal community. The correspondence should encourage goodwill.

Looking back over the correspondence file in a closed case will clearly show you how individual letters and memos create a chronological record of the events as they occur. Correspondence may, for example, create a record to help an attorney and client see the opponent's unwillingness to comply with the rules of the court. Keeping the "historical record" view of correspondence in mind, work to create a paper trail that reflects the following attributes:

- courtesy,
- discipline,

- timeliness,
- professional tone, and
- appropriate language.[3]

4.2 / Basic Parts of a Letter

The letter building process requires a strong foundation. You must understand the variety of possible letter formats and the main parts of a letter as well as basic grammar. Even if you have been writing letters for some time, you may benefit from a brief review in the elements and structure of a letter.

A letter has fifteen basic parts or elements, some of which are optional. In Form 4.1, numbers have been assigned to each letter element, following the structure of the list below:

1. Sender's Address,
2. Date,
3. Recipient's Address,
4. Re: Line,
5. Salutation,
6. Body,
7. Closing,
8. Firm Name,
9. Signer's Name,
10. Signer's Title,
11. Identifying Initials,
12. Enclosures,
13. "Carbon" Copy,
14. Computer File Locator, and
15. Subsequent Page Identification.

Each letter part or element will be addressed in more detail in the following sections.

4.3 / Sender's Address

For business letters, the sender's address is found in the firm's letterhead. (Personal letters should be written on personal stationery, which sometimes includes the sender's home address already printed.) Some letter-heads are centered, others are flush right, flush left, or inhabit the margins on either side. The letterhead contains much useful information, including the firm's

- name,
- address,
- telephone and fax number, and
- telex or E-mail numbers, if appropriate.

The type of letterhead structure will dictate the letter format used to achieve an aesthetically pleasing look. (*See* §4.18, "Types of Letter Formats.") The positioning of letterhead information on the page also conveys the image the firm wants to present. Administrators, marketing specialists, and partners spend a lot of time developing the letterhead "look" to convey the desired image.

Individual attorneys at the firm may be listed on either side of the letter-head information or below it. Some states allow firms to list paralegals on the firm letterhead as long as the paralegals are clearly identified. Make sure that you use current letterhead that lists the names of all attorneys in the office, and does not include those who are no longer with the firm.

4.4 / Date of the Letter

Always date your letter the day it will be mailed. There are *no* exceptions to this rule. The date can begin one space directly below the letterhead, but it looks better when separated by two or three lines.

The proper form for listing the date can follow either the more common structure of "September 11, 1995," or the military (or European) style, "11 September 1995." Either form is acceptable. Whichever one you use, however, *be consistent*.

Note the lack of punctuation in "11 September 1995," which is a standard format in the military and has become popular in some law offices. Many attorneys feel this style reflects increased precision and may be clearer to comprehend, especially when used for international correspondence.

The date of a letter is anything but inconsequential. Attention to detail is the name of the game in this business, so remember the following:

- do not spell out the number of the day after the month (e.g., September First),
- do not use ordinal numbers to express the date (e.g., September 1st, 2nd, 3rd, or 4th), and
- do not use abbreviations such as "Sept. 1, 1995" or "9/1/95."

Abbreviations are extremely informal and convey a lack of attention to detail. While abbreviations may save time, they can damage the professional impression you want to create and nurture.

4.5 / Recipient's Address

The recipient's address section of a letter actually consists of several items:

- the recipient's name,
- the recipient's job title or position,
- the name of the firm or organization, and
- the correct address, including suite number and zip code.

Spell and punctuate all words in the address exactly as the recipient would spell and punctuate them. It is extremely important to address every letter correctly and precisely.

- Use an individual's full name with the appropriate forms of address. For example, use *Mr. Robert Jones* and *Ms. Cynthia Jones,* as opposed to *Bob Jones* and *Cindy Jones,* unless your relationship to the recipient has already proceeded to less formal modes of address.

- If you know the job title or position of the recipient, list this information directly below the person's name. If you are writing to a judge, magistrate, or other personage, use the proper form of address. For example, a letter to *Judge Robert Jones* should be addressed to *The Honorable Robert Jones.*

- List the company or firm name exactly as you see it on letterhead or business cards. For example, if a firm's name is listed on the letterhead as "Smith Jones Johnson & Wilson" (no commas between names), that is exactly how it should be listed in a letter to a person at that firm. Likewise, if a company calls itself "Carpets&" (no space before the ampersand), *do not* insert a space before the ampersand, even though that is the more common usage.

- The recipient's name and address on the envelope should be an exact copy of the spelling and punctuation on the letter. Double-check to make sure; it doesn't help to address a letter correctly if the envelope contains errors.

- The address information must be correct and complete for the post office to deliver the envelope and its contents. It certainly helps to include the extended zip code (nine digits) in the recipient's address whenever you have that information.

- It is acceptable to abbreviate terms such as "Street" and "Boulevard." In addition, the post office recommends using standard two-letter state abbreviations such as "CA" instead of spelling out the state name "California."

- It is acceptable, but not mandatory, to type the company name in capital letters to set if off from the rest of the address. This last item is a point of preference, but either way, the usage of capital letters (or not) should be consistent from one letter to another.

Pay special attention to the unique spelling of names and nicknames. My firm once had a client whose name was Jo, not Joseph, Josephine, or Joe, but *Jo*. Fortunately, she laughs each time she receives a letter addressed "Dear Mr." Not everyone has such a good sense of humor upon finding their name misspelled.

4.6 / Use of the Re: Line

How the *re:* line is used in letters varies from firm to firm. Consult existing client files for letters written by others to see how this element is used by your firm. Generally, however, the *re:* line should identify, in a few words, the subject matter of the letter. This information may include

- the case name,

- case number,

- the recipient's identification, and

- your internal file number or identification.

The *re:* line is typically underlined to set it apart from the rest of the letter.

When responding to correspondence, note all the information used on the writer's *re:* line. Use the claim number or date of accident if it is included. Nearly all offices maintain their files by file number as well as client name, so make it a habit to include as much information as you can to help the recipient locate the appropriate file.

4.7 / Salutation

Unless you and the recipient routinely address each other by first names, use a formal form of address. *Mr.* and *Ms.* are now the most common and acceptable forms of address, but you may have occasion to use *Mrs.* or *Miss,* if the recipient of your letter prefers that usage.

Sometimes, you may not know the exact name of the recipient. If you have the title of the person you are writing to but no name, you could address the letter by incorporating the name of the department in your address: *Dear Human Resource Representative,* for example. While this is acceptable, it is not the preferred solution to this problem. Instead, call the firm or company to whom you are writing and ask for the name of the person who should receive your correspondence. Be sure to double-check the spelling and job title.

If calling for this information is an impossibility, you may use *Dear Sir or Madam.* Always include both genders in this form of address. If you simply use *Dear Sir,* you run the risk of possibly offending the recipient before he or she even gets a chance to read the body of the letter.

Salutations in a letter to multiple recipients can take several forms:

- If you are addressing a male and a female concurrently, you can use *Dear Mr. Jones and Ms. Smith* or *Dear Ms. Smith and Mr. Jones.*

- For a letter addressed to two men, it is acceptable to use *Dear Messrs. Jones and Smith.*

- In a letter addressed to two women, use *Dear Ms. Jones and Smith.*

- If your letter is addressed to more than two parties, acceptable forms include the following:
  - *Dear Gentlemen,*
  - *Dear Ladies,*
  - *Dear Ladies and Gentlemen,* or
  - *To Whom It May Concern.*

Listing each and every name, when there are more than two, is not strictly necessary and may not be appreciated. In some instances, an attention line or *re:* line is used in lieu of the salutation line. While this may be acceptable, most law firms prefer to use *Dear Sir or Madam.*

In Form 4.1, the particular designation of *Marcus Novick, Ph.D.* was chosen to create a point. You can see that *Dr. Novick* is the salutation used, *not Mr. Novick* or *Mr. Marcus Novick, Ph.D.* When you use a title after a name, do not also use the title of Mr., Ms., or the like. Use one or the other, not both.

After you've gotten the recipient's proper name and title, use either comma or colon to end the salutation. Commas to end salutations tend to be favored in personal letters, but a colon is used most often in business correspondence. However, the choice of punctuation will depend on your firm's preferences. As with all other style points, consistency is the key. When in doubt, refer to one of the sources listed in "Reference Books on Writing and Language Use" found at the back of this book.

4.8 / Body of the Letter

The body of a letter begins two spaces down from the salutation and is generally single spaced. The body contains your main purpose for writing. The three basic elements of this section include the introduction, factual information, and closing:

- The introduction should *introduce* the topic or purpose of your letter. It must logically lead into the body of the letter.
- The body should then describe the action or reaction concerning your *topic and directives*. Elaborate on your purpose and include information that supports your contentions. Briefly and simply summarize the issue(s).
- The *conclusion* should include what you want the reader to do or what you will be doing next.

See Chapter 1, particularly §1.4, for more detailed discussions of this subject.

4.9 / Closing Phrase

Business letters can utilize both formal and informal closings. Your firm's style will dictate which language to use. The most frequently used letter closing language follows:

- *Respectfully yours* (very good for letters to judges or arbitrators),
- *Very truly yours,*
- *Sincerely,*
- *Sincerely yours,* and
- *Yours very truly.*

Whichever closing phrase you choose, note that only the *first* word is capitalized; the remaining words are in lower case. Place a comma at the end of the phrase.

4.10 / Firm Name in the Signature Block

After the closing in the signature block, it is acceptable but *not* mandatory to type the firm or company name in capital letters. This is yet another point of personal preference. Whichever choice you make, the usage (or not) of capital letters should be consistent from one letter to another. If your firm does prefer to list its name, this information can be listed in two different places:

- on the line directly below the closing phrase, or

- after skipping a line.

Be sure to leave sufficient space for a signature below the firm name and above the typed name of the signatory.

In this book, the firm name is included in Form 4.1, as an example of the placement of this element. But you will *not* find it used in other sample letters throughout the remainder of the text.

4.11 / Signer's Name

Below the space for the sender's signature, list your full name, or if you are drafting a letter for someone else, that person's name. If appropriate, also list a job title or other indication of position (e.g., Esq., CLA, etc.). The author's name may be typed in all capital letters or upper and lower case.

When also listing a job title or status information like *Legal Assistant* or *Esq.* on the same line as the author's name, separate the author's name from the title by a comma. On the other hand, if the title is listed on the line below the author's name, it is *not* necessary to include any punctuation after the name. Both forms depend entirely on personal and firm preferences.

4.12 / Signer's Title

Listing the signer's name on the firm's letterhead paper without also including a job title generally implies that the signer is an attorney. When preparing your own correspondence, you must disclose your status as a paralegal so the recipient of the letter is properly informed of your position, and does not mistakenly assume that you are an attorney. By including your job title, you state clearly that you are corresponding as a legal assistant or paralegal. (*See* §3.3 for a thorough discussion of this subject.)

4.13 / Identifying Initials

Identifying initials are placed on the letter to indicate the author and typist (if any). The upper case initials identify the writer and the lower case initials identify the typist.

- If you (initials *PAR*) draft a letter on behalf of an attorney (initials *ATY*), and your secretary (initials *SEC*) transcribes it, the identifying initials in this case would read *ATY/PAR/sec*.

- If you finalized the word processing document as well as drafted the letter for the attorney, the appropriate identifying initials would be *ATY/PAR* or *ATY/PAR/wp*.

- If you draft the letter for your own signature and your secretary transcribes it, the identification would be *PAR/sec*.

- If you both drafted and finalized the word processing version of a letter for your own signature, either *PAR* alone or *PAR/wp* would be appropriate identification.

You can utilize this knowledge on letters you receive to identify the person you wish to speak with and respond to. If a letter was drafted by an individual other than the signer, you can ask to speak to that person. Usually this person is often another paralegal. It is more efficient to speak with the person who researched the underlying issues and is most familiar with all the facts.

4.14 / Enclosures or Attachments

If you are including other documents with your letter, indicate this information at the bottom of the letter. List the title of the enclosed document following the word *Enclosure:* or *Attachment:*. Use the word *Attachments:* when faxing a letter with other documents attached. Use *Enclosures:* when actually enclosing other materials in the same envelope as your letter. Use a colon preceding the listing of enclosures or attachments.

If you use a form letter structure, you can place the *Enclosures:* notation on the letter. If there are no enclosures, you can either type *none* on your form or delete the line before printing the final letter.

It is prudent to spot check your outgoing mail to make sure that the appropriate enclosures really are enclosed. This is especially important when you are dealing with sensitive documents.

4.15 / "Carbon" Copies

When a copy of a letter is sent to another party (*cc: William Jones, Esq.*), include this information right above the *Enclosures:* line. When the original letter is sent with enclosures, copies of these may or may not be attached to the courtesy copy of the letter.

- If enclosures are being included with the copy, indicate this information as follows: *cc w/enc: William Jones, Esq.*

- If the original of the letter has enclosures but these enclosures are not included with the copy, indicate this fact using the following structure: *cc w/o enc: William Jones, Esq.*

Blind copies (those sent to other people without the original recipient being notified) are often noted in the file with a note attached to the file copy showing this status (for example, *bcc: Mr. Eric Smith*).

Some law firms *cc:* the client on all outgoing correspondence regarding that client's legal matters. Other firms require discretion in judging who gets copies of specific documents. Check your firm's policies for the appropriate action to take.

4.16 / Computer File Locator Information

It is necessary to identify the computer file containing a letter so that anyone else in the office can locate it for revision or modification. Your word processing department will probably have a format for file identification. If it does, follow that format carefully and consistently.

If there is no office format, make sure your file and directory names are clear enough to locate the document. The name of a directory can identify the type of documents it contains such as *ltr* for letters or *pld* for pleadings. If you store information on disks, documents can be identified by disk number, drive identification number, and directory name.

4.17 / Subsequent Page Identification

If a letter is longer than one page, the second and any succeeding pages must be numbered and identified. This information is usually provided in the top lefthand corner of the subsequent pages

- list the name of the recipient,
- the date, and
- the page number (you can either spell out the number or use a numeral).

Although it is acceptable to also include the recipient's job title or company name in the subsequent page information, this is not necessary.

Skip two to three lines before commencing the continued text for the subsequent page. Generally, skip at least one line between *each* part or element of the letter until you reach the letter's closing. Below that, leave a minimum of four lines for the signature, and more if the author's signature is large and space permits. Then put in the signer's name, skip a line, and then indicate the author's job title, and so on. Continue to skip a line between each following element.

If the vertical placement of your letter looks odd on the page, add a few lines between the date and the recipient's name and address to create a more balanced effect.

1.   **DeLost, Ernst, Miessner, Powell & Wilcox**
                                    Attorneys at Law
                                   1257 Main Street, Suite 900
                                    Los Angeles, CA 90066
                                       (310) 555-6000

2.   [DATE]

3.   Marcus Novick, Ph.D.
          Senior Engineering Advocate
          Technological Advances
          3827 Yarmouth Avenue
          Los Angeles, CA 90066

4.   Re: ABC Corp v. 123 Corp
                      Case no.: 1234567
                      Our file number: 1234.56

5.   Dear Dr. Novick:

6.   I enjoyed meeting with you today to discuss the problem-solving po-
          tential of our "newsletter" efforts. All the class members will benefit
          from timely updates on the pending litigation. I look forward to re-
          ceiving additional information about the points we discussed.

             Thank you again for your interest and help. Please do not hesitate to
          call me if you have any questions.

7.   Sincerely,

8.   DELOST, ERNST, MIESSNER, POWELL & WILCOX

                                             [SIGNATURE]

9.   Angela Shapiro
10.   Senior Paralegal
11.   ALS/wp

12.   Enclosures: none

13.   cc: William Jones, Esq.

14.   wp/alw1.ltr

15.   Marcus Novick, Ph.D.
          [DATE]
          Page 2

          [TEXT CONTINUES]

                          Form 4.1. Basic Parts of a Letter

4.18 / Types of Letter Formats

You will encounter several ways to format letters. Some are more aesthetically pleasing than others, but everyone has personal preferences. The most common letter format types include

- popular block,
- modified block, and
- full block.

These formats may sometimes be referred to by different names, but you will be able to recognize them easily.

Before finalizing a letter, consult your firm's policy manual, supervising attorney, paralegal manager, word processing supervisor, or your secretary about the letter format either preferred or mandated by the firm. Some firms employ no rigid standards for letter formats, while others require that specific guidelines be followed exactly. Remember to check your firm's policies and procedures for answers to the following questions:

- Should the letter use indented or block style?
- What typefaces can be used?
- How should the *re:* line information be presented?
- What information must be included in the salutation and closing?

Pay particular attention to the formats of those letters which you anticipate using as a standard form.

- Examine the final draft for overall placement of text on the page. A very short letter should occupy the center portion of the page. Do *not* bunch text too close to the top or the bottom.

- Be aware of spacing gaps, either because of poor hyphenation or because you are using an "insert the word" form.

- When creating a letter for use in a mass mailing, use the time saved by generic formatting to make the personalization appear genuine. This is easily accomplished using the mail merge features of most word processing programs.

Most people can quickly spot a carelessly prepared "form letter" and will not continue reading.

4.19 / Popular Block Format

In the popular block format, every line of the body of the letter starts at the left margin. Elements that are either centered or placed elsewhere on the page include:

- date,
- closing,
- firm name (if appropriate),
- signer's name, and
- signer's title.

The last four items listed above are typically indented to start somewhere between the left margin and the center of the page, although this may vary.

The date may be centered, as in Form 4.2. The other indented items all start at the same distance from the left margin. This distance will vary based on personal preference or the style rules of your firm.

In addition, clients sometimes require specific formats for letters addressed to them. Including information such as file numbers allows clients to more easily retrieve needed information or files for responding to your correspondence. For example, most insurance companies require firms to include the policy number in the *re:* lines of letters, along with a date of loss and the insured's name.

Pay very close attention to the fundamental rules for letter format and be consistent in their application. For example, if you choose to indent the first line of the letter's first paragraph, do so for each paragraph.

4.20 / Modified Block Format

The modified block format is very similar to the popular block style. But you'll find two significant differences. Both the *re:* line and the first line of each paragraph are indented, as shown in Form 4.3. People who use the modified block format prefer having the first sentence in a paragraph indented because it creates a more apparent break between thoughts.

All the sample letters used after this chapter utilize a centered letterhead and the modified block letter format. The format you choose will depend on what works best with your letterhead design, your firm's policies, and your own judgment. While you may be able to exercise discretion in selecting a letter format, remember to be consistent with your choices.

4.21 / Full Block Format

In the full block format, all letter elements found below the letterhead start at the left margin, as shown in Form 4.4. This format may be gaining popularity because it is pleasing to the eye and its simplicity makes it very easy to follow. As with other areas of style, your firm's internal policies will determine whether you have the option to format letters this way.

DeLost, Ernst, Miessner, Powell & Wilcox
Attorneys at Law
1257 Main Street, Suite 900
Los Angeles, CA 90066
(310) 555-6000

[DATE]

Marcus Novick, Ph.D.
Senior Engineering Advocate
Technological Advances
3827 Yarmouth Avenue
Los Angeles, CA 90066

Re: ABC Corp v. 123 Corp
    Case no.: 1234567
    Our file number: 1234.56

Dear Dr. Novick:

I enjoyed meeting with you today to discuss our "newsletter" efforts.
All the class members will benefit from timely updates on the pending
litigation. I look forward to receiving additional information about the
points we discussed.

Thank you again for your interest and help. Please do not hesitate to
call me if you have any questions.

                        Sincerely,

                        Angela Shapiro
                        Senior Paralegal

[AUTHOR/TYPIST]
Enclosures: none
cc: William Jones, Esq.
[DOCUMENT LOCATOR CODE]

Form 4.2. The Popular Block Letter

DeLost, Ernst, Miessner, Powell & Wilcox
Attorneys at Law
1257 Main Street, Suite 900
Los Angeles, CA 90066
(310) 555-6000

[DATE]

Marcus Novick, Ph.D.
Senior Engineering Advocate
Technological Advances
3827 Yarmouth Avenue
Los Angeles, CA 90066

    Re: ABC Corp v. 123 Corp
       Case no.: 1234567
       <u>Our file number: 1234.56</u>

Dear Dr. Novick:

  I enjoyed meeting with you today to discuss our "newsletter" efforts.
All the class members will benefit from timely updates on the pending
litigation. I look forward to receiving additional information about the
points we discussed.

  Thank you again for your interest and help. Please do not hesitate to
call me if you have any questions.

       Sincerely,

       Angela Shapiro
       Senior Paralegal

[AUTHOR/TYPIST]
Enclosures: none
cc: William Jones, Esq.
[DOCUMENT LOCATOR CODE]

Form 4.3. The Modified Block Letter

DeLost, Ernst, Miessner, Powell & Wilcox
Attorneys at Law
1257 Main Street, Suite 900
Los Angeles, CA 90066
(310) 555-6000

[DATE]

Marcus Novick, Ph.D.
Senior Engineering Advocate
Technological Advances
3827 Yarmouth Avenue
Los Angeles, CA 90066

      Re: ABC Corp v. 123 Corp
         Case no.: 1234567
         Our file number: 1234.56

Dear Dr. Novick:

I enjoyed meeting with you today to discuss our "newsletter" efforts.
All the class members will benefit from timely updates on the pending
litigation. I look forward to receiving additional information about the
points we discussed.

Thank you again for your interest and help. Please do not hesitate to
call me if you have any questions.

Sincerely,

Angela Shapiro
Senior Paralegal

[AUTHOR/TYPIST]
Enclosures: none
cc: William Jones, Esq.
[DOCUMENT LOCATOR CODE]

Form 4.4. The Full Block Letter

End Notes

[1]The National Association of Legal Assistants, Inc., *NALA Manual for Legal Assistants,* §1.0823 (2d ed. 1992).
[2]Id., §1.0823(a).
[3]Id., §1.0823(d).

F*ive*

MEMOS AND REPORTS

5.1 / How Memos Are Used

5.2 / Formal and Informal Memos

Form 5.1. Basic Interoffice Memo Structure

5.3 / Effective Presentation of Memo Content

5.4 / Reports to Supervising Attorneys and Managers

5.5 / Requests for Information, Status Reports, and Cover Memo

Form 5.2. Forms Supply Request Memo

Form 5.3. Reminder Memo for Case Status Reports

Form 5.4. Effective Use of Humor in Requesting Information

Form 5.5. Short Form Assignments Status Report

Form 5.6. Detailed Assignments Status Report

Form 5.7. Report of Witness Location Efforts

Form 5.8. Cover Memo with Accompanying Reports

5.6 / Using Memos to Convey Complex Information

Form 5.9. Report Analyzing Possible Document Coding Project

5.1 / How Memos Are Used

Memoranda (the plural form of memorand*um*) are more commonly and simply referred to as *memos*. Contrary to popular belief, their use is not limited to interoffice communications. Memos can supplement or even become reports to clients and other outside parties. The size of memos can vary from a one-line information request to a multiple-page report. In addition to requesting or transmitting information and instructions, a file memo can be used to document continuing progress and updated information.

Memos, like letters, are permanent and lasting evidence of an event or activity. The guidelines for writing memos are virtually the same as those you employ for letter writing. This is particularly important to remember when preparing a memorandum report that may travel outside the office.

Of course, interoffice memos are not the only way you can communicate with others in your firm. Face-to-face communication will work much better in some instances. However, memos can be a very effective medium when used appropriately.

5.2 / Formal and Informal Memos

The most informal type of memo is one that is handwritten. For example, when you are running out of supplies, you can quickly note down the date, the name of the person to whom the request is addressed, the list of supplies you need, and your signature. This streamlined method of communication can be acceptable in this situation.

On the other hand, if you are writing a report to document an event or writing a memo to an attorney, you need to be more formal. This is true even on those rare occasions when such information may be handwritten due to urgency. For example, if the attorney is in a deposition and needs the information *now,* you might write this memo by hand, but maintain a degree of formality by using a memo form such as the one found in Form 5.1.

The extra time taken to prepare each memo in an appropriate, formal style and level of detail will ultimately save everyone extra work. A memo reporting on a meeting or hearing for the supervising attorney's immediate review will often be sent directly to the client. If that initial memo was not prepared properly, you would have to do a separate report for the client. Avoid double work by taking more care in the first place. Often, file memos (or "memos to the file") will be used in addition to other reports.

Minimally the memo form should include the following information: *To, From, Date,* and *re:* lines. Additional lines of information might be included for the firm's file number, the name of the case or client, or other identifying facts to orient the reader to the subject.

5.3 / Effective Presentation of Memo Content

Not only should a memo adhere to the basic rules of effective letter writing (*see* Chapter 1 for a complete discussion), it also should quickly attract the reader's interest. Otherwise, memos tend to be forgotten or lost on people's desks. Of course, if the initial memo did not prompt the hoped-for response, additional memos can be sent as reminders, but soon, all you're doing is creating a paper nightmare.

Memos generated inside an organization sometimes receive less attention than letters received from outside sources. Even so, memos can be a key to

MEMORANDUM

To: [ATTORNEY]

From: [PARALEGAL]

Date: [DATE]

Re: [SPECIFY IDENTIFYING INFORMATION]

   I am writing this memo in response to your request for information about....

Form 5.1. Basic Interoffice Memo Structure

effective in-house communications. In law firms, memos are frequently used to document particular occurrences for the file, and help to create the historical record of events.

Get the reader interested enough to encourage reading the entire document. Be clear, organized, and spare in your use of words. This approach will help maintain the reader's attention throughout the memo.

- Use the first line to gain the reader's interest.
- Sustain the interest by communicating in a lively way. Don't be afraid to be creative to make your point.
- State your facts in order of *importance,* not necessarily in chronological order.
- Get to the point and clearly write what you need the reader to know.
- Stop writing once you say all you need to say.

5.4 / Reports to Supervising Attorneys and Managers

You will frequently need to produce reports for your supervising attorneys or paralegal managers. These reports in the form of memos may address any number of topics, but the most common will detail information about

- pending projects and assignments,
- answers to particular questions,
- time estimates for completing projects, and
- analysis of documents, case files, or other matters.

These types of information and activity reports should be reported using a memo form, provided on a timely basis, and include all information available at the time the report is written. If you do not have all the information you need to respond or report completely, say so in your report. Keep in mind the following factors as you write:

- Reports are important to the person requesting them, no matter how mundane or bothersome they may seem to you.
- Be thorough in your reply without becoming repetitious.
- Show interest and enthusiasm.
- Use each report-writing opportunity to show off your writing, analysis, and organization skills.

Timely report writing is one measure of your performance. Even if the quality of your reports is stellar, that fact will be obscured if the reports are late.

5.5 / Requests for Information, Status Reports, and Cover Memos

The forms supply request found in Form 5.2 is a very simple memo, but two features should be highlighted. Note that this memo thanks the recipient for complying with the author's request in advance. This memo is also very specific in the request it makes. The required deed forms are precisely identified. When asking for specific items (like forms), it is *not* good practice to assume that the reader will know exactly what you want.

A great example of a memo requesting and outlining requirements for completing status reports is found in Form 5.3. While offering help, it firmly states an upcoming deadline and the need to comply with this deadline. This message has a tongue-in-cheek quality that no doubt diffused some of the tension surrounding this issue. Also note the author's use of underlining to attract attention to important information.

A very good illustration of how humor can be used effectively is Form 5.4. This is a follow-up memo to the earlier status report request found in Form 5.3. Notice that the writer doesn't wait for the body of the memo to make a point. Instead, she strikes out with a real attention grabber on the *re:* line.

Form 5.5 shows a short form report listing the basic elements of certain assignments. It was written in response to a request for specific information. Form 5.6 is a portion of a status report using a prescribed format that can vary from firm to firm or according to the supervising attorney's needs.

There will be times when you need to give a chronological detailed description of your actions on a particular assignment. It is important to include every detail. Remember that the person requesting the information has a reason for asking, which may not be clear to you. Form 5.7 is an example of this kind of report. Note how deliberately specific the memo is in offering the requested information in a step-by-step chronicle.

From time to time, you may be asked to prepare a cover memo (or transmittal memo), which summarizes certain information or documents. In some cases, the cover memo will be a summary of the content of attached documents. If so, readers of your cover memo may *never* read the underlying documents and rely solely on your *summary*.

On the other hand, the cover memo may provide information relevant to the attached documents but not extracted from them. Form 5.8 shows an example of the latter type of cover memo.

All cover memos should be clear, accurate, and concise. Remember that your observations and suggestions, in addition to required reports, can be very helpful to your firm.

5.6 / Using Memos to Convey Complex Information

Obviously memos are used to request information, documents, or action. But it is important to remember that memos are used to convey a substantial amount of complex information that is crucial for effective workload management.

MEMORANDUM

To: [NAME]

From: [PARALEGAL]

Date: [DATE]

Re: Real Estate Forms

Here is a list of forms that we need for the Real Estate Department form files:

Grant Deed—Exemptions from Documentary Transfer Tax

Deed of Partial Reconveyance

Deed of Full Reconveyance

Jurats—Joint Venture

Power of Attorney

Substitution of Trustee under Deed of Trust

I usually order all forms from [NAME] Title Company; however, these particular forms are not on their list of available forms. Do you have any idea where I can order them?

I'm trying to keep the form file well stocked because practically everyone with the firm uses these files. I would appreciate any help you can give me.

Form 5.2. Forms Supply Request Memo

MEMORANDUM

To: Litigation Associates

From: Angela Shapiro, Senior Paralegal

Date: [DATE]

Re: <u>Litigation Case Status Reports for July 16–31</u>

Yes, it's that time again, the occasion you all look forward to every two weeks. It's time for litigation case status reports for the period of [DATE]. I'd like to receive <u>all reports by [DATE]</u>, so the information provided to the Litigation Assignments Committee is, at least, somewhat timely.

I'm happy to report a significant increase in the number of people providing status reports since my initial request. Only four people sent in reports for [DATE]. But a grand total of ten—count 'em ten—people sent in reports for [DATE]. Admittedly, only two of those reports were received before [DATE] (the last one straggled in on [DATE]), but it's the thought that counts.

I do appreciate the effort shown by the two associates who recently sent me reports for the [DATE] period. But please keep in mind that the Committee is <u>not</u> interested so much in <u>historical information</u> as it is in information about your <u>current workload</u>.

I'm also working on the suggestions you offered to make this an easier process. I'm looking into creating a shorter, pre-printed form, that could be accessed in the computer, with each person's active cases. This is a good idea.

Meanwhile, however, <u>PLEASE RETURN YOUR [DATE] REPORT TO ME BY [DATE].</u>

Form 5.3. Reminder Memo for Case Status Reports

MEMORANDUM

To: Litigation Associates

From: Angela Shapiro, Senior Paralegal

Date: [DATE]

Re: <u>So, You Forgot to Send in Your Litigation Case Status</u>
             <u>Report</u>

Well, I'm sure that everyone actually completed their status reports,
but simply forgot to send in them in, right? I am beginning to wonder if
the upward trend I detected earlier was simply coincidental, however.

Be that as it may, here's another opportunity to make up for your lost
or totally forgotten August reports. IT'S TIME TO SEND IN YOUR REPORTS
COVERING [DATE] TO [DATE]. <u>The cut-off date is [DATE]</u>.

I've noticed that some of you are still using the <u>old</u> form. You can
tell if you have an old report form if:

(1)   you haven't sent in a report in ages, and are simply using the
         dusty forms your secretary found in the back of a file draw-
         er, or

(2)   the form has a category for estimating your time requirements
         for the <u>next 90 days</u>.

If you've been using this form, please <u>stop</u>. The <u>future 90-day report-</u>
<u>ing requirement was dropped some time ago</u>.

Since I'm not sure who still has copies of the old report, I've attached a <u>current</u> version of the form for your use. Please note that this
form now has a place for listing <u>which time period is covered</u> by the
report. There is usually a substantial overlap between current reports
and those from the previous period. I added this category so I could
tell them apart. Those of you requesting computer reports recently
should have received this current version. Enjoy!

Form 5.4. Effective Use of Humor in Requesting Information

MEMORANDUM

To: Angela Shapiro, Senior Paralegal

From: Mark C. Williams

Date: [DATE]

Re: Assignments Information Requested

I am currently working full time on the following assignments:

(1)   *Smith v. Jones:* Assembling documents designated by the client
       and others. Office services is doing the actual pulling and
       copying.

(2)   *Johnson v. ABC Company:* Gathering documents for Deanna De-
       Lost's review for our Second Designation, which are due on
       [DATE].

       Also preparing a list of Designations, indicating information
       about when they were received and when objections must be
       filed.

(3)   *Firm's Work-Product Database:* This on-going computer project
       is proceeding on schedule. We should have several categories
       of documents, including Motions for Summary Judgment, loaded
       into the database by next month.

Form 5.5. Short Form Assignments Status Report

MEMORANDUM

To: Angela Shapiro, Senior Paralegal

From: Mark C. Williams

Date: [DATE]

Re: Case Status Report

I. Matters on which I am currently working:

Client & Matter	Supervising Attorney	Description of Project	Estimated hours next 2 weeks	Estimated hours to complete
[FILE NUMBER & NAME]	W. Jones	Updating Corporate Minute Book	5	10-15
[FILE NUMBER & NAME]	W. Jones	Follow up on Corporate Formation	5-7	10-12
[FILE NUMBER & NAME]	W. Jones	Organization of Corporate Files—5 Corps	8	ongoing

II. Matters I anticipate working on in the next 30 days:

Client & Matter	Supervising Attorney	Description of Project	Estimated hours to complete
[FILE NUMBER & NAME]	S. Beacham	Follow up on Corporate Formation	10-14
[FILE NUMBER & NAME]	W. Jones	Acquisition of bond for insurance adjuster	5

Form 5.6. Detailed Assignments Status Report

III. Comments:

How many hours are on your time sheet for the last two weeks?

    Billable   _____

    Nonbillable   _____

    TOTAL   _____

How has your workload been for the last two weeks?

    Too heavy   _____

    Just right   _____

    Too light   _____

Additional comments: _____

_____

_____

_____

_____

Form 5.6. Detailed Assignments Status Report *(Continued)*

MEMORANDUM

To: Anthony Wilcox, Esq./FILE

From: Sandra Wilson, Paralegal

Date: [DATE]

Re: Carl Baker Matter

I tried to contact Mr. Baker by phone countless times during the week of [DATE]. I left two messages on his answering machine, but he did not return my calls. While I was out of the office, my secretary reached his answering machine on three separate occasions. On the third attempt, she concluded that the answering machine appeared full. When I returned on [DATE], I tried five more times to contact the witness and received a "busy" signal each time.

Today, at approximately 1:30 P.M., Mr. Baker answered his phone "hello." I identified myself as a paralegal and asked if we could set up a mutually agreeable time in which to effect service of the subpoena for the deposition on [DATE].

He explained that he had just returned from out of town and was about to leave for [LOCATION] when I called. He said that he would return on the [DATE]. Approximately five minutes later, my secretary dialed Mr. Baker's number and reached his answering machine.

During my conversation with the witness, he reported that his business address was [ADDRESS].

This report concludes my efforts to locate this individual. It appears to me the deposition date will not work out with this witness. In view of the scheduling problem which exists, please advise as to further action.

Form 5.7. Report of Witness Location Efforts

MEMORANDUM

To: [NAME]

From: [PARALEGAL]

Date: [DATE]

Re: <u>Litigation Case Status Reports</u>

Enclosed are copies of 18 litigation case status reports for the current reporting period. I'm assuming this very low total is primarily due to the holidays. It is likely a few more reports will arrive later this week.

Also enclosed for your review is a summary report and a checklist of associates providing reports. Please note the [OTHER LOCATION OF FIRM'S OFFICES] associates are no longer listed. Of course, those associates recently voted into the partnership have also been deleted. (Several of them responded to my congratulations by saying, "Thank God I don't have to do those damned reports anymore!")

The following associates have not provided reports despite repeated reminders sent to their secretaries:

[ASSOCIATE'S NAME]
[ASSOCIATE'S NAME]
[ASSOCIATE'S NAME]
[ASSOCIATE'S NAME]
[ASSOCIATE'S NAME]
[ASSOCIATE'S NAME]
[ASSOCIATE'S NAME]
[ASSOCIATE'S NAME]

However, I am happy to report that [ASSOCIATE'S NAME] has provided a report for the first time since August.

Form 5.8. Cover Memo with Accompanying Reports

Form 5.9 is a portion of a memo that assesses the need to create a computerized database for documents pertaining to a specific case. It summarizes all the relevant data, weighs the pros and cons of the proposed project, and estimates the effort and costs involved. It is a very good example of a complete, clear, and concise presentation of a potentially confusing subject.

When writing memos of this nature, it is a good idea to test a draft of your material on a couple of readers before sending out your final version. As you go through this exercise a number of times, you may develop a skill for accurately predicting your recipients' responses.

MEMORANDUM

To: [SUPERVISING ATTORNEY]   cc: [PARTNER]

From: [PARALEGAL]   [PARTNER]

Date: [DATE MEMO SENT]

Re: [CASE NAME]— Computerized Retrieval of Produced Documents

As you know, there are several ways to organize documents produced in litigation. Documents can be maintained:

- in the order in which they were produced,

- in chronological order, or

- arranged by some key feature, as in this case, the tract and lot number of the houses involved.

Any of these organizational methods can be handled by hard-copy filing and retrieval.

If the third approach mentioned above is selected, documents can be segregated by the particular tract/lot numbers referenced in each document. Copies of the appropriate documents can be filed in folders for each specific tract/lot. Before separating the documents into their respective folders number them first. This way, the order of production (if this is important) can easily be determined by the range of numbers used for each batch of produced documents.

You may also wish to create a separate copy set of all documents in chronological order. In this case, the documents are separated into tract and lot number and can be maintained in chronological order within each folder.

While certainly workable, there are some problems with this system. First, in the file drawer I reviewed, I noticed several documents with references to multiple tract and lot numbers. (There was one type of document in particular that listed approximately 20 tract/lot combinations.) Assuming this pattern continues, all multiple listing documents will have to be copied first, in an amount equal to the tract/lots listed before being placed in the separate tract/lot folders. These documents should probably be separated from the rest of the document population at the time of review for later copying and filing.

Second, after the folders of documents are created, maintaining the documents in the correct folder and chronological order will be fairly time consuming. Depending on how often specific documents must be pulled from the folders (as opposed to copying the entire folder), the need for frequent refiling can present opportunities for errors. Misfiled documents are, in effect, lost documents.

Form 5.9. Report Analyzing Possible Document Coding Project

Third, having only folders of similar tract/lot numbered documents doesn't allow for a review of particular types of documents or information across tract and lot numbers. For example, you may be interested in the frequency of complaints or which repair companies were used most often. With the hard-copy approach, you can retrieve those documents only by referring to specific tract/lots with any ease.

On the other hand, you could accomplish all the above (maintain order of production, chronological order, and tract/lot number order) by creating a document retrieval database. The database can be created by:

- deciding on the specific categories of information needed:

    - date of document,
    - production number of document,
    - tract and lot numbers, and
    - document type, etc.

- selecting pertinent information from each produced document (perhaps 10 to 12 information fields), and

- entering that information into a database structure.

With a database approach, you can search across documents for information. In addition, you can note in the computer record when the document was pulled for depositions or withheld due to privilege. Then you don't have to create separate lists to refer to if only a hard-copy/folder approach is used. The hard copies of the documents selected via the computer search can be pulled and copied. Since the actual hard-copy documents are maintained in number order, the likelihood of misfiling documents is decreased.

There are two key assumptions to determine when estimating the cost of the database. The estimates will not be accurate if any of the assumptions are wrong. The two key assumptions are:

(a)   the number of pages per document (which determines the total documents in the document population), and

(b)   the speed at which the documents can be coded.

I've outlined some general calculations to use in determining the cost of creating a computer database for our firm.

(1)   The document population consists of 4 file drawers of documents.

(2)   In my experience, each full file drawer usually contains the equivalent of 2 bankers' boxes of documents. Four file drawers, then, is equivalent to 8 boxes of documents.

(3)   Each banker's box can hold approximately 2,000 pages of documents. Eight boxes of documents will contain 16,000 pages....

Form 5.9. Report Analyzing Possible Document Coding Project *(Continued)*

ADMINISTRATIVE LETTERS

6.1 / Importance of Administrative Duties

6.2 / Finding Vendors

6.3 / Vendor Requests for Proposal (RFP)
    Form 6.1. Request for Proposal to Vendor

6.4 / Complaint Letters
    Form 6.2. Complaint Letter

6.5 / Letters Denying Payment
    Form 6.3. Denial of Payment

6.6 / Letters Requesting Payment
    Form 6.4. Request for Payment from Opposing
    Counsel

6.7 / Letters of Appreciation
    Form 6.5. Short Letter of Appreciation to Vendor
    Form 6.6. Letter of Appreciation to Vendor

6.8 / Letters to Professional Colleagues
    Form 6.7. Response to a Survey Request
    Form 6.8. Notice and Invitation to Association
    Meeting

6.1 / Importance of Administrative Duties

Work assignments that are administrative in nature are both necessary and important to a firm, even though most such responsibilities are not billable on an hourly basis to clients. Even so, handling administrative assignments can provide you with an opportunity to learn a wide variety of information about law firm management and structure. These assignments can also help develop management skills that may ultimately gain you more upward mobility.

Paralegals often deal with vital administrative issues such as working with outside service providers. They may also become involved in bill collection efforts and related issues. This chapter discusses letters that might be written in connection with the following activities:

- locating appropriate vendors,
- complaint letters,
- letters of appreciation,
- letters regarding payment, and
- letters to professional colleagues.

In addition, many legal assistants become involved in the screening of potential support staff. You will find an extensive discussion about recruiting staff and other employment matters in Chapter 7.

6.2 / Finding Vendors

Companies that provide specialized legal services—such as court reporters to transcribe depositions—are chosen on the basis of their ability to meet the firm's needs at an acceptable price. It may be your job to find the best vendor for a specific situation in which your firm needs outside support. Of course, research is the first step in selecting the vendor that will do the best job. However, before you can begin interviewing vendors, you will need to know:

- what exactly does your firm need, and
- if possible, what is the budget for the project?

You can find the right product or service supplier more effectively by understanding the precise needs of a particular project. It is not always possible to determine exact requirements at the outset of a project, and circumstances may change. As a result, it is wise to collect all available information a vendor may offer. Once you know what you are looking for, you should do the following:

- Compile a list of companies that provide the particular service you want. Trade journals, directories, and the firm's records are great sources of information.
- Obtain initial information from each company over the phone or by letter. Ask for information about the services provided by the vendor, and the prices for those services.
- If time permits, send letters outlining your specific requirements to each vendor with a request for a bid.

Your research will show the scope of services each company provides and bring you up to date on any new use of technology or other information germane to your firm's need for services. For example, court reporting companies now typically include software with transcripts to aid in-house production of deposition summaries and abstracts for trial. Temporary personnel services may not only provide temporary document clerks and paralegals but may also offer investigative services and exhibit coding and copying.

6.3 / Vendor Requests for Proposal (RFP)

Requests for Proposal (RFP) from vendors provide a thorough, if time-consuming, way to select vendors for the services you need. When you are preparing requests for proposals, keep the following points in mind:

- Tell the vendor your requirements and your budget.
- Be specific in asking for the information you want.
- Request a specific deadline for a response.
- Always leave the door open for additional information.

You will find a sample request for proposal (RFP) in Form 6.1.

It can only help you and the vendor if you are up front about your requirements and budget limits. This will assist the vendor in determining whether it can provide the services you need within your required budget. It will also help to eliminate any possibility of wasted time.

Be specific when asking for the information you want. Most vendors hesitate to discuss costs until they feel you are likely to use *their* services. If you don't ask for prices, you may receive only an overview about the company and its services. Specify a reasonable deadline for a response, and include a telephone number where you can be reached. The vendor may require additional information from you to provide an accurate bid.

If the ultimate decision-maker will be someone other than you, make that clear in your letter. Otherwise, it will be assumed that you are the contact for a decision.

Keep in mind that a sophisticated portfolio of a company's services does not necessarily mean that it is the best service provider for you. A wonderful company may lack a glamorous presentation because it gets so much business by word of mouth, due to its demonstrated superior service.

If you haven't received a response and the deadline is approaching, call the vendor to see if that company intends to bid. However, you should think about whether you really want to do work with a vendor who is not responsive from the outset.

DeLost, Ernst, Miessner, Powell & Wilcox
Attorneys at Law
1257 Main Street, Suite 900
Los Angeles, CA 90066
(310) 555-6000

[DATE]

Paragon Court Reporters
2741 First Street, Suite 341
Alameda, CA 91300

    Re: <u>Request for Proposal</u>

Dear Account Representative:

Our office represents a client in an action that is currently set for
trial on [DATE] in the [COURT NAME AND LOCATION]. It will be necessary
to depose several individuals in the states of [NAMES OF STATES] during
the period of [SPECIFY TIME PERIOD].

Because of the limited time period, we will need to establish deposition rooms in those states and coordinate attendance of counsel from
our office. We will also need an ample amount of document coding services at the depositions. Please let me know if you will be able to ful-
fill these requirements.

Also, please include information about any additional services you may
offer, such as videotaping. At this time, I am waiting for an estimate
on the exhibit documentation and will provide you with that information
for you to include in your estimate.

Please submit your proposal in writing, including your price estimates
for each task, on or before [DATE]. Responses which do not include the
specific information requested will not be considered. Thank you for
your time.

             Sincerely,

             Angela Shapiro
             Senior Paralegal

[AUTHOR/TYPIST]
[DOCUMENT LOCATOR CODE]

Form 6.1. Request for Proposal to Vendor

6.4 / Complaint Letters

Today, the best advertising comes from word of mouth. The last thing any business can afford is to have someone "advertise" a problem with their company. However, you will encounter situations that warrant writing a letter of complaint. Generally, complaint letters serve two purposes:

- They are the appropriate vehicle to help get your complaint rectified.

- They help all companies become aware of problems or inconsistencies in their business.

More and more businesses today seek to excel in the quality of service or product they provide. These companies will appreciate a clear statement of the facts so that any deficiencies can be corrected promptly. If you do not communicate your dissatisfaction, the problem may never be apparent, and an otherwise stable business relationship may slowly slip away.

According to *Effective Letters in Business,* complaint letters typically contain four elements.

- An explanation of what is wrong, including specific facts to help the reader understand the problem.

- A statement that explains the loss or inconvenience that resulted.

- An attempt to motivate action by appealing to the recipient's sense of fair play, honesty, or pride. Don't threaten loss of business at the first error.

- An explanation of what you need or want in order to rectify the situation.[1]

Introduce yourself, describe the problem and then ask for the solution you think is fair.

Without being accusing, be specific about the cause of your complaint and how any errors or shortcomings can be rectified. As with all forms of correspondence, it is important to remember the general rules of effective letter writing, like keeping the recipient in mind. (*See* Chapter 1 for a thorough discussion of these rules.) After all, how would you respond if the tables were turned, and you were on the receiving end of a nasty letter that does not clearly discuss the problem at hand?

Form 6.2 contains all the appropriate elements of a complaint letter, along with a request for continuing goodwill. It seems that both parties are at fault: one for an employee's belligerent behavior and the other for lack of diligence in locating information. While the explanation *is* lengthy, it does state the facts clearly and calmly in an honest and open manner.

DeLost, Ernst, Miessner, Powell & Wilcox
Attorneys at Law
1257 Main Street, Suite 900
Los Angeles, CA 90066
(310) 555-6000

[DATE]

Priscilla Courtwright
Accounting Administrator
Paragon Court Reporters
2741 First Street, Suite 341
Alameda, CA 91300

PERSONAL AND CONFIDENTIAL

Dear Ms. Courtwright:

Since I am the paralegal supervisor for our firm, I generally do not handle accounting matters for our office. However, I became involved in this matter when I was informed that one of your employees, Janet Smith, had harassed our receptionist, several secretaries, and three paralegals in my department. I was told that she "threatened their lives" over a misplaced file from your office.

When I first spoke to Janet on the telephone, I calmly asked her to tell what prompted this complaint from my staff. She immediately said that she would leave a message with me so I could get in touch with the appropriate person. I calmly explained to her that I *was* the appropriate person.

I then told her I felt her previous outbursts were out of line, based upon the situation. I also said I would do everything in my power to locate her missing file and return it to her.

I mentioned that her company was not on our firm's approved vendor list. This means that no tracking system is in place to locate missing documents, files, tapes, etc.

I explained that there was also a problem with our computer system. Not only had we recently moved our offices, but at that time, I was preparing to leave for vacation. However, I made it clear I would do everything in my power to locate her case file and call her as soon as we found it.

Janet telephoned early the next day and demanded that I give her the status of the search. I told her I had placed a "request for information" through our accounting department with a "super expedite" request. I said I would call her as soon as I had any information.

Janet called back a few moments later. In a rude tone (again), she demanded to know who she needed to speak with in order to find "my (expletive) file."

Form 6.2. Complaint Letter

Priscilla Courtwright
[DATE]
Page 2

Ms. Courtwright, I handle many matters on behalf of this office and quite frankly I have never encountered such a rude individual! It is not our office policy to allow anyone—for any reason—to raise their voice to a client, regardless of the situation. Our office strives to build long-lasting relationships with our vendors to assure a quality work for our clients. In this respect, I believe Janet acted with a severe lack of judgment.

I respectfully request that Janet not call our office again. Her method of communication, especially in a situation as trivial as this one, is harassing, disruptive, and disturbing to our personnel. I believe she feels that what she is doing is perfectly acceptable, and that she intends to continue this behavior.

Finally, once I have a chance to evaluate your company's services with those on our approved vendor list, I would like to get together to discuss a working arrangement. In the meantime, I'd like to maintain our relationship. Please give me a call so we can discuss a mutually acceptable remedy.

In my effort to appease your office, I asked my assistant manager, Robert Rogers, to conduct the file search while I'm away. The search began last week and should bring results in a few days. I would appreciate hearing from you when I get back, or I will contact your offices to discuss this matter further.

Sincerely,

Angela Shapiro
Senior Paralegal

[AUTHOR/TYPIST]
cc: Bob Rogers
[DOCUMENT LOCATOR CODE]

Form 6.2. Complaint Letter *(Continued)*

6.5 / Letters Denying Payment

Sometimes, you may need to *deny* payment for service or supplies. For example, the product or service received may not have been to your specifications. In such cases, particularly when the item at issue concerns services, restitution by the vendor may be impossible. Anytime you are in the position of denying payment, it is a delicate situation that should be handled carefully.

The tone employed in such a letter is critical. You won't want to point the finger of blame for something that may have been just an honest mistake. And even if the problem is more serious, you may not want to destroy the business relationship.

- Identify the job or project, along with the relevant facts.
- Clearly state that you are not making payment.
- Briefly explain the reason.

The sample letter in Form 6.3 may be helpful in preparing this type of correspondence. Notice how it follows the suggestions given above for writing a denial of payment letter.

It is usually best to resolve the issue by telephone and then send a letter as confirmation. Always keep a copy of the letter with the original billing statement. Be sure to also send the firm's accounting department a copy of your letter, so they won't pay the statement in error a few months later.

6.6 / Letters Requesting Payment

You may be asked to *request* payment from a vendor, client, or opposing counsel. In this case, it is most important to address this request to the appropriate individual: the person who can authorize payment and preferably who will sign the check. You should call in advance to confirm the name of that person.

When requesting payment from *a client,* always have the draft letter approved by at least two partners and the person who assigned this task to you. The goodwill of the attorney–client relationship is paramount, regardless of the account situation. It is likely that one of these three people will tell you not to send the request and may handle the request-for-payment situation another way.

Frequently, a request for payment involves either the splitting of legal costs or costs to be paid by the prevailing or losing party. A simple request for payment to opposing counsel is shown in Form 6.4. You should follow up on this type of letter with a telephone call in three days.

(You will find sample letters to ask for payments that become due at the end of trial in Chapter 8. In addition, Chapter 17 contains some excellent letters for use in collecting judgments and fines.)

DeLost, Ernst, Miessner, Powell & Wilcox
Attorneys at Law
1257 Main Street, Suite 900
Los Angeles, CA 90066
(310) 555-6000

[DATE]

Joyce Palmer
Paralegals for Projects
1936 Tamarach Road
Santa Monica, CA 90402

Re: *Morrison v. Ferber* Trial Documents

Dear Ms. Palmer:

As I mentioned earlier this morning, I received [NAME]'s time sheet
on [DATE] for time worked on [DATES]. This is over two months after the
cut-off date for approval of time sheets.

Per our agreement about the management of this project, I cannot approve this extremely late claim for time worked. As a result, I will
not be processing this invoice for payment.

I hope that this mistake will not occur again, because I do value our
working relationship. If you have any questions, feel free to contact
me at [PHONE].

Thank you,

Angela Shapiro
Senior Paralegal

[AUTHOR/LIST]
cc: Accounting/Laura
[DOCUMENT LOCATOR FILE]

Form 6.3. Denial of Payment

If the response to your letter requesting payment evades the issue, you may have to seek assistance from the firm's accounting department. The party you initially contacted may have no intention of paying. If so, you can spend much time and effort trying to collect, and you still may not succeed. Send just one demand letter and make no more than two follow-up calls before referring this account to the appropriate person in the firm who handles collections.

6.7 / Letters of Appreciation

Occasionally, you are so impressed with a vendor that you want to acknowledge that company's stellar performance. A letter of appreciation is a great way to nurture relationships of superior quality. Whether you are trying to build a new business relationship or maintain a longstanding one, this type of letter is very simple to draft.

- state your opinion,
- explain the particular situation, then
- extend your thanks.

Successful letters of appreciation are brief, simple, and sincere. Forms 6-5 and 6-6 show two different versions of such letters.

6.8 / Letters to Professional Colleagues

Most legal assistants will frequently find occasions to write letters to—and respond to inquiries from—colleagues and professional organizations. Since corresponding with colleagues can add to your network of professional contacts, write these letters with care. When you have received correspondence, reply promptly, especially if you are asked for information.

Surveys are one type of information request that merits prompt attention. See Form 6.7 for a sample letter which replies to a questionnaire. Notice that this letter also requests a copy of the survey results once they have been compiled (a very good idea).

Respond to requests for information even if you find that you cannot supply what has been requested. You may not have the time, or you may have nothing to contribute, particularly if the information requested falls outside your specialty area. In these cases, write a letter stating the reason you cannot respond. *Never* just ignore correspondence. After all, you don't want to give your colleagues a bad impression.

New paralegals interested in making professional contacts are often advised to join their local paralegal association.[2] If you get involved with an association, you may need to send association-related correspondence, such

DeLost, Ernst, Miessner, Powell & Wilcox
Attorneys at Law
1257 Main Street, Suite 900
Los Angeles, CA 90066
(310) 555-6000

[DATE]

Andrew S. Mitchell
Attorney at Law
3356 Manhattan Boulevard
Hermosa Beach, CA 04471

          Re: <u>Omsley v. Bartok</u>

Dear Dr. Mitchell:

  Enclosed is the original affidavit of court costs for the *Omsley v. Bartok* case that was settled recently. We are now requesting your client's reimbursement of these costs.

  Make the check for these costs payable to [NAME], in the amount of $[AMOUNT], at your earliest possible convenience.

  Thank you for your prompt attention to this matter. If you have any questions, please feel free to call.

                         Sincerely,

                         Scott Powell, Esq.
[AUTHOR/TYPIST]
Enclosures: affidavit
[DOCUMENT LOCATOR CODE]

Form 6.4. Request for Payment from Opposing Counsel

DeLost, Ernst, Miessner, Powell & Wilcox
Attorneys at Law
1257 Main Street, Suite 900
Los Angeles, CA 90066
(310) 555-6000

[DATE]

Richard Farrell
Corporate Bank
875 East Robinson Road
Los Angeles, CA 90068

        Re: <u>GHL Industries v. Adamston Corp.</u>

Dear Mr. Farrell:

   I just wanted to take a moment and thank you for your prompt assistance in resolving those "Problem Transmittals."

   Your commitment to a quick resolution of these issues has allowed us
to be equally expedient in answering the vendor's questions. [NAME] has
kept me well informed on this and expressed her total satisfaction in
working these issues out with you.

   Again, thank you for your assistance.

                              Sincerely,

                              Mark C. Williams
                              Legal Assistant
[AUTHOR/TYPIST]
[DOCUMENT LOCATOR CODE]

Form 6.5. Short Letter of Appreciation to Vendor

DeLost, Ernst, Miessner, Powell & Wilcox
Attorneys at Law
1257 Main Street, Suite 900
Los Angeles, CA 90066
(310) 555-6000

[DATE]

Richard Farrell
Corporate Bank
875 East Robinson Road
Los Angeles, CA 90068

Re: <u>Congratulations on a job well done!</u>

Dear Mr. Farrell:

I want to let you know about our success so far with the bank searches provided by your company, [NAME OF COMPANY]. I have never been more
satisfied than I have been with you and your staff. Even though our request was limited with respect to [SPECIFIC ENTITY NAME], you and your
staff did a great job in determining the current status of the company, its principal, and business ventures.

I would like to thank everyone who assisted our company in the location of assets to offset our judgments. In these difficult times of
charge-offs and bankruptcies, it's good to know that your company is
there to help from coast to coast and abroad. Your staff has helped make
the difference in recoveries of judgments.

If I can be of assistance, please feel free to contact me.

Sincerely,

Paul Ernst, Esq.

[AUTHOR/TYPIST]
[DOCUMENT LOCATOR CODE]

Form 6.6. Letter of Appreciation to Vendor

as notices of meetings scheduled by the organization. Form 6.8 illustrates a sample meeting notice and invitation.

The guidance found in *Letters for All Occasions* outlines the key attributes that help create effective invitations:

- make the notice clear by including the date, time, and purpose;

- make sure that the invitation's content is gracious and pleasing; and

- let recipients know what is expected of them and what they can expect.[3]

It helps to personalize each letter for people on a mailing list by using the mail-merge features of word processing programs.

As with other forms of correspondence, if you receive a notice of a meeting or other gathering, it is important to respond, whether or not you plan to attend this particular function. Unanswered correspondence creates an impression of inefficiency, and this is *not* how you want to be perceived.

End Notes

[1]Robert L. Shurter and Donald J. Leonard, *Effective Letters in Business*, p. 105 (1984).

[2]There are two national professional groups for practicing paralegals: the National Association of Legal Assistants (NALA), and the National Federation for Paralegal Associations (NFPA). Most states have at least one local paralegal association, and large states may have three or four throughout the state, often found in the largest cities.

[3]Alfred Stuart Myers, *Letters for All Occasions*, p. 73 (1993).

DeLost, Ernst, Miessner, Powell & Wilcox
Attorneys at Law
1257 Main Street, Suite 900
Los Angeles, CA 90066
(310) 555-6000

[DATE]

George Barnes
Paralegal Administrator
Llewellyn, Jones & Young
3742 Rogers Court, Suite 7503
Dallas, TX 42851

        Re: [NAME] Survey

Dear Mr. Barnes:

   Enclosed is my response to your [NAME] survey. I hope you find my answers helpful to your needs.

   I am definitely looking forward to seeing the results of the entire
survey. The more information that is available, the better, as far as
I'm concerned.

   It was nice talking with you, even if it was only over the phone.
Please feel free to call if you have any follow-up questions.

                            Sincerely,

                            Angela Shapiro
                            Senior Paralegal

[AUTHOR/TYPIST]
Enclosures: survey
[DOCUMENT LOCATOR CODE]

Form 6.7. Response to a Survey Request

DeLost, Ernst, Miessner, Powell & Wilcox
Attorneys at Law
1257 Main Street, Suite 900
Los Angeles, CA 90066
(310) 555-6000

[DATE]

Stephanie L. Ross
Paralegal Administrator
Roberts, Giene, Abers & Lopez
3957 Albany Drive, Suite 488
Los Angeles, CA 90713

        Re: [NAME OF ASSOCIATION] Meeting

Dear Ms. Ross:

  Please accept this invitation to attend the next meeting of the [NAME] Chapter of the [ASSOCIATION NAME].

  This meeting promises to be an exciting one because we need to select a new chairperson for the chapter. We will also discuss the regional meeting in [PLACE] on [DATE]. The meeting will be held:

   ·   at the offices of [NAME OF MEETING PLACE AND ADDRESS, IF NOT ON LETTERHEAD],

   ·   on [DATE] at [TIME].

  I've also enclosed a list of possible topics that may be discussed at future chapter meetings. From the length of the list, it looks as if it will take at least a year to address everything!

  I certainly look forward to meeting you and discussing the issues that concern us all. Please don't hesitate to call if you have any questions. My direct number is [PHONE].

                Sincerely,

                Mark C. Williams
                Legal Assistant
[AUTHOR/TYPIST]
Enclosure: List of Discussion Topics
[DOCUMENT LOCATOR CODE]

Form 6.8. Notice and Invitation to Association Meeting

RECRUITING AND EMPLOYMENT

7.1 / Overview of Employment-Related Correspondence

7.2 / Rejection Letters to Prospective Employees

Form 7.1. Long Form Rejection Letter

Form 7.2. Short Form Rejection Letter for Advertised Position

Form 7.3. Short Form Response to an Unsolicited Inquiry

Form 7.4. Letter Returning Materials Provided During Interview

Form 7.5. Letter Indicating Interest Without Commitment

Form 7.6. Short Letter Inviting Future Discussion

7.3 / Accepting a Candidate for Employment

Form 7.7. Letter Requesting Reference Information

Form 7.8. Letter Expressing Interest in a Candidate

Form 7.9. Memo Announcing Hiring of Temporary Employee

Form 7.10. Memo Announcing Arrival of New Employee to All Staff

7.4 / When You Are in the Job Market

Form 7.11. Letter Expressing Interest in Employment

Form 7.12. Thank You Letter After Interview

Form 7.13. Change of Position/Address Notification

7.5 / Notes of Appreciation and Policy Memos to Staff

Form 7.14. Memo Setting Forth New Policy

Form 7.15. Memo Extending Congratulations for Good Performance Reviews

Form 7.16. Short Form Letter of Recommendation

Form 7.17. Detailed Letter of Recommendation
Form 7.18. Confirmation of Employment Letter

7.1 / Overview of Employment-Related Correspondence

As a legal professional, you should expect, at some point in your career, to be involved in recruiting and screening staff for your firm. On the flip side of the employment picture, you will need to look for employment at various times throughout your career. This chapter covers both aspects, finding people to employ and finding employment for yourself. In the employment process—both reviewing applications and applying for jobs—correspondence plays a major role.

A gracious volleyball game of sorts begins when a candidate sends a letter of inquiry. Remember to always keep the company in a positive light and to be gracious whether or not you intend to hire a particular candidate. Sections 7.2 and 7.3 of this Chapter discuss the following occasions when correspondence is required:

- rejecting someone's application for employment,
- advising the recipient that he or she is still under consideration, but no decision has been made,
- replying when another person introduces or refers an applicant to you for consideration,
- sending a congratulatory letter once a particular applicant has been hired,
- advising other applicants who interviewed for the position about the firm's employment decision.[1]

In addition, in §7.4 you will find letters useful in your own job search activities. Finally, §7.5 addresses the occasions when you, as a manager or supervisor, need to address the staff members who report to you, either to encourage effective work habits or detail policy issues.

7.2 / Rejection Letters to Prospective Employees

Always treat individuals applying for employment with courtesy and respect. Remember what it feels like to be the applicant and be told a position you want is not available. Regardless of the reason, the effect of rejection can be anything from disappointing to devastating. On a more pragmatic level, keep in mind that roles can reverse. The applicant you are interviewing today may be a prospective employer for you in the future. Even in a large city, the legal community tends to be a small world. This is especially true within a specialized practice area.

From any perspective, the task of rejecting applicants for employment is a delicate one. Remember two basic principles when rejecting an inquiry about employment:

- respond directly to the request, and
- be as courteous as possible in crafting your reply.

Applicants may be seeking a specific advertised position or making a general employment inquiry that has not been solicited by the firm. Both situations require the same degree of tact. Most rejection letters follow this four-step pattern:

- A neutral statement of appreciation for the inquiry about employment.
- A brief, courteous explanation of why the inquiry is being declined.
- If appropriate, include in the closing paragraph of your letter a constructive suggestion for additional job possibilities.[2]

Although rejection is never appreciated, the fact that it is done graciously always will be. Forms 7.1, 7.2 and 7.3 illustrate various versions of a rejection letter.

After a prospective candidate is interviewed but not hired, a follow-up letter is a courteous gesture. Form 7.4 discusses the return of the candidate's writing samples in a short, tactful letter. Time permitting, this is an excellent way to present the firm in a positive light even if this particular candidate was not hired.

For occasions when your firm is not seeking additional staff and you receive an employment inquiry from an individual with outstanding qualifications, Form 7.5 shows a thoughful response. It encourages the applicant to remain interested in the firm and to stay in touch, without making any promises. The highlighting of noteworthy accomplishments helps to communicate that the writer is truly impressed with the applicant's background. Most of all the letter is *sincere*.

It is important to keep a file of information such as the letter and resumé submitted by this applicant. Not only is maintaining this information sometimes required by labor and employment laws, but in the future, you may want to get back in touch with some of these applicants. Keeping rejected resumés on file gives you a ready resource to check first. Who knows, you may find that a person rejected for an earlier position is exactly right for the one open now.

When you are not actively recruiting for specific positions, the approach of the letter found in Form 7.6, in which the writer invites future discussion, is a good one. It is both courteous and efficient, and provides encouragement to the recipient by stating when the writer will be available to discuss possible opportunities with the applicant. If the letter's recipient is still interested at that time, he or she will follow up.

DeLost, Ernst, Miessner, Powell & Wilcox
Attorneys at Law
1257 Main Street, Suite 900
Los Angeles, CA 90066
(310) 555-6000

[DATE]

Sharon Halbertson
34799 Dorry Crescent
Los Angeles, CA 91349

Re: <u>Application for Employment</u>

Dear Ms. Halbertson:

Thank you very much for writing to our firm about possible employment opportunities. We carefully reviewed your resumé and we are most impressed with your background and past accomplishments. Unfortunately, we are unable to offer you a position at the present time.

It is always a pleasure to hear from someone with such an strong background. However, it does make for difficult choices when our job openings are limited and a number of very able people apply. In view of the keen competition for openings, please do not feel this decision reflects negatively on your fine qualifications.

The time and effort you have taken to express your interest in [FIRM] is very much appreciated. We wish you success in securing a position that is rewarding, stimulating, and compatible with your career interests.

Sincerely,

Angela Shapiro
Senior Paralegal

[AUTHOR/TYPIST]
[DOCUMENT LOCATOR CODE]

Form 7.1. Long Form Rejection Letter

DeLost, Ernst, Miessner, Powell & Wilcox
Attorneys at Law
1257 Main Street, Suite 900
Los Angeles, CA 90066
(310) 555-6000

[DATE]

Anna Phillips
924 Ocean Avenue
Orlando, OH 45678

    Re: <u>Advertised Paralegal Position</u>

Dear Ms. Phillips:

Thank you for your interest in our law firm and for submitting your resumé for the litigation paralegal position.

While your experience is impressive, we have selected a another candidate whose background more specifically fits the requirements of this position.

I wish you good luck in your future endeavors.

    Sincerely,

    Angela Shapiro
    Senior Paralegal

[AUTHOR/TYPIST]
[DOCUMENT LOCATOR CODE]

Form 7.2. Short Form Rejection Letter for Advertised Position

DeLost, Ernst, Miessner, Powell & Wilcox
Attorneys at Law
1257 Main Street, Suite 900
Los Angeles, CA 90066
(310) 555-6000

[DATE]

Sharon Halbertson
34799 Dorry Crescent
Los Angeles, CA 91349

Re: Interest in Employment

Dear Ms. Halbertson:

Thank you very much for writing to our office about possible employment opportunities. We appreciate your interest in becoming employed as
a paralegal. However, we are unable to offer you a position at this time.

We wish you the best of luck in securing a position that will meet
your expectations.

Thank you very much for your interest in [FIRM].

Sincerely,

Angela Shapiro
Senior Paralegal

[AUTHOR/TYPIST]
[DOCUMENT LOCATOR CODE]

Form 7.3. Short Form Response to an Unsolicited Inquiry

DeLost, Ernst, Miessner, Powell & Wilcox
Attorneys at Law
1257 Main Street, Suite 900
Los Angeles, CA 90066
(310) 555-6000

[DATE]

Sharon Halbertson
34799 Dorry Crescent
Los Angeles, CA 91349

        Re: <u>Return of Writing Samples</u>

Dear Ms. Halbertson:

  Enclosed are the writing samples that you so kindly provided. I certainly enjoyed meeting you and I am sorry the position did not work out.

  I appreciate your interest in [FIRM], and wish you the best of luck in your future endeavors.

                Sincerely,

                Angela Shapiro
                Senior Paralegal

[AUTHOR/TYPIST]
Enclosures: writing samples
[DOCUMENT LOCATOR CODE]

Form 7.4. Letter Returning Materials Provided During Interview

DeLost, Ernst, Miessner, Powell & Wilcox
Attorneys at Law
1257 Main Street, Suite 900
Los Angeles, CA 90066
(310) 555-6000

[DATE]

Lawrence Tambor
1234 Highway Two
Phoenix, AZ 12345

Re: <u>Your Letter Seeking Employment</u>

Dear Mr. Tambor:

Thank you for expressing interest in a legal assistant position with our firm. Your letter was forwarded to me for review by [NAME] because I am the firm's Manager of the Legal Assistant Department.

I am impressed with your educational achievements—a triple major is quite an accomplishment. It also appears that your experience with [ENTITY] has provided you with a fairly good idea of the responsibilities and tasks of the legal assistant position.

While I cannot say with certainty what my specific staffing requirements will be, I do anticipate needing to hire additional legal assistants for the firm's litigation department in the near future. If you have an interest in this area of law and in the possibility of relocating to [CITY], please give me a call at [PHONE NUMBER].

I look forward to speaking with you.

Sincerely,

Angela Shapiro
Senior Paralegal

[AUTHOR/TYPIST]
[DOCUMENT LOCATOR CODE]

Form 7.5. Letter Indicating Interest Without Commitment

DeLost, Ernst, Miessner, Powell & Wilcox
Attorneys at Law
1257 Main Street, Suite 900
Los Angeles, CA 90066
(310) 555-6000

[DATE]

Sharon Halbertson
34799 Dorry Crescent
Los Angeles, CA 91349

        Re: <u>Application for Employment</u>

Dear Ms. Halbertson:

  Your letter of interest was referred to me by [NAME].

  At this point, I do not know what the staffing requirements for the
coming year will be for the legal assistant staff at [FIRM]. But I will
be happy to discuss the position with you after your arrival in [CITY].

  I will be away from the office until after the first of the year.
Please feel free to contact me then.

                Sincerely,

                Marjorie Miessner, Esq.

[AUTHOR/TYPIST]
[DOCUMENT LOCATOR CODE]

Form 7.6. Short Letter Inviting Future Discussion

7.3 / Accepting a Candidate for Employment

When an applicant becomes a serious candidate for a position, that person's references should be checked before you schedule a final interview with the partner or associate attorney who makes the final decision. Form 7.7 shows a letter requesting verification of the experience the candidate has described in his or her resumé.

After a candidate's references and recommendations have been checked, and you are confident these meet the requirements of the firm's decision maker, sending a letter expressing interest in a candidate, such as the one in Form 7.8, might be appropriate. Note that no promises are made, but this letter does give the applicant a better understanding of the firm's hiring process.

When an individual joins a firm, it is necessary to inform the staff of the status of the new employee and to extend a welcome. The department in which that person will be working should be provided more detailed information to understand the new employee's capabilities and assigned functions. When colleagues are adequately informed, a new member of the team can be utilized appropriately. Memos introducing the new employee to their specific department tend to be more detailed as in Form 7.9. In addition to extending a welcome, this memo explains what responsibilities will be assigned to the new employee.

It is a good idea to attach a resumé, as was done in this case, to help explain the employee's background. Another possibility would be to attach a memo summarizing the person's background. Although this sample letter involves a temporary employee, you should also provide similar information to introduce a permanent employee to the department.

Letters introducing new employees to the entire staff are generally short. Form 7.10 shows a short memo of introduction. Generally, only those staff members who will be working directly with the new employee need to know all the details about the person's background and duties.

7.4 / When *You* Are in the Job Market

When *you* are applying for a position, the cover letter you write may be the most important part of your presentation. First impressions last a long time, so you want to make a positive, long-lasting one. In cover letters which introduce you to a potential employer, you must accomplish several goals.

- "Sell" yourself as a potential employee. Be confident but not arrogant in describing your abilities.

- Highlight your background and experience in relation to the requirements detailed for the *position*.

- Emphasize how you can provide needed assistance to the company. Do not focus solely on how much the job would mean to you.

DeLost, Ernst, Miessner, Powell & Wilcox
Attorneys at Law
1257 Main Street, Suite 900
Los Angeles, CA 90066
(310) 555-6000

[DATE]

Joan Sherman
Attorney at Law
3599 Ashley Place, Suite 700
Los Angeles, CA 91349

        Re: Reference Check for [NAME OF APPLICANT]

Dear Ms. Sherman:

   [NAME OF APPLICANT] recently interviewed in our office for the [PO-
SITION TITLE] position. You were included on a list of references provided by [NAME OF APPLICANT]. I am in the process of verifying background information and request your immediate assistance and response.

   [NAME OF APPLICANT] worked with you as a [POSITION TITLE] from [DATE]
to [DATE]. [HIS/HER] responsibilities included [LIST KEY TASKS APPLI-
CANT DESCRIBED].

   Since time is of the essence in completing this background check,
please feel free to call me with your response.

                Sincerely,

                Angela Shapiro
                Senior Paralegal

[AUTHOR/TYPIST]
[DOCUMENT LOCATOR CODE]

Form 7.7. Letter Requesting Reference Information

DeLost, Ernst, Miessner, Powell & Wilcox
Attorneys at Law
1257 Main Street, Suite 900
Los Angeles, CA 90066
(310) 555-6000

[DATE]

Shaun Galvin
37916 Windham Drive
Los Angeles, CA 90351

        Re: <u>Possible Employment Opportunity</u>

Dear Mr. Galvin:

   Thank you so much for dropping off your impressive array of writing
samples. I copied the form memorandum to keep with your resumé.

   I believe we will need to hire additional staff for a large case
rather soon. Because the attorneys need assistance with a variety of
tasks, including drafting discovery documents, I think your background
will be appropriate for this case. If the meeting scheduled for this
week confirms that a number of people will in fact be needed, I will
probably ask you to come in for an interview with the attorneys on the
case.

   Please keep in mind nothing definite has been decided yet. If you are
still interested in [FIRM], please let me know.

                    Sincerely,

                    Angela Shapiro
                    Senior Paralegal

[AUTHOR/TYPIST]
[FILE LOCATOR CODE]

Form 7.8. Letter Expressing Interest in a Candidate

MEMORANDUM

To: Litigation Department Attorneys

From: Angela Shapiro, Senior Paralegal

Date: [DATE]

Re: New Temporary Employee

   Attached is the resumé for Marie Chen, a temporary Legal Assistant hired to work on the [NAME] project. In addition to three years' experience working for New York area law firms, Marie has worked in the construction industry and is familiar with this terminology.

   Marie will begin working tomorrow. I've asked her to arrive at 9:30, per [ATTORNEY'S] request. I hope that in the afternoon Marie and I can get together to have a brief orientation session.

   Given her years of experience, I have set her billing rate at $[AMOUNT]. The charge from the temporary agency will be $[AMOUNT]. Because the agency pays overtime, the charge for all regular overtime will be $[AMOUNT].

   Please let me know if you have any questions.

Form 7.9. Memo Announcing Hiring of Temporary Employee

MEMORANDUM

To: All Employees of DEMP&W

From: Angela Shapiro, Senior Paralegal

Date: [DATE]

Re: <u>New Employee Welcome</u>

Please take a moment to stop by, introduce yourself, and welcome Carlos Sanchez, our new legal assistant who's moving in to the office next to me. Initially, Carlos will be working on the [NAME] project, but he will also be available to help out on other projects after he gets settled in.

Please keep in mind that Carlos will need at least a week to adjust to his new surroundings. Try to remember the way *you* felt during *your* first week and treat Carlos accordingly. As soon as he gets oriented to the firm's policies and procedures, Carlos can begin working on projects.

I'm sure Carlos will make significant contributions to the work of the Legal Assistant Department.

Form 7.10. Memo Announcing Arrival of New Employee to All Staff

· Never conceal vital facts. Dates of employment—and sometimes salary information—can be easily discovered by employers.[3]

Form 7.11 is a sample cover letter used to apply for a position that had been advertised.

After you have been interviewed by a prospective employer, thank the interviewer for taking the time to meet with you. This act of courtesy can create a tremendous amount of goodwill. On one occasion, the person I had interviewed prepared a simple handwritten note of thanks on a printed card and left it with the receptionist right after the interview had concluded. I can't tell you how impressed I was by this gesture. For those seeking a more formal approach, Form 7.12 is a good start.

When you move to a new position—whether it is at the same firm or a new one—it is important to advise colleagues, membership associations, vendors, and any other business contacts of the change. You should provide your new job title and telephone extension if you are continuing to work for the same firm. If you move to a different firm, however, be sure to include the new firm's name and address in your letters of notification. Form 7.13 shows a very short and simple letter announcing such a change.

7.5 / Notes of Appreciation and Policy Memos to Staff

If you have moved into a managerial position, either as head of a department or supervisor of other staff members, you know how important it is to maintain a positive work environment. The people you work with or those who work for you will appreciate the time you take to write a note of thanks for their contributions.

Of course, policies and work procedures must also be communicated, and sometimes, it is best to do so in writing. The time required to write such communications is well worth avoiding the chaos or uncertainty that may develop if you don't. For example, you may need to know the whereabouts of certain members of the firm's support staff even if you do not have direct supervisory authority. If you find you seldom know of your secretary's or another support person's availability, use a memo like the one found in Form 7.14.

As a department manager or team supervisor, it is a good idea to let people in the department know their contributions are appreciated. Form 7.15 is an example of this type of "appreciation memo." While such notes of appreciation may come at any time, you will not want to forget the following occasions:

· For a particular job well done.

· To the person who keeps things running smoothly, yet is rarely recognized.

· For years of service anniversaries.

125 Appleseed Street, Apt. 10
Los Angeles, CA 90039
(310) 555-6000

[DATE]

Joanna Stanley
Legal Assistant Manager
Palmer, Brown & Jessop
377 Alpers Drive, Suite 788
Los Angeles, CA 91349

Re: Application for [TITLE OF PROSPECTIVE POSITION]

Dear Ms. Stanley:

I understand that your firm recently considered applicants for a paralegal position. If the position is still available, I would like the opportunity to meet with you to discuss my qualifications. Enclosed you will find my resumé, along with copies of articles I have written about [SPECIALTY], a list of references, two letters of recommendation, and a list of continuing education seminars I have attended.

Of course, a letter and resumé can serve only as an introduction to one's professional achievements and qualifications. I have over five years of experience in this field and possess strong management and communication skills. I am looking for a position to take advantage of my skills and to utilize my extremely high level of energy and enthusiasm.

I look forward to discussing what I can bring to a position with your company. Salary requirements are entirely negotiable at this time. Please feel free to telephone me at my office number, keeping in mind the confidential nature of the contact.

Thank you for your consideration.

Sincerely,

Paula Kendall

Form 7.11. Letter Expressing Interest in Employment

                                        125 Appleseed Street, Apt. 10
                                            Los Angeles, CA 90039
                                               (310) 555-6000

                                                             [DATE]

Joanna Stanley
Legal Assistant Manager
Palmer, Brown & Jessop
377 Alpers Drive, Suite 788
Los Angeles, CA 91349

        Re: Meeting of [DATE]

Dear Ms. Stanley:

   It was a pleasure to meet with you yesterday to discuss how my qualifications might match with the needs of your firm. I was very impressed
with the increased responsibilities handled by legal assistants at
[FIRM] and definitely would like to meet with the attorneys to discuss
this position further.

   Please do not hesitate to call if you have any questions or need more
information. Thank you very much for the time and consideration you have
already given me; I look forward to hearing from you soon.

                        Sincerely,

                        Paula Kendall

Form 7.12. Thank-You Letter After Interview

DeLost, Ernst, Miessner, Powell & Wilcox
Attorneys at Law
1257 Main Street, Suite 900
Los Angeles, CA 90066
(310) 555-6000

[DATE]

Laurel Bernard
Computer Peripherals
2140 West 67th Street
Los Angeles, CA 90062

        Re: Notice of New Office Location

Dear Dr. Bernard:

 As of May 11, 1995, I will move to a new position as the Lease Administrator for the [NAME] Project. I am leaving my current position at
[FIRM NAME] effective today. You can now contact me at:

            Lease Management Company
            9962 Aspen Road
            Zephyr Cove, NV 89448
            (702) 555-7022.

 Please change your records to reflect this new information. As usual,
thanks very much for your assistance.

            Sincerely,

            Angela Shapiro
            Senior Paralegal
[AUTHOR/TYPIST]
[DOCUMENT LOCATOR CODE]

Form 7.13. Change of Position/Address Notification

· For promotions.

· For retirements.

If you hold an official management position, you may also be called upon to prepare letters of recommendation such as the brief letter in Form 7.16. The most important rule to remember in writing letters of recommendation is to state the facts accurately. Your letter of recommendation will be most effective if you can include concrete examples of good performance, not just general platitudes. A good example is found in Form 7.17.

If you receive requests for reference letters about former employees of your firm, verification of former employment is a normal part of the recruiting process. Responses such as the one in Form 7.18 should provide only the information requested, most often:

· a job description, and

· dates of the individual's employment.

Of course, if you feel that the person in question did a stellar job, say so.

End Notes

[1] See also L.E. Frailey, *Handbook of Business Letters*, p. 611 (1989), for both additional information and a different approach to some of these letters.

[2] Robert L. Shurter and Donald J. Leonard, *Effective Letters in Business*, p. 93 (1984).

[3] See, e.g., Alfred Stuart Myers, *Letters for All Occasions*, p. 133 (1993). *See also* Andrea Wagner and Chere B. Estrin, "Where Do I Go from Here?" *Career Choices for Experienced Legal Assistants*, pp. 219–229 (1992); Andrea Wagner, *How to Land Your First Paralegal Job*, pp. 73–87 (1992); and Chere B. Estrin, *Paralegal Career Guide*, §515 (1992).

MEMORANDUM

To: [NAME OF SUPPORT STAFF MEMBER]

From: [YOUR NAME]

Date: [DATE MEMO SENT]

Re: <u>Your Availability</u>

<u>Please notify me (or my secretary) as soon as possible</u> when you anticipate being out of the office on business, due to illness, or coming to work late. This information is vital.

Leave a message for me or [NAME OF SECRETARY] at the message desk. Be sure to tell the person taking that message to deliver it to my office immediately.

Your cooperation is appreciated.

Form 7.14. Memo Setting Forth New Policy

MEMORANDUM

To: Litigation Department

From: [YOUR NAME]

Date: [DATE MEMO SENT]

Re: <u>Congratulations!</u>

Congratulations on receiving such encouraging performance evaluations from the attorneys you have been working with in [GEOGRAPHIC SECTION].

The three reviews by [LIST REVIEWERS] all note your willingness to work hard and your enthusiasm about the job. These are indeed welcome traits. I have enclosed copies of these forms for your review.

Keep up the good work!

Form 7.15. Memo Extending Congratulations for Good Performance Reviews

DeLost, Ernst, Miessner, Powell & Wilcox
Attorneys at Law
1257 Main Street, Suite 900
Los Angeles, CA 90066
(310) 555-6000

[DATE]

To Whom It May Concern:

    Re: [NAME OF EMPLOYEE]

   [NAME OF EMPLOYEE] was employed as a proofreader in the local office of [FIRM NAME] from [DATE] to [DATE].

   [NAME OF EMPLOYEE] performed his duties exceptionally well. In addition to proofreading, he performed various duties to aid the legal assistants. He's a team player, willing to help others and do whatever is necessary to get the job done.

   Unfortunately, due to economic reasons, [NAME OF EMPLOYEE] was laid off on [DATE]. We wish him well and know that he will be an asset to any law firm or company.

        Sincerely,

        Deanna DeLost, Esq.

[AUTHOR/TYPIST]
[DOCUMENT LOCATOR CODE]

Form 7.16. Short Form Letter of Recommendation

DeLost, Ernst, Miessner, Powell & Wilcox
Attorneys at Law
1257 Main Street, Suite 900
Los Angeles, CA 90066
(310) 555-6000

[DATE]

To Whom It May Concern:

        Re: <u>Recommendation of [NAME OF EMPLOYEE]</u>

   It is my distinct pleasure to have worked with [NAME OF EMPLOYEE], an
Administrative Assistant for [FIRM]. Because I frequently consult with
[NAME OF ATTORNEY], I have had many opportunities to observe the work
of [NAME OF EMPLOYEE].

   [NAME OF EMPLOYEE] has many skills and abilities, and she really ex-
cels at using computers. For example, when working on the acquisition
of a computer network for [FIRM], I asked [NAME OF EMPLOYEE] to serve
as the primary systems supervisor, so I could function as backup only.
Because [NAME OF EMPLOYEE] is a fearless computer user and takes great
joy in problem solving on her own, my role in maintaining the computer
system has been quite minimal (which is exactly what I wanted).

   [NAME OF EMPLOYEE] also possesses excellent organizational, procedural, and analytical skills. To illustrate these attributes, I'd like to
tell you about a mailing list project handled by [NAME OF EMPLOYEE].
This project began with a simple goal: Mail a marketing flyer, reply
card, and envelope to [FIRM'S] master list of customers. Of course, it
all had to be done in less than a week.

   On its face, this task looked as if it would be no problem. Except
for one small detail: There was *no* master mailing list in existence.
Each attorney's secretary had indeed put together a list of the attorney's own clients, but no one created these files using the same (or
even similar) formats.

   So, mailing lists from several different people had to be reformat-
ted into a standard structure, merged into one list, the duplicates
purged, and the remaining names and addresses sorted into zip code
order. And all through word processing software only, *not* a database
program! Then, after a master mailing list was created, [NAME OF EM-
PLOYEE] oversaw the work of the mailing house to make sure the mailing
got out on time (it did).

   Even though she was under incredible stress and had a very short deadline, [NAME OF EMPLOYEE] handled this difficult project with great
aplomb. Of course, this particular project required tact, planning, organization, patience, analysis of problems, and people management
skills, but hardly a week goes by when [NAME OF EMPLOYEE] does not successfully handle similarly demanding tasks.

Form 7.17. Detailed Letter of Recommendation

Recommendation of [NAME OF EMPLOYEE]
[DATE]
Page 2

[NAME OF EMPLOYEE] is very intelligent, hardworking, a quick study,
and eager to learn. And, she is quite ready to take on increased responsibilities. Because [NAME OF EMPLOYEE] also has a legal background
and has gained extensive knowledge of the legal practice in her current job, I highly recommend her for any paralegal or law firm administrative position.

Please don't hesitate to call if you have any questions.

Sincerely,

Angela Shapiro
Senior Paralegal
[AUTHOR/TYPIST]
[DOCUMENT LOCATOR CODE]

Form 7.17. Detailed Letter of Recommendation (*Continued*)

DeLost, Ernst, Miessner, Powell & Wilcox
Attorneys at Law
1257 Main Street, Suite 900
Los Angeles, CA 90066
(310) 555-6000

[DATE]

Joanna Stanley
Legal Assistant Manager
Palmer, Brown & Jessop
377 Alpers Drive, Suite 788
Los Angeles, CA 91349

          Re: [NAME OF FIRM'S FORMER EMPLOYEE]

Dear Ms. Stanley:

   As you requested, [NAME OF FORMER EMPLOYEE] was employed as [GIVE FOR-
MER TITLE] from [DATE] to [DATE]. [HIS/HER] duties included [DESCRIBE
BRIEFLY].

   Please feel free to contact me if you need more information.

                    Sincerely,

                    Angela Shapiro
                    Senior Paralegal

[AUTHOR/TYPIST]
[DOCUMENT LOCATOR CODE]

Form 7.18. Confirmation of Employment Letter

LITIGATION

8.1 / The Paralegal Role

8.2 / Accepting a New Client

8.3 / Rejecting a Client

8.4 / Preparing for Discovery

8.5 / Searching for Documents

8.6 / Lack of Response to Discovery

8.7 / Confirming Extensions of Time to Respond

8.8 / Assisting the Client to Respond

8.9 / Depositions

8.10 / Working with Witnesses

8.11 / Preparing for Trial

8.12 / During the Trial

8.13 / Settlement

8.14 / Other Frequently Used Letters

Form 8.1. Acknowledging File and Documents to the Client

Form 8.2. Acknowledging Documents from Another Law Firm

Form 8.3. Acknowledging Documents Received for Review

Form 8.4. Acknowledgement with Outline of Fee Structure

Form 8.5. Rejection of a Potential Client

Form 8.6. Letter to Client Describing Demurrer

Form 8.7. Helping the Client to Organize Documents

Form 8.8. Memo to Attorney Before Trial

Form 8.9. Document Search

Form 8.10. Failure to Respond to Discovery

Form 8.11. Confirmation of Granting of Extension of Time to Respond

Form 8.12. Confirmation of Extension of Time to Respond to Discovery

Form 8.13. Obtaining Client Answers to Interrogatories

Form 8.14. Short Form Transmittal of Discovery to Client

Form 8.15. Transmittal of Discovery to Client with Instructions

Form 8.16. Sending Notice of Deposition to Client

Form 8.17. Scheduling a Predeposition Meeting with Client

Form 8.18. Scheduling Depositions

Form 8.19. Deposition Transcript Review

Form 8.20. Deposition Transcript Review

Form 8.21. Providing the Court with a Deposition as an Exhibit

Form 8.22. Letter to Witness

Form 8.23. Request to Postmaster for Forwarding Address

Form 8.24. Scheduling Expert Deposition

Form 8.25. Deposition of Opposing Party's Expert Witness

Form 8.26. Long Form Subpoena Letter to Witness with On-Call Agreement

Form 8.27. Short Form Subpoena Letter to Witness with On-Call Agreement

Form 8.28. Informing the Client of a Settlement Conference

Form 8.29. Informing the Client of the Trial Date

Form 8.30. Getting Client Contact Information Before Trial

Form 8.31. Letter to Client About Scheduled Mediation

Form 8.32. Arranging for Receipt of Daily Trial Transcripts

Form 8.33. Settlement Letter to Opposing Counsel

Form 8.34. Settlement Letter to Client with Release for Signature

Form 8.35. Release Letter for Client's Signature

Form 8.36. Short Transmittal Letter

Form 8.37. Transmittal Form Letter

Form 8.38. Letter to a Clerk of the Court

Form 8.39. Transmittal of Several Documents to a
Clerk of the Court
Form 8.40. Letter to Magistrate
Form 8.41. Instructions for Service of Summons and
Complaint
Form 8.42. Instructions for Service of Subpoena
Form 8.43. Thank-You Letter to Witness After Trial

8.1 / The Paralegal Role

A litigation paralegal's overall objective is to help prepare a case for trial. In this mode, paralegals often review files and summarize their contents. They may work directly with investigators, witnesses, experts, and clients in preparation for trial testimony.

While paralegal litigation specialists rarely participate in what is termed "transactional work," those who do routinely have occasion to get involved in litigation. Litigation reaches into most practice areas. Corporate, copyright, and other specialties may also be litigation heavy despite their "transactional" heritage.

Litigation paralegals draft pleadings—both antagonistic and responsive—and participate in all areas of discovery and trial. Specifically, paralegals can draft many of the following documents:

· complaints,

· answers,

· demurrers,

· interrogatories,

· requests for documents, and

· requests for admissions.

In addition, when working on large matters, paralegals may also oversee teams of people handling the sorting, numbering, and organizing of massive amounts of exhibits for both depositions and trials.

8.2 / Accepting a New Client

Initial correspondence between an attorney and prospective client initiates the attorney–client relationship. Whether or not the attorney decides to accept a particular case, the attorney and the firm need to be presented in a positive and professional light through this initial correspondence. Before beginning any action on behalf of a new client the attorney must

· discuss the matter with the potential client, and

· determine if it is appropriate to represent the client.

Once that has been accomplished the responding correspondence must be prepared, either accepting or rejecting the matter. In the event of acceptance, the terms of the business relationship should be defined. As outlined in *Managing Litigation: The Insider's Guide,* by Rick Wallace, the initial correspondence should:

· Include a statement clearly stating the client agrees to retain the attorney.

· Identify all the attorneys, client contacts, and managers for the case.

· Introduce yourself and your role as the paralegal.

· Identify all associate, paralegal, or other staff members assigned to work on the matter.

· Note that both you and the attorney are available to the client, as needed.

· Clearly define the scope of services to be performed. For example, "We will represent you with regard to the lawsuit titled . . . ."

· Specifically state the fees, billing cycle, and fee calculation method, as set by the attorney.

· Outline the firm's expenses. Does the firm charge expenses on a strict pass-through basis or are some marked up? Do the fees include telephone, meals, faxes, photocopies, overtime, word processing, and computer time?

· State that the client will be informed via monthly or bimonthly progress reports and mention to whom the reports will be directed. These reports should be written, not oral.

· Include updates on strategy plans, a fresh assessment of the potential for settling the litigation, and a running tally of litigation costs.[1]

The acknowledgment letter can provide some security for the client, conveying that you are on the case and ready to roll. After the paralegal has prepared a letter explaining the attorney plans to represent the client, it is *signed by the attorney* and mailed to the client. Ideally, the acknowledgment letter should be sent out the day the file is received. If immediate action is necessary, it should be discussed in this correspondence.

The client may be expected to do something in the very near future. Form 8.1 lets the client know a declaration will be arriving within a week. It allows the client time to plan, either to be available to review and sign the document or to elect a different declarant.

Forms 8.1 through 8.5 all show the initial correspondence to a new client. However, they vary in format and style. Use Forms 8.2 and 8.3 when

- accepting documents for review to determine if the attorney can take on a specific matter, or
- acknowledging receipt of materials after the attorney accepts a case.

You will probably have to prepare these same types of letters on many occasions, especially just before and during trial, on a rush basis. It is a good idea to have a general acknowledgment form with blank lines that can be filled in quickly when the need arises. Form 8.4 is such a form letter which acknowledges receipt of the action, and sets forth a brief action plan, and outlines a typical fee structure and payment schedule. As a paralegal, you cannot design fee structure or accept a client on behalf of the firm, therefore, this type of letter is also *signed by the attorney*.

Many procedures in litigation follow a predetermined course. For example, if you file a complaint you expect an answer, a demurrer, or the opposing party may take a default judgment. A client may not understand the difference between a demurrer and a complaint. The actions and procedures related to a case need to be explained to the client. Form 8.5 shows a comprehensive letter describing a demurrer, including its purpose and the firm's planned action.

8.3 / Rejecting a Client

In some instances, your firm will *not* want to accept a case. There may be several reasons for deciding not to represent a client. The letter rejecting a potential client's case clearly states the reason and is sent promptly. According to *Managing Litigation: The Insider's Guide,* this rejection letter should include any of the following points that might apply to the specifics of the case:

- State the attorney will not be representing the client in the matter.
- Describe how and when the client asked to be represented and what the attorney was asked to do.
- Describe what the attorney has done for the client (i.e., "reviewed documents," "discussed the case by telephone," "meeting with witness").
- If the attorney has given preliminary advice or opinions, state they were preliminary only. Further, the letter should state the advice or opinions given were not based on a thorough analysis. Explain that the client may not rely on the attorney's opinions, but should seek other counsel for advice.

- If a critical statute date is approaching and time is short, don't delay the rejection. Make every effort to leave the rejected client time to obtain another attorney.

- In the letter, include any statute dates pertinent to the case. If you don't have enough information to evaluate statute of limitations information, include a statement to that effect.

- While you are not required to tell a client why the attorney is rejecting the case, you may, if the attorney chooses, give the reason for doing so (e.g., conflict of interest). Cite any appropriate statute that applies to the case rejection decision.

- Include all original documents given to the attorney by the prospective client with the letter.

- Send the letter by certified mail, return receipt requested.[2]

The example in Form 8.6 explains that due to excessive costs because of the location of the matter at hand the firm cannot take on the case. Any potential client appreciates an honest response and will very likely consider the firm at some future date for litigation matters within its geographical area.

In other instances where a case is rejected the attorney may feel another counsel may be more appropriate for the client or another method of recovery may be more suitable, such as small claims court or mediation. Clients don't necessarily realize that the cost of litigation may be greater than the potential sums to be recovered.

Regardless of the attorney's motivation for rejecting a case, it is important to inform the potential client quickly. Speed is not just a matter of courtesy. The client may need to take specific actions before a certain time limit expires and should be given enough time to make alternate plans.

8.4 / Preparing for Discovery

Informal discovery may begin before the attorney talks to the client in the initial interview. From the start you need to be prepared to assist the attorney. Use the following checklist for a quick reminder of informal discovery items.

- The attorney conducts the initial client interview.

- Initial documentation from the client must be collected.

- If the attorney envisions any Freedom of Information Act requests, you will have to move fast. FOIA requests often take a very long time for completion.

- The attorney asks your assistance in gathering public records, using the many computer systems available for on-line analysis.

- The attorney may visit the site or sites involved in the litigation and take snapshots.

- On-line databases may be searched for pertinent information on the case, any technical subjects touched by the case, the parties and opposing counsel, as well as the judge or arbitrator.[3]

During the months before trial it is your responsibility to determine the amount of assistance the attorney will require. Plan effectively so each task is executed within its designated time period. It is up to you, *not the attorney,* to estimate accurately how much time it takes to summarize a deposition or assemble a trial notebook. If your scheduling is realistic, you can minimize the stress a trial can generate.

A memo to the supervising attorney, using a checklist such as the one in Form 8.7, is an excellent way to begin planning. Whenever possible use checklists to keep track of your tasks. You must anticipate unexpected events and plan for them in order to give yourself enough time to produce a quality product at each stage.

To provide the best possible service to a client you need to keep them informed. Send copies of documents and correspondence received and produced to the client. The amount of paper involved can be so voluminous the client can have difficulty finding key pieces of information at crucial times. Remember, the client needs time to answer interrogatories, prepare for depositions, or provide details in other situations where accuracy is vital. You can help your client a great deal by suggesting a system for organizing all the material concerned.

Form 8.8 tells the client what to expect and suggests a filing system to prevent excessive volumes of paper from becoming uncontrollable. It is important to give the client assistance, otherwise much of the documentation and work you invest can appear to have little value through the client's eyes.

8.5 / Searching for Documents

In your request specify the documents you want and include any background information to assist in the search. Attach a copy of the reference you have, such as an application, record request, or questionnaire, if any exists. Also note any other sources already searched. The actual document request must include:

- the date the request is initiated,
- the due date,
- the requesting attorney,

- the grounds upon which you are entitled to the documents, and

- the legal assistant that is the contact person.

If a release is required, attach a copy. If the entity that has the documents requires the release to be notarized, make sure that it is.

Before sending the letter, find out the name of the person who should receive your request and their exact mailing address. This is especially important if you are dealing with a government agency because it helps to reduce delays. Form 8.9 shows an example. According to *Managing Litigation: The Insider's Guide* by Rick Wallace:

> The key concepts of drafting document requests are planning, timing, and precision drafting. Document requests that aren't carefully drafted are open to interpretation by opposing counsel. Use the following guidelines as a quality control checklist when you are drafting document requests.
>
> - From the discovery plan, establish a list of targets for the document-production request.
>
> - During drafting, refer to the discovery plan and all the elements used to create the plan (facts and issues analysis, sample jury instructions, informal discovery).
>
> - Review all previous discovery to make sure all relevant material has been requested.
>
> - Consider whether there are any protective orders that limit discovery in the case.
>
> - Read the relevant statutes and local rules regarding timing and notice.
>
> - Set a location for production of the documents.
>
> - Determine your document strategy, based on the number of documents. Do you want to inspect the documents and choose select items for copying? Or do you prefer to receive copies of all the documents?
>
> - Set up a mutually agreeable method for copying the documents (e.g., on site photocopying or microfilming, having documents sent out to a local copy service).[4]

8.6 / Lack of Response to Discovery

If the opposing party does not respond to discovery, a letter citing the applicable code must be sent to the party. In essence, this letter should offer a final opportunity to respond. Form 8.10, a California example, contains all the elements necessary for further action.

8.7 / Confirming Extensions of Time to Respond

In the name of professional courtesy it is not uncommon for attorneys to extend the time limits for responding to various pleadings. How often they do this and how much extra time they will allow usually depends on the firm's internal policy.

Whether your firm asks for an extension or grants one, you will often be asked to write a letter to opposing counsel to confirm an extension and to document the file. Forms 8.11 and 8.12 illustrate confirmations of granting and receiving extensions. Such a letter should be sent out the same day the extension is verbally granted.

8.8 / Assisting the Client to Respond

It is your responsibility to obtain client answers to discovery questions. Astute use of your communication skills can help the client provide the necessary information in a timely manner. A good example of a letter to a client formally requesting discovery information is Form 8.13. Note these important elements:

· correct name of the people and/or companies involved,

· the letter's intent,

· the requirements,

· time and place, if necessary,

· what the letter writer wants from the recipient (in this case, draft answers), and

· an offer of help if the client has any questions.

Overall it is your responsibility to ensure that you and the client complete each task on time. When interrogatories request documents, telephone the client about three days after sending out the request for responses. Determine if obtaining the documentation will present a problem or cause a delay. Rather than waiting until the last minute, find out potential problems and work out solutions as soon as possible.

It is also part of your job to make sure the client's responses to interrogatories are relevant and understandable. You cannot assess whether or not the information is true. However, you can educate the client about the importance of complete and accurate answers and the consequences of not providing these.

Form 8.14 is an excellent example of a simple transmission especially appropriate if the attorney has already held a conference with the client about the importance of responses. Form 8.15 is more specific. It includes a warning about incorrect information and requests a meeting after the client has drafted the responses. This is a very good approach, since the information can be clarified or revised during that meeting.

8.9 / Depositions

The paralegal's role is critical in achieving a smooth transition of events from discovery to trial. This is quite evident when the paralegal organizes depositions. As a precursor to trial you will

- · send out notices,
- · set deposition dates and times,
- · attend depositions,
- · transmit transcripts to witnesses for review, and
- · summarize those same transcripts (very likely).

While your client will be aware of the duty to appear at a noticed deposition, it is your firm's responsibility to make sure the client does not forget and is prepared for the event. Many attorneys meet with the client at the office, review testimony, and put the client's mind at ease. The client and attorney then travel together to the deposition location if it is outside the office.

Form 8.16 is a transmittal of the official notice to the client. Form 8.17 is a letter confirming the deposition date, time, and place and establishes a meeting prior to the deposition. The attached information tells the client what to expect and how to prepare for the event.

In some situations you will have to contact many different parties to schedule depositions. If you do not get cooperation, you have the right to issue a soft ultimatum as long as it is a reasonable one. Form 8.18 shows an example.

After a deposition the witness must review the original transcript and make any necessary changes before signing it in front of a Notary Public; otherwise, incorrect testimony may be lodged with the court. Forms 8.19 and 8.20 illustrate letters to convey this information.

If you provide the court with a deposition as an exhibit, you will need to use a signed original in accordance with the appropriate Rules of Court. Form 8.21 is a sample that may be helpful when you need to lodge a deposition with the court.

8.10 / Working with Witnesses

Paralegals are often entrusted with the task of locating and contacting witnesses for trial. It is very important to sit down with the attorney and discuss the background of each witness.

To locate the people you need, you may work with an investigator or skip tracer. They will need all the available information, especially when witnesses are hostile.

When faced with the actuality of testifying, witnesses can begin acting less than enthusiastically about the prospect. You should first make telephone contact whenever possible to feel out that person's disposition and then follow up with a letter. It is common practice to confirm telephone discussions by letter. Sometimes you cannot make contact by telephone and a letter becomes your only recourse. Form 8.22 is a sample letter in such a situation.

If the post office returns a letter because the address is outdated, you can obtain a forwarding address by mailing Form 8.23 with the appropriate fee. Mail this to the postmaster at the city, state, and zip code of the addressee. Following this method, you will usually get an almost immediate response.

Expert witnesses provide testimony supporting your client's and the opposing party's claims. When working with expert witnesses

- know when your supervising attorney is available,

- set aside time to examine opposing counsel's experts, and

- when writing to expert witnesses, include possible deposition dates and times, such as in Form 8.24.

If there are few experts in your client's particular case, a letter such as the one in Form 8.25 will suffice. When there are numerous experts, it is helpful to set aside blocks of time as in the example. Be sure to follow up with a telephone call to set the actual date.

When you are responsible for seeing that each witness is available for trial ,you do not want to turn a friendly witness into a hostile one by having them wait for hours, or even days, around the courtroom. Convey your intent to make their experience as convenient as possible. The party can agree to be *on-call,* meaning they will be available upon reasonable notice by telephone.

The best way to set up an on-call agreement is in a spirit of cooperation. Form 8.26 is a long version of a subpoena letter with an on-call agreement; Form 8.27 is a shorter version. The version you use will depend on your and your supervising attorney's judgment.

Once a subpoena is served, send a letter to get the individual to agree to appear at the time and place listed on the subpoena. Don't assume a witness will automatically show up in court after being subpoenaed.

Witness fees are negligible, so witnesses often feel inadequately compensated. Some people just don't want to go near a courtroom. Your telephone calls and letters to potential witnesses can solidify the relationship between them and your office.

8.11 / Preparing for Trial

Part of your firm's responsibility is to prepare the client to appear in a favorable light when attending any type of hearing. Some clients may need advice regarding manner of dress, depending upon their profession and life style. All clients need to understand the events they attend and what is expected of them.

Most firms have information sheets to include with letters conveying the dates, times, and places of hearings. Form 8.28 is a letter telling the client when a settlement conference is scheduled. The information sheet is attached.

Clients must be advised of trial dates and any rescheduling. If there is any chance the client will need to attend settlement conferences and other hearings, the dates of these must be communicated well in advance.

Form 8.29 shows a succinct letter conveying the trial date with a copy of the actual order. Follow up with a telephone call to make sure the client is completely aware of this date, time, and place.

8.12 / During the Trial

Usually, the client must be available for the full duration of the trial. Most juries like to see parties to an action actively involved in their case. It is not a good idea for your client to be absent from the trial.

You must have current contact information for the client at all times before and during the trial—including every phone number at which the individual or individuals can be reached at all times of the day. Form 8.30 shows a short informational letter. It should always be followed by a telephone call.

If the matter is being mediated or arbitrated instead of going to trial, various rules will govern the procedures. You will need to notify and inform your client. Form 8.31 very simply outlines hearing information, transmits general information about mediation, and lets the client know the firm will be in touch.

During trial, attorneys may want to review the daily transcripts to help prepare for the next day's witnesses. In larger matters you may have a team of attorneys and paralegals, who are not in the courtroom, scrutinizing the case. To obtain daily transcripts you must usually make arrangements with the court reporter in advance.

Check with the court's clerk to find out the procedure for obtaining what are called "dailies." In most cases the court reporter will need to know in advance that a daily transcript will be required. A format like the one in Form 8.32 can be used for this purpose.

8.13 / Settlement

Many issues scheduled for trial settle on the stairs to the courthouse or on the car phone on the way to court. If you are involved in the settlement, you may be called upon to transmit release agreements, compromise agreements, or the dismissal. Form 8.33 is an example of a letter in this situation.

Sometimes a case is settled before litigation begins. The release can be set forth in letter form and transmitted to the client for signature. Form 8.34 outlines the settlement agreement and asks the client to sign the release. Form 8.35 sets forth the intentions of all parties to release one another from any and all liability.

8.14 / Other Frequently Used Letters

Certain types of letters are written almost on a daily basis in most law firms. But the most frequently used letter, especially in litigation, is the transmittal. The decision to use a preprinted form or a customized letter is usually made by the firm. Form 8.36 is an example.

Form 8.37 can be used with or without a computer. Its function is to identify enclosures and indicate why they are being sent. Information can either be typed or handwritten on this preprinted form.

You will also need to write many letters to court clerks, most often transmitting pleadings for filing with the court. Because clerks receive thousands of complaints and other pleadings each day, they will appreciate kind words and your attention to detail. In corresponding with court clerks

- Always list the case information clearly in the letter's *re:* line.

- If you know the location of the file or the department in which the case is being heard, include this information.

- List each document enclosed and tell the clerk what you want done with each one.

- Always include a self-addressed, stamped envelope for a reply.

Most correspondence to the court will be transmitting and requesting documents and/or pleadings. Form 8.38 is a sample of what the letter should look like. Form 8.39 shows how the letter should be formatted when transmitting more than one item.

Correspondence to a judge or magistrate must convey neutrality and must be technically correct. Never use a letter to a court official to express an opinion. Be especially polite and attempt to list all relevant facts while leaving out extemporaneous information as in Form 8.40.

In some cases, instructions for service of documents must be set forth in letter form and signed by an attorney. It does not matter whether a marshal, sheriff, or registered process server will complete service. The information provided on the completed proof of service will be based directly on your instructions. Be precise.

List all names exactly as stated on the document to be served. In a summons and complaint, as discussed in Form 8.41, even a long name (especially if it is long and confusing), or a corporate name must be listed in full, exactly as on the summons. In the event you are serving a subpoena, Form 8.42 may be helpful.

Most witnesses are tremendously interested in the case and its outcome. For you, as a legal professional, hearings and trials may be everyday events. But to people outside the legal field, these occurrences can be exceptionally interesting. It is always a good idea, especially because of the appeals process, to thank witnesses for their cooperation. Form 8.43 is a great way to express these sentiments.

DeLost, Ernst, Miessner, Powell & Wilcox
Attorneys at Law
1257 Main Street, Suite 900
Los Angeles, CA 90066
(310) 555-6000

[DATE]

Eleanor Sedgewick
Chief Operating Officer
Donaldson Pen Company
243 Admiral Road, Suite 1020
Los Angeles, CA 90099

Re: [IDENTIFY MATTER]

Dear Ms. Sedgewick:

We have received your file and documents in regard to the above-entitled matter. Our office will immediately [EXPLAIN FIRST STEP]. We will send a declaration for you to sign within the week.

[NAME], the paralegal assigned to this matter, is available to answer any questions you may have. Additionally, [HE/SHE] will provide you with updates, as necessary. Of course, please do not hesitate to contact me directly should you have any questions.

Sincerely,

Scott Powell, Esq.

[AUTHOR/TYPIST]
[DOCUMENT LOCATOR CODE]

Form 8.1. Acknowledging File and Documents to the Client

DeLost, Ernst, Miessner, Powell & Wilcox
Attorneys at Law
1257 Main Street, Suite 900
Los Angeles, CA 90066
(310) 555-6000

[DATE]

Eleanor Sedgewick
Chief Operating Officer
Donaldson Pen Company
243 Admiral Road, Suite 1020
Los Angeles, CA 90099

Re: [IDENTIFY MATTER]

Dear Ms. Sedgewick:

The following documents have been hand-delivered to me by [FIRM] with reference to the above referenced cause of action:

[LIST ITEMS]

DATED: _____   SIGNED: _____

ACKNOWLEDGED RECEIVED: _____

Sincerely,

Angela Shapiro
Senior Paralegal

[AUTHOR/TYPIST]
[DOCUMENT LOCATOR CODE]

Form 8.2. Acknowledging Documents from Another Law Firm

DeLost, Ernst, Miessner, Powell & Wilcox
Attorneys at Law
1257 Main Street, Suite 900
Los Angeles, CA 90066
(310) 555-6000

[DATE]

Eleanor Sedgewick
Chief Operating Officer
Donaldson Pen Company
243 Admiral Road, Suite 1020
Los Angeles, CA 90099

        Re: [IDENTIFY MATTER]

Dear Ms. Sedgewick:

  We have received the materials you sent us regarding the above-referenced claim. After reviewing these materials we will be in touch with you.

  Thank you for forwarding this claim to us.

                    Sincerely,

                    John B. Watson
                    Legal Assistant
[AUTHOR/TYPIST]
[DOCUMENT LOCATOR CODE]

Form 8.3. Acknowledging Documents Received for Review

DeLost, Ernst, Miessner, Powell & Wilcox
Attorneys at Law
1257 Main Street, Suite 900
Los Angeles, CA 90066
(310) 555-6000

[DATE]

Mr. Alec Sutherland
1936 Papermill Road
Mission Springs, CA 90067

Re: [IDENTIFY MATTER]

Dear Mr. Sutherland:

You have asked us to represent you in recovering $[AMOUNT] plus interest accrued from [DATE], owed to you for professional services rendered to [NAME]. We will be happy to do so.

We will attempt to have [OBLIGOR] enter into a promissory note to be secured by Deed of Trust. The executed Deed of Trust will then be recorded with the County Auditor and create a lien on real property. However, if [OBLIGOR] does not cooperate, we are prepared to file a collection suit to recover the funds.

Our firm requires clients to deposit a retainer prior to commencing legal action. As discussed at our meeting on [DATE], please forward a $[AMOUNT] retainer directly to my attention.

We also need to declare, at the outset of a new matter, the attorney fee and cost arrangements involved. Our office bills at an hourly basis for services performed. All fees are adjusted periodically, usually in January of each year.

My services are presently billed at $[AMOUNT] per hour; I will be in charge of this matter. Paralegal [NAME] will provide services as well at a $[AMOUNT] per hour billable rate.

In addition to our legal fees, you will be charged for expenses incurred or advances made by us on your behalf. These expenses include but are not limited to:

· word processing costs,
· filing fees,
· special mailing or courier,
· photocopying, and
· postage.

We will consult with you about any extraordinary costs before incurring them on your behalf.

Form 8.4. Acknowledgment with Outline of Fee Structure

Mr. Alec Sutherland
[DATE]
Page 2

Generally, we send out bills on a monthly basis. Bills briefly describe the matter and services performed and separately identify fees
for legal services and expenses incurred on your behalf. Typically, the
period described by each bill is for the previous month. Some expenses
and charges may not be billed until several months after the date the
expenses were incurred. We cannot determine such expenses as long-dis-
tance telephone charges until we are billed.

Our invoices are payable within thirty (30) days of the billing date.
Past-due amounts bear interest at the rate of twelve (12) percent per
annum. If you ever have any questions regarding any aspects of your
bill, please let me know. Your silence will indicate agreement with the
bill.

You will receive copies of all significant correspondence, memoranda,
and other documents relating to you in this matter. You have authorized
us to take all actions that we deem advisable on your behalf. We will
do this and, at the same time, make every effort to limit the fees and
costs to those that are necessary.

If this agreement, on the terms and conditions set forth above, is
satisfactory to you, please sign your name where indicated below on the
enclosed copy of this letter. Please return the signed copy as well as
your $[AMOUNT] retainer to me in the enclosed envelope.

We look forward to working with you on this and other matters.

                        Sincerely,

                        Paul Ernst, Esq.

Acknowledged, accepted, approved, and agreed.

    Date: _____   Signed: _____

[AUTHOR/TYPIST]
[DOCUMENT LOCATOR CODE]

Form 8.4. Acknowledgment with Outline of Fee Structure *(Continued)*

DeLost, Ernst, Miessner, Powell & Wilcox
Attorneys at Law
1257 Main Street, Suite 900
Los Angeles, CA 90066
(310) 555-6000

[DATE]

Joseph R. Martin
1945 Berks Boulevard
Suite Three
Shillington, PA 19613

    Re: [IDENTIFY MATTER]

Dear Mr. Martin:

  Please be advised that we cannot accept the within action for commencement of litigation. This is in Northern Solano County, Northern
California, and not in our litigation area. The costs and travel necessary would exceed the amount of recovery. It would not be cost effective to litigate outside the county in which the action was filed.

  We are sorry we are unable to help you at this time. If you need further information or assistance in regard to this matter, please do not
hesitate to contact me.

              Sincerely,

              Majorie Miessner, Esq.

[AUTHOR/TYPIST]
[DOCUMENT LOCATOR CODE]

Form 8.5. Rejection of a Potential Client

DeLost, Ernst, Miessner, Powell & Wilcox
Attorneys at Law
1257 Main Street, Suite 900
Los Angeles, CA 90066
(310) 555-6000

[DATE]

Eleanor Sedgewick
Chief Operating Officer
Donaldson Pen Company
243 Admiral Road, Suite 1020
Los Angeles, CA 90099

　　　　Re: [IDENTIFY MATTER]

Dear Ms. Sedgewick:

After studying the pleading filed by [NAME OF OPPOSING PARTY], I believe we should test the legal sufficiency of the complaint by filing a
demurrer. I will forward the demurrer and a copy of our Points and Authorities memorandum to you.

A demurrer is a technical device by which the court accepts the facts
pleaded as true and rules only on points of law. The objective is to
urge the court to find the plaintiff's pleading not legally sufficient.

Should the court adopt our position, the plaintiff is usually given
a chance to amend. That is, unless the court is convinced the legal the-
ory cannot survive attack. This is rare on the first occasion.

We hope to have the matter on calendar and heard on [DATE AND TIME].
Since this is purely a legal matter, you don't need to be present in
court. But you may attend the hearing if you wish to.

Please understand there will be many cases on the court's calendar,
and we cannot determine exactly what time the matter will be called. If
you plan to be present in court, please call my secretary a few days
before the hearing date to make sure the matter has not been continued
to a later date. If there is any problem with the proposed hearing date,
please let me know.

　　　　Sincerely,

　　　　Anthony Wilcox, Esq.

[AUTHOR/TYPIST]
[DOCUMENT LOCATOR CODE]

Form 8.6. Letter to Client Describing Demurrer

DeLost, Ernst, Miessner, Powell & Wilcox
Attorneys at Law
1257 Main Street, Suite 900
Los Angeles, CA 90066
(310) 555-6000

[DATE]

Lisa Campinella
1936 Papermill Road
Mountain View, CO 80301

Re: [IDENTIFY MATTER]

Dear Mrs. Campinella:

It is helpful to the success of your case if you keep the materials you receive from our office in an organized fashion.

We suggest that letters and memos be kept in chronological order in a separate file. Easy access tends to reduce the time required for attorney-client conferences.

It is our practice to send you copies of all legal documents including those pertaining to discovery and motions filed with the court. Since these tend to be voluminous, we strongly suggest they be kept in a separate file from the letters and memos. Clients report this system helps them in providing information needed to answer and prepare for:

- interrogatories,
- requests for admission,
- depositions,
- settlement conferences, and
- trial testimony.

If you have any questions, please feel free to call me.

Sincerely,

Angela Shapiro
Senior Paralegal

[AUTHOR/TYPIST]
[DOCUMENT LOCATOR CODE]

Form 8.7. Helping the Client to Organize Documents

MEMORANDUM

To: [ATTORNEY]

From: [PARALEGAL]

Date: [DATE MEMO SENT]

Re: [IDENTIFY CASE]

According to the General Calendar, the last day to lodge the following is [DATE]:

- Objections to Jury Instructions,
- Jury Statement,
- Pretrial Report, and
- Opposition to Motions in Limine.

There is a Final Settlement Conference/Mandatory Settlement Conference on [DATE] in the above-referenced matter.

To provide you the needed paralegal support, please indicate on the list below what assistance you will need, and return this form to me at your earliest convenience. Thanks for the attention.

_____ Prepare exhibits
_____ Shepardize and cite check brief/legal memorandum
_____ Prepare subpoena/notice/stipulation
_____ Draft motions: for continuance, for transfer, to dismiss, to strike
_____ Prepare hearing/exhibit/case notebook
_____ Draft requests for admission/production
_____ Draft answers to interrogatories
_____ Summarize answers to interrogatories
_____ Prepare notices of depositions
_____ Prepare subpoena duces tecum
_____ Draft declaration/affidavit
_____ Prepare memorandum of costs
_____ Prepare damages calculations
_____ Prepare writ of attachment

Comments: _____

_____

_____

Form 8.8. Memo to Attorney Before Trial

DeLost, Ernst, Miessner, Powell & Wilcox
Attorneys at Law
1257 Main Street, Suite 900
Los Angeles, CA 90066
(310) 555-6000

[DATE]

Leslie Morris
123 Koritnice Way
Orlando, OH 45678

Re: [IDENTIFY MATTER]

Dear Ms. Morris:

Pursuant to the attached release form, please provide our office with the following documents:

[LIST]

The case identification is [PROVIDE IDENTIFICATION] and the incident occurred on [DATE].

Trial has been set in this matter which sets forth a deadline date of [DATE]. Pursuant to [CITE AUTHORITY] you must submit this information on or before [DATE].

Thank you for your help. Please feel free to telephone me, reversing charges, if you require anything further.

Sincerely,

Angela Shapiro
Senior Paralegal

[AUTHOR/TYPIST]
Enclosure: Release
[DOCUMENT LOCATOR CODE]

Form 8.9. Document Search

DeLost, Ernst, Miessner, Powell & Wilcox
Attorneys at Law
1257 Main Street, Suite 900
Los Angeles, CA 90066
(310) 555-6000

[DATE]

Gerald P. Meridith
Haskell, Wood, Alpert, Franks & Kayman
1135 University Avenue, Suite 1700
Los Angeles, CA 90033

    Re: [IDENTIFY MATTER]

Dear Mr. Meridith:

As you will recall, this office represents defendant, [NAME], in the above-captioned action. As you are aware, we served your office with [TYPE OF DISCOVERY] on [DATE]. To date, we have not received any answer to the discovery. Please allow this letter to act as a meet and confer session in the hope of resolving this dispute without the necessity of court intervention.

As you know, California Code of Civil Procedure §2030 (h) provides that a party must serve responses to interrogatories within 30 days of the date the interrogatories are propounded. You will further recall that Civil Procedure Code §2030 (k) specifically states:

> If a party to whom interrogatories have been directed fails to serve a timely response, that party waives any right to exercise the option to produce writings under subdivision (f), as well as any objection to the interrogatories, including one based upon privilege or the production of work product under section 2018 ¼

Accordingly, based upon the above-referenced sections, you have now waived your right to object to all discovery previously propounded to you in this action. We request that your responses to this discovery be served upon us, without objections, within ten (10) days of the date of this correspondence. If these responses are not received by that time, I will have no other alternative but to proceed with the filing of a motion to compel at which time a request for sanctions will be made. However, I am confident that we can avoid court intervention in resolving this dispute.

Thank you for your anticipated courtesy and cooperation in this regard.

    Sincerely,

    Scott Powell, Esq.

[AUTHOR/TYPIST]
[DOCUMENT LOCATOR CODE]

Form 8.10. Failure to Respond to Discovery

DeLost, Ernst, Miessner, Powell & Wilcox
Attorneys at Law
1257 Main Street, Suite 900
Los Angeles, CA 90066
(310) 555-6000

[DATE]

Gerald P. Meridith
Haskell, Wood, Alpert, Franks & Kayman
1135 University Avenue, Suite 1700
Los Angeles, CA 90033

           Re: [IDENTIFY MATTER]

Dear Mr. Meridith:

   This letter confirms that we have agreed to an extension for you to
file answers to interrogatories and documents in response to our request
for production. The extension is for thirty (30) days from the current
due date.

   We will require that you file objections timely, pursuant to the
rules.

   I understand the extension of time was requested because you are currently in trial in [PLACE].

                    Sincerely,

                    Sandra Wilson
                    Litigation Coordinator

[AUTHOR/TYPIST]
[DOCUMENT LOCATOR CODE]

Form 8.11. Confirmation of Granting of Extension of Time to Respond

DeLost, Ernst, Miessner, Powell & Wilcox
Attorneys at Law
1257 Main Street, Suite 900
Los Angeles, CA 90066
(310) 555-6000

[DATE]

Joseph R. Martin, Esq.
1945 Berks Boulevard
Suite Three
Shillington, PA 19613

     Re: [IDENTIFY MATTER]

Dear Mr. Martin:

  This correspondence confirms our telephone conversation wherein you graciously extended the time for our discovery responses from the date due of [DATE], for two (2) weeks, up to and including [DATE].

  As you requested, the attorney will contact you in regard to a possible settlement of this matter prior to the discovery deadline.

  Please feel free to contact me should you have any questions in the meantime.

                    Sincerely,

                    Mark C. Williams
                    Legal Assistant

[AUTHOR/TYPIST]
[DOCUMENT LOCATOR CODE]

Form 8.12. Confirmation of Extension of Time to Respond to Discovery

DeLost, Ernst, Miessner, Powell & Wilcox
Attorneys at Law
1257 Main Street, Suite 900
Los Angeles, CA 90066
(310) 555-6000

[DATE]

Eleanor Sedgewick
Chief Operating Officer
Donaldson Pen Company
243 Admiral Road, Suite 1020
Los Angeles, CA 90099

Re: [IDENTIFY MATTER]

Dear Ms. Sedgewick:

The attorney representing Mr. [NAME] has served us with a set of written questions called interrogatories. Unless we request an extension of time, we are required to answer each of these questions within thirty (30) days, or, in this case, by [DATE]. A copy of the interrogatories is enclosed with space available for your answer under each question.

We have a duty to answer these questions as long as the questions:

(1)   are relevant to the subject of the lawsuit,
(2)   appear reasonably calculated to lead to the discovery of admissible evidence, and
(3)   do not involve privileged communication and discussion of strategy between us.

We can object and not answer questions which are:

(1)   unreasonably repetitive, or
(2)   unduly burdensome or expensive and can be obtained from some other less burdensome or less expensive source.

We can also seek a protective order from the court and not answer questions that appear designed to embarrass you or to protect a trade secret or other confidential information.

Please provide me with draft answers to as many factual questions as possible within two weeks, or by [DATE]. We will then edit and supplement the answers and get them back to you for final review before you sign them. Some of these questions are legal rather than factual in nature and will be answered by us. Our failure to cooperate with this discovery process can result in dire consequences, such as the trial court excluding certain evidence, or even dismissal of our lawsuit.

Form 8.13. Obtaining Client Answers to Interrogatories[5]

Eleanor Sedgewick
[DATE]
Page 2

   If you have any questions concerning this procedure, please contact
me promptly.

                              Sincerely,

                              Angela Shapiro
                              Senior Paralegal
[AUTHOR/TYPIST]
[DOCUMENT LOCATOR CODE]

Form 8.13. Obtaining Client Answers to Interrogatories[5] *(Continued)*

DeLost, Ernst, Miessner, Powell & Wilcox
Attorneys at Law
1257 Main Street, Suite 900
Los Angeles, CA 90066
(310) 555-6000

[DATE]

Eleanor Sedgewick
Chief Operating Officer
Donaldson Pen Company
243 Admiral Road, Suite 1020
Los Angeles, CA 90099

Re: [IDENTIFY MATTER]

Dear Ms. Sedgewick:

Please read through the attached requests for admissions from [NAME] and answer them by stating that you either admit or deny each of the facts stated.

We are under a deadline for responding. Please return the enclosed document to me by [DATE].

If you have any questions or comments, please do not hesitate to give us a call.

Sincerely,

Robert Evans
Legal Assistant

[AUTHOR/TYPIST]
Enclosures: Requests for Admission
[DOCUMENT LOCATOR CODE]

Form 8.14. Short Form Transmittal of Discovery to Client

DeLost, Ernst, Miessner, Powell & Wilcox
Attorneys at Law
1257 Main Street, Suite 900
Los Angeles, CA 90066
(310) 555-6000

[DATE]

Alec Sutherland
1936 Papermill Road
Mountain View, CO 80301

Re: [IDENTIFY MATTER]

Dear Mr. Sutherland:

The copies of defendant [NAME]'s interrogatories and request for production concerning your case are enclosed. As you know, you must answer the questions and provide the items from the list if you have them.

It is imperative that you answer each question as fully as possible. Under the rules, both need to be returned to the defendant by a certain date. After you have done so, please call me for an appointment to come in and review the answers and sign the required verification pages.

A recent case was dismissed by the judge because the plaintiff misled the court when answering questions like the ones enclosed. Please be sure you fully answer each question.

IT MAY BE DAMAGING TO YOUR CASE IF WE DO NOT COMPLETE THESE ANSWERS IN LESS THAN TWENTY (20) DAYS.

Please contact me by [DATE]. Do not hesitate to call if you have any questions.

Thank you for your immediate attention to this matter.

Sincerely,

Angela Shapiro
Senior Paralegal

[AUTHOR/TYPIST]
Enclosures: Interrogatories
            Request for Production
[DOCUMENT LOCATOR CODE]

Form 8.15. Transmittal of Discovery to Client with Instructions

DeLost, Ernst, Miessner, Powell & Wilcox
Attorneys at Law
1257 Main Street, Suite 900
Los Angeles, CA 90066
(310) 555-6000

[DATE]

Eleanor Sedgewick
Chief Operating Officer
Donaldson Pen Company
243 Admiral Road, Suite 1020
Los Angeles, CA 90099

    Re: [IDENTIFY MATTER]

Dear Ms. Sedgewick:

   A Notice to Take Oral Deposition by Videotape of [NAME] is enclosed.
The deposition is scheduled for [DATE AND TIME], pursuant to our agreement.

   The deposition will take place at [PLACE] in accordance with the enclosed Notice.

   Thank you for your attention to this matter.

                    Sincerely,

                    Angela Shapiro
                    Senior Paralegal

[AUTHOR/TYPIST]
Enclosure: Notice
[DOCUMENT LOCATOR CODE]

Form 8.16. Sending Notice of Deposition to Client

DeLost, Ernst, Miessner, Powell & Wilcox
Attorneys at Law
1257 Main Street, Suite 900
Los Angeles, CA 90066
(310) 555-6000

[DATE]

Eleanor Sedgewick
Chief Operating Officer
Donaldson Pen Company
243 Admiral Road, Suite 1020
Los Angeles, CA 90099

        Re: [IDENTIFY MATTER]

Dear Ms. Sedgewick:

  This letter is to confirm your deposition scheduled for [DATE] at our
office.

  We also scheduled a predeposition meeting for you on [DATE AND TIME].
Please contact [NAME] if you have any problems with the schedule.

  I enclose a list of deposition suggestions for your reference. I look
forward to visiting with you.

                 Sincerely,

                 John B. Watson
                 Paralegal
[AUTHOR/TYPIST]
Enclosure: Deposition Suggestions
[DOCUMENT LOCATOR CODE]

Form 8.17. Scheduling a Predeposition Meeting with Client

DeLost, Ernst, Miessner, Powell & Wilcox
Attorneys at Law
1257 Main Street, Suite 900
Los Angeles, CA 90066
(310) 555-6000

[DATE]

Gerald P. Meridith
Haskell, Wood, Alpert, Franks & Kayman
1135 University Avenue, Suite 1700
Los Angeles, CA 90033

    Re: [IDENTIFY MATTER]

Dear Mr. Meridith:

  We have attempted to schedule the depositions of the employees from the [NAME PARTY] on several occasions.

  This letter is to follow up your conversation with [ATTORNEY]. He again requested deposition dates for the employees. As I understand it, you agreed to schedule the depositions next week. Please contact [ATTORNEY] or me with the names and dates on or before [DATE].

  If we do not hear from you by [DATE], we will send Notices for [STATE MONTH].

  Thank you for your attention to this matter.

            Sincerely,

            Mark C. Williams
            Legal Assistant

[AUTHOR/TYPIST]
[DOCUMENT LOCATOR CODE]

Form 8.18. Scheduling Depositions

DeLost, Ernst, Miessner, Powell & Wilcox
Attorneys at Law
1257 Main Street, Suite 900
Los Angeles, CA 90066
(310) 555-6000

[DATE]

Eleanor Sedgewick
Chief Operating Officer
Donaldson Pen Company
243 Admiral Road, Suite 1020
Los Angeles, CA 90099

                Re: [IDENTIFY MATTER]

Dear Ms. Sedgewick:

   The original and a copy of your oral deposition taken on [DATE] are
enclosed for your review. Please read through the transcript very carefully and note any corrections on a separate sheet of paper. It is necessary that you sign the original in front of a Notary Public. If you
do not have access to a notary in your area, we have several in our office. We are under a strict time deadline, so it is imperative you sign
and return the deposition immediately.

   I recommend you keep your copy of the deposition to review in the
event we go to trial. I enclose a self-addressed, stamped envelope for
your convenience in returning the signed original to our office.

   If you have any questions, please do not hesitate to contact me. Your
prompt attention to this matter will be greatly appreciated.

                Sincerely,

                Robert Evans
                Legal Assistant
[AUTHOR/TYPIST]
Enclosures: Original and copy of deposition transcript
[DOCUMENT LOCATOR CODE]

Form 8.19. Deposition Transcript Review

DeLost, Ernst, Miessner, Powell & Wilcox
Attorneys at Law
1257 Main Street, Suite 900
Los Angeles, CA 90066
(310) 555-6000

[DATE]

Eleanor Sedgewick
Chief Operating Officer
Donaldson Pen Company
243 Admiral Road, Suite 1020
Los Angeles, CA 90099

Re: [IDENTIFY MATTER]

Dear Ms. Sedgewick:

The original transcript of your deposition is enclosed for your review. Please read the transcript, and if any changes are necessary in your answers, please mark out the incorrect portions and insert the corrections. Initial each correction in the righthand margin.

After reviewing the transcript, please sign under penalty of perjury. Return the transcript, in the envelope provided for your convenience, directly to our office.

If the transcript is not signed and returned to [NAME] within thirty (30) days of submission to you, it will be deemed you have failed to sign the transcript. At the time of trial a copy signed by the reporter will be filed with the court, along with a declaration stating that you have not signed your deposition transcript.

Thank you very much for your cooperation.

Sincerely,

John B. Watson
Paralegal

[AUTHOR/TYPIST]
Enclosure: Deposition transcript
[DOCUMENT LOCATOR CODE]

Form 8.20. Deposition Transcript Review

DeLost, Ernst, Miessner, Powell & Wilcox
Attorneys at Law
1257 Main Street, Suite 900
Los Angeles, CA 90066
(310) 555-6000

[DATE]

County Courthouse
Criminal Division
9 Greetwar Junction
Railway, MO 52379

Attention: Department 32 Clerk

        Re: [IDENTIFY MATTER]

Dear Clerk of the Court/Department 32:

   I understand that you will handle the deposition and exhibits in accordance with the Federal Rules.

   Enclosed please find the original deposition of [NAME], and the original set of deposition exhibits. The original deposition has been signed
by [NAME].

                        Sincerely,

                        Angela Shapiro
                        Senior Paralegal
[AUTHOR/TYPIST]
Enclosures: Deposition
            Deposition Exhibits
[DOCUMENT LOCATOR CODE]

Form 8.21. Providing the Court with Deposition as an Exhibit

DeLost, Ernst, Miessner, Powell & Wilcox
Attorneys at Law
1257 Main Street, Suite 900
Los Angeles, CA 90066
(310) 555-6000

[DATE]

Douglas LeFevre
3906 Halderman Blvd.
Suite 800
Sacramento, CA 90046

　　Re: [IDENTIFY MATTER]

Dear Mr. LeFevre:

　As a matter of introduction, I am the legal assistant who has been asked to coordinate witnesses for trial in the above-entitled matter. [NAME] is currently involved in litigation against [NAME] due to [ISSUE]. The litigation is in the discovery phase and our in-house attorneys are trying to educate themselves about the history that led up to the contract dispute.

　You were identified as one of the individuals knowledgeable in that area. Staff attorney [NAME] asked me to contact you and to set up an interview date for him. Please let me know if it would be convenient for you to meet him during the week of [DATES]. My direct line is [PHONE]. Please feel free to call me should you have any questions.

　Thank you, in advance, for your cooperation.

　　　　　　　Sincerely,

　　　　　　　Sandra Wilson
　　　　　　　Litigation Coordinator

[AUTHOR/TYPIST]
[DOCUMENT LOCATOR CODE]

Form 8.22. Letter to Witness

DeLost, Ernst, Miessner, Powell & Wilcox
Attorneys at Law
1257 Main Street, Suite 900
Los Angeles, CA 90066
(310) 555-6000

[DATE]

Postmaster
[CITY, STATE AND ZIP CODE OF OLD ADDRESS]

    Re: [CASE NAME]
       [ANY OTHER STANDARD OFFICE INFORMATION]

Dear Postmaster:

  Please begin a search and provide us with the forwarding address on the following:

       [NAME
       PREVIOUS ADDRESS AND ZIP]

  I have enclosed a check for $[AMOUNT]. A self-addressed, stamped envelope is included for a convenient reply.

       Sincerely,

       Angela Shapiro
       Senior Paralegal

[AUTHOR/TYPIST]
Enclosures: Check
       Envelope
[DOCUMENT LOCATOR CODE]

Form 8.23. Request to Postmaster for Forwarding Address

DeLost, Ernst, Miessner, Powell & Wilcox
Attorneys at Law
1257 Main Street, Suite 900
Los Angeles, CA 90066
(310) 555-6000

[DATE]

Albert Keswick, Ph.D.
ASC Environmental Consulting
26 Center Road
Los Angeles, CA 90055

Re: [IDENTIFY MATTER]

Dear Dr. Keswick:

This letter is to let you know we are setting aside Mondays and Tuesdays through October for depositions of our experts in this case.

Please let me know when you can be available on those dates. Your deposition will be taken there at your office.

Thank you for your attention to this matter.

Sincerely,

Paul Ernst, Esq.

[AUTHOR/TYPIST]
[DOCUMENT LOCATOR CODE]

Form 8.24. Scheduling Expert Deposition

DeLost, Ernst, Miessner, Powell & Wilcox
Attorneys at Law
1257 Main Street, Suite 900
Los Angeles, CA 90066
(310) 555-6000

[DATE]

Gerald P. Meridith
Haskell, Wood, Alpert, Franks & Kayman
1135 University Avenue, Suite 1700
Los Angeles, CA 90033

Re: [IDENTIFY MATTER]

Dear Mr. Meridith:

This will confirm our telephone conversation this morning that you will make your expert, [NAME], available for his deposition as soon as possible.

Thank you for your cooperation in this matter.

Sincerely,

Anthony Wilcox, Esq.

[AUTHOR/TYPIST]
[DOCUMENT LOCATOR CODE]

Form 8.25. Deposition of Opposing Party's Expert Witness

DeLost, Ernst, Miessner, Powell & Wilcox
Attorneys at Law
1257 Main Street, Suite 900
Los Angeles, CA 90066
(310) 555-6000

[DATE]

Andrea Wilkins
754 Kings Road, Apt. 3
Los Angeles, CA 90056

Re: [IDENTIFY MATTER]

Dear Ms. Wilkins:

You have been subpoenaed to testify at the trial in the above-entitled case. As you will not be called to testify on the first day of the trial, it would cause unnecessary trips to the courthouse (and a lot of waiting around), if you were to appear in court on the date listed in your subpoena. Many times there are delays in the commencement of a trial and it is impossible to determine now the exact date and time you will testify.

California Code of Civil Procedure §1985.1 [CITE RELEVANT CODE FOR YOUR LOCALE] provides:

Any person who is subpoenaed to appear at a session of court, or at the trial of an issue therein, may, in lieu of appearance at the time specified in the subpoena, agree with the party at whose request the subpoena was issued to appear at another time or upon such notice as may be agreed upon. Any failure to appear pursuant to such an agreement may be punished as a contempt by the court issuing the subpoena.

If you will call my office we will cooperate with you in making arrangements for you to be "on call." This way, you will not have to appear in court on the dates specified in the subpoena, or wait in court until you are needed to testify.

We are asking your cooperation in contacting our office at your earliest possible convenience, so we may discuss your availability for appearance at trial.

Should we not hear from you within the next five (5) days, we shall have no alternative but to contact our process server in order to personally serve the subpoena upon you, in order to protect our client's interests in this matter.

Form 8.26. Long Form Subpoena Letter to Witness with On-Call Agreement

Andrea Wilkins
[DATE]
Page 2

   Thank you for your attention. Please sign and return the enclosed
original documents immediately in the envelope provided for your convenience.

   Please feel free to contact the undersigned directly with any questions you may have.

                              Sincerely,

                              Sandra Wilson
                              Litigation Coordinator
[AUTHOR/TYPIST]
Enclosure: Agreement to be On-Call
[DOCUMENT LOCATOR CODE]

Form 8.26. Long Form Subpoena Letter to Witness with On-Call Agreement *(Continued)*

[TOP OF NEXT PAGE]

TO [THE PERSON SERVED]:

This subpoena requires your attendance in court on the day trial has been set to begin in _____ v. _____, Case no.: _____, on _____ [DATE]_____ at _____ A.M./P.M., in _____ [ADDRESS]_____. However, due to the congestion of court calendars, the trial seldom begins on the first day and frequently the case trails from day to day, until it can be assigned to an available courtroom.

If you appear on the date set forth in the subpoena, it is likely that the court will order you to reappear on another date when the courtroom is available. You can avoid this inconvenience by agreeing to be "on-call." We agree to give you as much advance notice as possible as to when your appearance in court will be required.

In order to be placed "on-call," you must sign below and indicate your name, address, and telephone numbers where you can be reached days and evenings. Then, you must return this agreement to [NAME] in the envelope provided.

AGREEMENT TO BE ON-CALL

Because a subpoena has been served upon me, I hereby agree to be on-call and agree to appear when notified by telephone to do so.

Name: _____

Address: _____

_____

Telephone Number: Days: _____

Evenings: _____

Dated: _____ Signed: _____

Form 8.26. Long Form Subpoena Letter to Witness with On-Call Agreement (Continued)

DeLost, Ernst, Miessner, Powell & Wilcox
Attorneys at Law
1257 Main Street, Suite 900
Los Angeles, CA 90066
(310) 555-6000

[DATE]

Gloria Rutger
12 Anticure Lane
Pottsville, OR 23456

        Re: [IDENTIFY MATTER]

Dear Ms. Rutger:

   You have been served with a subpoena to appear as a witness at the
above-entitled trial. Because of the congestion of the court calendar, it
is difficult to predict the exact time you will be called to testify.

   To inconvenience you as little as possible, we are permitted to make
an arrangement with you so you will not have to appear at the time specified in the subpoena if you agree to appear at a later time upon receipt of a phone call. We will try to give you notice, at least a day
in advance, as to when you will be needed to testify. The trial will
either start shortly after the above date, or it may be moved to a later
date if a courtroom is not available.

   If you agree to the above arrangement, please date and sign the enclosed copy of this letter and return it in the enclosed self-addressed
envelope. If you do not agree to this arrangement, you will be required
to appear at the time and place stated in the subpoena.

                     Sincerely,

                     Anthony Wilcox, Esq.
[AUTHOR/TYPIST]

   I, the undersigned, hereby agree to appear at the court indicated in
the enclosed subpoena, dated [DATE OF SUBPOENA], upon receipt of a telephone call or written notice. I may be reached or a message may be left
at the following telephone numbers:

                                        _____

Dated: _____   Signed: _____
                                           [TYPE WITNESS' NAME]
[DOCUMENT LOCATOR CODE]

Form 8.27. Short Form Subpoena Letter to Witness with On-Call Agreement

DeLost, Ernst, Miessner, Powell & Wilcox
Attorneys at Law
1257 Main Street, Suite 900
Los Angeles, CA 90066
(310) 555-6000

[DATE]

Eleanor Sedgewick
Chief Operating Officer
Donaldson Pen Company
243 Admiral Road, Suite 1020
Los Angeles, CA 90099

Re: [IDENTIFY MATTER]

Dear Ms. Sedgewick:

As we discussed in our telephone conversation today, your case has been set for a settlement conference on [DATE AND TIME]. The conference will take place at [NAME OF FIRM AND ADDRESS].

As you know, the conference is an attempt to successfully resolve this matter without the necessity and risk of going to trial.

Please be at our office no later than [TIME].

Enclosed are some information sheets for your reference. Please do not hesitate to contact us if you have any questions.

Sincerely,

Angela Shapiro
Senior Paralegal
[AUTHOR/TYPIST]
Enclosure: Information Sheet
[DOCUMENT LOCATOR CODE]

Form 8.28. Informing the Client of a Settlement Conference

DeLost, Ernst, Miessner, Powell & Wilcox
Attorneys at Law
1257 Main Street, Suite 900
Los Angeles, CA 90066
(310) 555-6000

[DATE]

Eleanor Sedgewick
Chief Operating Officer
Donaldson Pen Company
243 Admiral Road, Suite 1020
Los Angeles, CA 90099

        Re: [IDENTIFY MATTER]

Dear Ms. Sedgewick:

  This is to advise you the trial of the above-referenced case has been
rescheduled for [DATE]. I enclose a copy of the court's order for your
reference.

  Please do not hesitate to contact me if you have any questions or comments, or if you have any scheduling conflicts.

        Sincerely,

        Sandra Wilson
        Litigation Coordinator

[AUTHOR/TYPIST]
Enclosure: Order
[DOCUMENT LOCATOR CODE]

Form 8.29. Informing the Client of the Trial Date

DeLost, Ernst, Miessner, Powell & Wilcox
Attorneys at Law
1257 Main Street, Suite 900
Los Angeles, CA 90066
(310) 555-6000

[DATE]

Eleanor Sedgewick
Chief Operating Officer
Donaldson Pen Company
243 Admiral Road, Suite 1020
Los Angeles, CA 90099

Re: [IDENTIFY MATTER]

Dear Ms. Sedgewick:

The judge has set your case for trial the week of [DATE]. The Thursday before the week your case is set, the court will notify us if your case will be called to trial.

If the judge calls your case to trial, we will need to get in touch with you on short notice. You must inform us immediately of any changes in your residence or business addresses or telephone numbers.

THIS DOES NOT MEAN THAT YOU SHOULD BE IN OUR OFFICE ON THAT DATE OR MAKE ARRANGEMENTS TO TAKE OFF WORK AT THIS TIME IF YOU ARE PRESENTLY WORKING.

However, you MUST call and give us current telephone numbers so we can locate you if the judge calls your case to trial.

Sincerely,

Mark C. Williams
Legal Assistant

[AUTHOR/TYPIST]
[DOCUMENT LOCATOR CODE]

Form 8.30. Getting Client Contact Information Before Trial

DeLost, Ernst, Miessner, Powell & Wilcox
Attorneys at Law
1257 Main Street, Suite 900
Los Angeles, CA 90066
(310) 555-6000

[DATE]

Eleanor Sedgewick
Chief Operating Officer
Donaldson Pen Company
243 Admiral Road, Suite 1020
Los Angeles, CA 90099

        Re: [IDENTIFY MATTER]

Dear Ms. Sedgewick:

   This letter is to advise you that your case has been scheduled for
mediation on [DATE AND TIME].

   I enclose some information for your reference regarding the mediation
process.

   We will be in touch with you to make all the arrangements.

            Sincerely,

            Angela Shapiro
            Senior Paralegal
[AUTHOR/TYPIST]
Enclosure: Mediation Information
[DOCUMENT LOCATOR CODE]

Form 8.31. Letter to Client About Scheduled Mediation

DeLost, Ernst, Miessner, Powell & Wilcox
Attorneys at Law
1257 Main Street, Suite 900
Los Angeles, CA 90066
(310) 555-6000

[DATE]

Behi Nardel
U.S. County Courthouse
1000 State Street
Independence, CA 92344

        Re: [IDENTIFY MATTER]

Dear Ms. Nardel:

Please provide me with the forms necessary to receive daily transcripts from the trial in progress. I will return them to you immediately for processing.

This letter will also confirm that I would like to order the transcript for the hearing held in the above case on [DATE]. I believe the job number is [NUMBER].

Enclosed please find our firm's check in the amount of $[AMOUNT] made out to [PAYEE] for the deposit.

Please have the transcript preparation expedited. Thank you for your assistance in this matter.

                Sincerely,

                Angela Shapiro
                Senior Paralegal

[AUTHOR/TYPIST]
[DOCUMENT LOCATOR CODE]

Form 8.32. Arranging for Receipt of Daily Trial Transcripts

DeLost, Ernst, Miessner, Powell & Wilcox
Attorneys at Law
1257 Main Street, Suite 900
Los Angeles, CA 90066
(310) 555-6000

[DATE]

Gerald P. Meridith
Haskell, Wood, Alpert, Franks & Kayman
1135 University Avenue, Suite 1700
Los Angeles, CA 90033

                    Re: [IDENTIFY MATTER]

Dear Mr. Meridith:

   The signed and notarized Compromise Settlement Agreement, Release and
Indemnity Agreement are enclosed. I am also enclosing the signed Agreed
Order of Partial Dismissal with Prejudice for filing in connection with
the above-referenced matter. Please forward conformed copies to me after
you receive them from the clerk.

   Thank you for your cooperation in resolving this matter.

                    Sincerely,

                    Angela Shapiro
                    Senior Paralegal
[AUTHOR/TYPIST]
Enclosures: Compromise Settlement Agreement
            Release and Indemnity Agreement
            Agreed Order of Partial Dismissal with Prejudice
[DOCUMENT LOCATOR CODE]

Form 8.33. Settlement Letter to Opposing Counsel

DeLost, Ernst, Miessner, Powell & Wilcox
Attorneys at Law
1257 Main Street, Suite 900
Los Angeles, CA 90066
(310) 555-6000

[DATE]

Eleanor Sedgewick
Chief Operating Officer
Donaldson Pen Company
243 Admiral Road, Suite 1020
Los Angeles, CA 90099

        Re: [IDENTIFY MATTER]

Dear Ms. Sedgewick:

   After many conversations with the attorney for [NAME OF OPPOSING PARTY], they finally agreed to pay the settlement amount offered of $[AMOUNT]. The payment will be made in one installment on [DATE].

   Accordingly, I have enclosed a letter for your signature. Please return the signed release in the enclosed envelope. It will be forwarded to the attorney for [NAME OF OPPOSING PARTY] upon our receipt of the settlement funds.

   Please feel free to contact me should you have any questions.

                 Sincerely,

                 Angela Shapiro
                 Senior Paralegal

[AUTHOR/TYPIST]
Enclosure: Release
           Envelope
[DOCUMENT LOCATOR CODE]

Form 8.34. Settlement Letter to Client with Release for Signature

DeLost, Ernst, Miessner, Powell & Wilcox
Attorneys at Law
1257 Main Street, Suite 900
Los Angeles, CA 90066
(310) 555-6000

[DATE]

Juan Gomez
Finance Administrator
ABC Firing Company
3450 Altay Street
Bellevue, WA 89019

Re: [IDENTIFY MATTER]

Dear Mr. Gomez:

This letter shall confirm and memorialize our agreement today to fully resolve the claim of [NAME OF CLIENT], "[ABBREVIATED NAME]," against [NAME OF OPPOSING PARTY], "[ABBREVIATED NAME]," arising out of and in connection with the [IDENTITY OF MATTER AND DATE OF OBLIGATION].

[NAME OF OPPOSING PARTY] agrees to pay [NAME OF CLIENT] the sum of $[AMOUNT] on or before [DATE] and upon receipt of an executed copy of this letter agreement. [NAME OF CLIENT], upon receipt of such funds, releases, acquits, and discharges [NAME OF OPPOSING PARTY] from any and all claims, demands, debts, damages, liabilities, actions, causes of action, suits, claims for arbitration, arbitration demands, grievances, sums of money, accounts, covenants, agreements, contracts, benefits, and promises in law and equity which [NAME OF CLIENT] now has, or has ever had, or may have or obtain against [NAME OF OPPOSING PARTY], whether subject to dispute and whether known or unknown, suspected or unsuspected, of every character whatsoever (collectively "claims").

It is understood that [NAME OF CLIENT] makes such release and discharge of [NAME OF OPPOSING PARTY] on behalf of any and all persons, entities, associations, agents, employees, servants, officers, directors, corporations, subsidiaries, affiliates, successors and assigns, attorney's representatives, and partnerships connected with [NAME OF CLIENT].

It is further understood that the releases granted in this agreement include, but are not limited to, any claims, violations and breaches of any agreements, and any violations of law, and shall extend to all heirs, executors, administrators, persons, entities, associations, agents, employees, servants, officers, directors, corporation's subsidiaries, affiliates, successors and assigns, attorneys, representatives, and partnerships connected with or related to [NAME OF CLIENT].

Dated: _____   Signed: _____
                                            [TYPE CLIENT'S NAME]

Form 8.35. Release Letter for Client's Signature

DeLost, Ernst, Miessner, Powell & Wilcox
Attorneys at Law
1257 Main Street, Suite 900
Los Angeles, CA 90066
(310) 555-6000

[DATE]

Eleanor Sedgewick
Chief Operating Officer
Donaldson Pen Company
243 Admiral Road, Suite 1020
Los Angeles, CA 90099

        Re: [IDENTIFY MATTER]

Dear Ms. Sedgewick:

  Here are the copies you requested. If I can be of further assistance,
please don't hesitate to call me

                    Sincerely,

                    Angela Shapiro
                    Senior Paralegal

[AUTHOR/TYPIST]
Enclosures: [IDENTIFY]
[DOCUMENT LOCATOR CODE]

Form 8.36. Short Transmittal Letter

LAW FIRM NAME
ADDRESS & TELEPHONE NUMBERS

Date:

To:

Re:

Our file number:

Copies   Date   Description

[LIST THE SPECIFICS]

The above is/are transmitted with this notice:

[ ] For your approval	[ ] For necessary action
[ ] For signature and return	[ ] Per your request
[ ] Per our conversation	[ ] For review and comment
[ ] Approved	[ ] For correction
[ ] For distribution	[ ] Disapproved
[ ] For your file	[ ] For recordation
[ ] See remarks below	[ ] For payment
[ ] For your information	[ ] As noted below
[ ] No necessary action	[ ] For signature

Remarks: _____

_____

[CLOSING]
[FIRM NAME]
[signature]
[NAME AND TITLE,
IF NOT AN ATTORNEY]

Form 8.37. Transmittal Form Letter

DeLost, Ernst, Miessner, Powell & Wilcox
Attorneys at Law
1257 Main Street, Suite 900
Los Angeles, CA 90066
(310) 555-6000

[DATE]

[NAME]
[ADDRESS OF COURT]

        Re: [IDENTIFY MATTER]

Dear Clerk:

   An original and two (2) copies of [LIST DOCUMENTS] in the above-referenced action are enclosed.

   Please file the originals and one copy with the court, and return a file-stamped copy of each to me in the enclosed, self-addressed, stamped envelope I have provided for your convenience.

   By copy of this letter, I am serving counsel of record for [PARTIES] with a copy of the same.

   Thank you for your assistance in this matter. If you have any questions, please do not hesitate to call me.

                    Sincerely,

                    Angela Shapiro
                    Senior Paralegal

[AUTHOR/TYPIST]
[DOCUMENT LOCATOR CODE]

Form 8.38. Letter to a Clerk of the Court

DeLost, Ernst, Miessner, Powell & Wilcox
Attorneys at Law
1257 Main Street, Suite 900
Los Angeles, CA 90066
(310) 555-6000

[DATE]

[NAME]
[ADDRESS OF COURT]

        Re: [IDENTIFY MATTER]

Dear Clerk:

   The following documents are enclosed for entry in the above-referenced
matter:

   (1)   Original Motion and Declaration in Support of Order to Amend,
          etc.;
   (2)   Original and one copy of the Order to Amend;
   (3)   Original and one copy of each of the Amended Judgments;
   (4) $20 check for the court's fees; and
   (5)   Stamped, self-addressed envelope.

Please present the pleadings for amending the judgments to the judge for
entry.

   After filing the above, please return conformed copies of the Order
and Judgments in the enclosed, self-addressed stamped envelope. Thank
you.

                 Sincerely,

                 Angela Shapiro
                 Senior Paralegal

[AUTHOR/TYPIST]
[DOCUMENT LOCATOR CODE]

Form 8.39. Transmittal of Several Documents to a Clerk of the Court

DeLost, Ernst, Miessner, Powell & Wilcox
Attorneys at Law
1257 Main Street, Suite 900
Los Angeles, CA 90066
(310) 555-6000

[DATE]

Honorable Jane Smith
U.S. Magistrate
[ADDRESS]

        Re: [CASE INFORMATION]

Dear Magistrate Smith:

   In accordance with Local Rule 2.2(c) for the Northern District of
Texas, defendant must submit the documents delivered with this letter
under seal for your in camera inspection.

   Additionally, as directed in your letter to counsel dated [DATE], a
file-stamped copy of the defendant's response to plaintiff's motion to
compel discovery withheld on claim of privilege is being delivered to
you, and is filed this date with the Clerk for the Northern District of
Texas.

                    Sincerely,

                    John B. Watson
                    Legal Assistant

[AUTHOR/TYPIST]
Enclosures: [SPECIFY]
[DOCUMENT LOCATOR CODE]

Form 8.40. Letter to Magistrate

DeLost, Ernst, Miessner, Powell & Wilcox
Attorneys at Law
1257 Main Street, Suite 900
Los Angeles, CA 90066
(310) 555-6000

[DATE]

[NAME]
[ADDRESS]

Re: [IDENTIFY MATTER]

Dear Process Department:

Enclosed are three (3) copies of the summons and complaint in the above-entitled matter. Please take immediate action to serve the following:

[FULL NAME AS IT APPEARS ON THE SUMMONS AND COMPLAINT; VERY IMPORTANT BECAUSE THE PROOF OF SERVICE WILL LIST THIS INFORMATION EXACTLY AS STATED HERE]

[ADDRESS]

[AGENT FOR SERVICE IF APPLICABLE]

Subservice is acceptable if you provide us with a declaration regarding due diligence. We ask that you expedite action in this matter as we have an Order to Show Cause hearing date set on [DATE].

Sincerely,

Angela Shapiro
Senior Paralegal

[AUTHOR/TYPIST]
Enclosures: [LIST]
[DOCUMENT LOCATOR CODE]

Form 8.41. Instructions for Service of Summons and Complaint

DeLost, Ernst, Miessner, Powell & Wilcox
Attorneys at Law
1257 Main Street, Suite 900
Los Angeles, CA 90066
(310) 555-6000

[DATE]

[NAME]
[ADDRESS]

       Re: [IDENTIFY MATTER]

Dear Process Department:

   The courtesy subpoena I described by telephone last night is enclosed.
If you could, please see it is served on [NAME] at the address shown.
[NAME] will accept service but has requested the service agent call to
arrange a convenient time. Because of security measures in the building, the agent will also have to call [NAME] from the security gate.

   Should you have any unforeseen questions or difficulties, please contact [NAME] in our office at [NUMBER].

   Thank you for your help in this matter on such short notice.

                    Sincerely,

                    Mark C. Williams
                    Legal Assistant

[AUTHOR/TYPIST]
Enclosure: Subpoena
[DOCUMENT LOCATOR CODE]

Form 8.42. Instructions for Service of Subpoena

DeLost, Ernst, Miessner, Powell & Wilcox
Attorneys at Law
1257 Main Street, Suite 900
Los Angeles, CA 90066
(310) 555-6000

[DATE]

Andrea Wilkins
754 Kings Road, Apt. 3
Los Angeles, CA 90056

Re: [IDENTIFY MATTER]

Dear Ms. Wilkins:

This letter is to thank you for your assistance as a witness in the above-entitled case. I appreciate your willingness to make yourself available despite the inconvenience it undoubtedly caused.

In many ways, our justice system is totally dependent on the cooperation and support of witnesses who are willing to suffer inconvenience and sometimes hardship in responding and presenting information relevant to particular cases. Unfortunately, all too many people are unwilling to cooperate, which in turn raises serious questions about the continued vitality of what is, without question, one of the finest justice systems in the Western world.

I am pleased that no such problems were encountered in this case, and your participation and support for our legal system is gratefully acknowledged.

Sincerely,

Angela Shapiro
Senior Paralegal

[AUTHOR/TYPIST]
[DOCUMENT LOCATOR CODE]

Form 8.43. Thank-You Letter to Witness After Trial

End Notes

[1]Martin L. Dean and Anne Kemp, *Managing Litigation: The Insider's Guide,* §§1.29–1.30 (1991).

[2]Id. §1.24.

[3]Id. §§1.43–1.44.

[4]Id. §2.45.

[5]The body of this letter was originally printed in an article found in *Legal Assistant Today* magazine. See Michael K. Gaige, CLA, "Obtaining Thorough Answers to Interrogatories From Clients," *Legal Assistant Today,* pp. 111–112 (July/Aug. 1992).

Nine

CORPORATE LAW

9.1 / The Paralegal Role

    Form 9.1. Reservation of Corporate Name

    Form 9.2. Setting Up the Corporation

    Form 9.3. Information to and Request from Client

    Form 9.4. Filing a UCC-1

    Form 9.5. Preincorporation Information Request to Client

    Form 9.6. Information Letter Following Formation of Corporation

    Form 9.7. Stock Transaction Information Letter

    Form 9.8. Restricted Stock Letter

    Form 9.9. Dissolution Acknowledgement and Information to Client

    Form 9.10. Memorandum Re: Findings

9.1 / The Paralegal Role

Corporate legal assistants are also sometimes called business paralegals or business legal assistants. Titles vary even more, such as "portfolio specialist," "control officer," and "document analyst," when employed by a corporation as opposed to a law firm. According to *The Basics of Paralegal Studies* by David Lee Goodrich

Most of the work done by a paralegal in a firm which specializes in corporate law involves the preparation of paperwork. When a corporation is initially formed, it may be the responsibility of the paralegal to ascertain whether the name the client has chosen for the corporation is available, because a corporation will not be allowed to do business under a name that is deceptively similar to one that is already in use in the state. Articles of incorporation will have to be prepared and filed with the appropriate legal authorities so that the corporation can be properly chartered. Corporate bylaws, resolutions, minutes, and annual reports may need to be prepared for continuing clients.[1]

Paralegal responsibilities in this practice area involve a wide variety of tasks. The National Federation of Paralegal Associations includes the following specific tasks in its job description list:[2]

- Check availability and reserve corporate name.
- Draft and file articles of incorporation.
- Complete and file qualification of foreign corporations.
- Obtain good standing certificates from Secretary of State.
- Draft bylaws.
- Draft notices and minutes, or consents of organization meeting.
- Draft Subscription Agreements.
- Issue and transfer stock, prepare stock and shareholder registers, prepare and maintain analyses and charts of outstanding securities.
- Draft banking resolutions.
- Draft Shareholder Agreements.
- Draft Buy–Sell Agreements.
- Prepare necessary documents for opening of corporate bank account.
- Draft Employment Agreements.
- Complete and file any assumed name certificates.
- Complete and file election by small business corporation and subsequent shareholder's consents to such election.
- Complete and file application for employer identification number.
- Complete and file application for workers' compensation.
- Notify State Tax Commission of stock book location.
- Prepare and file DISC elections.
- Complete and file application for unemployment insurance.
- Complete and file application for employer withholding tax registration.
- Complete and file application for appropriate licenses to operate specific businesses.

- Complete and file trade name applications, copyright applications, and financing statements.

- Order minute book, stock book and seal.

- Draft and file application for proper licensing when forming professional or special purpose corporation.

- Draft response to auditor's request for information.

- Prepare and file annual reports.

- Maintain a tickler system for annual meetings.

- Draft notices, proxy materials, ballots, affidavits of mailing, and agendas for annual meeting and special meetings.

- Draft resolutions to be considered by directors.

- Draft oaths and reports of judges of election for annual meeting.

- Draft shareholder's and director's minutes.

- Draft written consents in lieu of meetings.

- Draft documents and correspondence necessary to effect dissolution and liquidation, consolidating merger, and sale of substantially all of the assets of corporations.

- Draft stock option plan, maintain stock option registers and related charts.

- Collect information, draft documents and correspondence necessary to adopt qualified profit sharing and pension plans, and related trust agreements and other documents. Submit such materials to IRS for determination letters.

- Draft and organize closing papers on corporate acquisitions.

- Draft lease agreements.

- Draft Articles of Merger or Consolidation, Plan of Merger or Consolidation.

- Draft closing checklists and closing memoranda.

- Prepare closing files and assist in closing.

- Draft articles of dissolution.

- Conduct due diligence investigation.

- Compile and index documents in corporate transactions.

- Draft partnership agreements and amendments.

- Draft statements of partnership and certificates of limited partnership.

- Draft certificates of amendment to certificates of limited partnership.

- Prepare and publish Notice of Substance of Certificates of General and Limited Partnership.
- Draft minutes of partnership meetings.
- Draft noncompetition agreements for selling partners.
- Draft Agreement for Dissolution of Partnership.
- Draft and publish Notice of Termination of Partnership (or Continuation of Successor Business).
- Draft certificates or cancellation of certificates of limited partnership.
- Draft and file trade name documents, amended trade name documents.
- Draft analysis in connection with tax planning, draft state and federal tax returns, and prepare for audit.
- Prepare documents for qualification to do business in foreign jurisdictions.
- Prepare necessary documents to amend and restate Articles of Incorporation and amend bylaws.
- File and terminate UCC Financial Statements with state and county offices.
- Search state and county offices for federal tax liens, UCC filings, deeds, mortgages, and judgments.
- Prepare and file DBAs (doing business as), certificates of trade names, and certificates of assumed names with the appropriate state office.
- Prepare and file governmental applications and reports.
- Collect information from, and verify filings with, the Secretary of State and other state and local agencies.
- Change registered office or agent.

Before mailing any documents, contact the person you are writing to by telephone to make sure that all appropriate documentation is included. This approach can expedite document return and reduce unnecessary delays.

The majority of correspondence is directed to either the incorporating client, an interdepartmental contact, or secretaries of state and government agencies, mostly explaining and transmitting required forms for processing and return. Some paralegals incorporate the document into the letter itself. The following letters reflect some types of correspondence frequently prepared by paralegals, either for their own signature or the attorney's.

DeLost, Ernst, Meissner, Powell & Wilcox
Attorneys at Law
1257 Main Street, Suite 900
Los Angeles, CA 90066
(310) 555-6000

[DATE]

Secretary of State
1340 "J" Street
Fresno, CA 04228

        Re: Reservation of Corporate Name [NAME]

Dear Secretary of State:

   In accordance with [CITE AUTHORITY], application is hereby made for a
Certificate of Reservation of the name [CORPORATE NAME TO BE RESERVED].

   Please reserve the above name for use by the corporation and send the
Certificate of Reservation to the undersigned in the stamped, self-addressed envelope enclosed for your convenience. I have enclosed a check
in the amount of $[AMOUNT] to cover your fees. Thank you for your as-
sistance in this matter.

                    Sincerely,

                    Angela Shapiro
                    Senior Paralegal

[AUTHOR/TYPIST]
Enclosures: [LIST]
[DOCUMENT LOCATOR CODE]

Form 9.1. Reservation of Corporate Name

DeLost, Ernst, Meissner, Powell & Wilcox
Attorneys at Law
1257 Main Street, Suite 900
Los Angeles, CA 90066
(310) 555-6000

[DATE]

Secretary of State
[ADDRESS]

        Re: [NAME OF CORPORATION]

Dear Secretary of State:

   On behalf of the above-captioned corporation, I am enclosing one original and three copies of the Articles of Incorporation and a check made
payable to your order in the amount of $[AMOUNT] to cover filing and
certification fees.

   Also enclosed is a Certificate of Reservation of Corporate Name no.
[SPECIFY], issued [DATE], on behalf of this corporation.

   Please file the original Articles of Incorporation and certify, and
return two copies of the articles to our messenger. Thank you for your
assistance in this matter.

                        Sincerely,

                        Mark C. Williams
                        Paralegal

[AUTHOR/TYPIST]
Enclosures: [LIST]
[DOCUMENT LOCATOR CODE]

Form 9.2. Setting Up the Corporation

DeLost, Ernst, Meissner, Powell & Wilcox
Attorneys at Law
1257 Main Street, Suite 900
Los Angeles, CA 90066
(310) 555-6000

[DATE]

Scott Samuels, Ph.D.
Senior Engineering Advocate
The High Sierra Telephone Company
8490 Lower Lakeside Road
Los Angeles, CA 90066

Re: [NAME OF CORPORATION]

Dear Dr. Samuels:

Your share certificate representing 100 shares of the common stock
[NAME] is enclosed. Please sign this certificate as both President and
Secretary and keep in a secure location.

Also enclosed is the corporation's minute book, which contains the Articles of Incorporation, Restated Articles of Incorporation, Bylaws, Organizational Minutes, and book of share certificates.

The corporation needs to be maintained on an annual basis with documentation of significant corporate accounts. Forms for annual meetings
are included in the "Forms" section of the minute book. Please call me
if we can be of any further assistance on this matter.

The purpose of the Uniform Commercial Code [UCC] is to establish a
coordinated code covering most of commercial law and to establish a
means of continuing revision to improve it and keep it up to date and
timely. The code requires a high standard of conduct for merchants by
imposing a duty to act in good faith. The UCC states the law for a major
part of all business transactions.

Sincerely,

John B. Watson
Legal Assistant

[AUTHOR/TYPIST]
Enclosures: [LIST]
[DOCUMENT LOCATOR CODE]

Form 9.3. Information to and Request from Client

DeLost, Ernst, Meissner, Powell & Wilcox
Attorneys at Law
1257 Main Street, Suite 900
Los Angeles, CA 90066
(310) 555-6000

[DATE]

Secretary of State
[ADDRESS]

    Re: [NAME OF CORPORATION]

Dear Secretary of State:

  I am enclosing four UCC-1 Financing Statements dated [DATE], wherein [NAME] is the debtor. Please file these UCC-1's with the [STATE] Secretary of State and conform the Acknowledgment copy, Secured Party copy, and Debtor copy.

  Please return the conformed copies to me via regular mail. I have enclosed a check made payable to the Secretary of State in the amount of $[AMOUNT] to cover their fees. Please call me if you have any questions.

               Sincerely,

               Mark C. Williams
               Legal Assistant

[AUTHOR/TYPIST]
Enclosures: [LIST]
[DOCUMENT LOCATOR CODE]

Form 9.4. Filing a UCC-1

DeLost, Ernst, Meissner, Powell & Wilcox
Attorneys at Law
1257 Main Street, Suite 900
Los Angeles, CA 90066
(310) 555-6000

[DATE]

Scott Samuels, Ph.D.
Senior Engineering Advocate
The High Sierra Telephone Company
8490 Lower Lakeside Road
Los Angeles, CA 90066

    Re: [NAME OF CORPORATION]

Dear Dr. Samuels:

  We would like to obtain some information from you so we can complete
the formation of your corporation. For this purpose, I am enclosing our
preincorporation questionnaire for you to complete.

  Should you have any questions or difficulties with completion of the
questionnaire, please feel free to contact me at my office.

  Upon completion, please return the questionnaire to the firm and to
my attention. Once again, should you have any questions regarding the
foregoing, please do not hesitate to contact me.

  Thank you for your cooperation.

          Sincerely,

          John B. Watson
          Legal Assistant

[AUTHOR/TYPIST]
Enclosures: [LIST]
[DOCUMENT LOCATOR CODE]

Form 9.5. Preincorporation Information Request to Client

DeLost, Ernst, Meissner, Powell & Wilcox
Attorneys at Law
1257 Main Street, Suite 900
Los Angeles, CA 90066
(310) 555-6000

[DATE]

Scott Samuels, Ph.D.
Senior Engineering Advocate
The High Sierra Telephone Company
8490 Lower Lakeside Road
Los Angeles, CA 90066

Re: [NAME OF CORPORATION]

Dear Dr. Samuels:

On [DATE], the Articles of Incorporation for the [NAME] Corporation were filed with and accepted by the Secretary of State of California, thus creating your new corporation. Enclosed are copies of the documents that are required to complete the formation of [NAME] Corporation.

What follows is a brief description of each document, along with instructions and other information regarding its completion. In addition, this letter discusses certain formalities about which you should be aware regarding your relationship to the new corporation.

(1) Appointment of Director(s)

The incorporator of a corporation is entitled to take certain preparatory steps in connection with the formation of a corporation after the articles of incorporation have been filed. This includes naming the initial director(s) of the corporation. In the enclosed Action by Sole Incorporator, I, as incorporator, am appointing you the initial director of the corporation. In addition, Section 40 of the enclosed Bylaws authorizes a Board of Directors consisting of [NUMBER] Director(s).

By the enclosed Acceptance of Appointment, the initial director accepts his appointment and election as a director of the corporation and discharges me from my capacity as incorporator.

(2) Section [SPECIFY]

Section [SPECIFY] reflects the actions that must be taken by the Board of Directors of the corporation in order to complete the formation of the corporation. As you will note, a number of items are contained in this document, including the adoption of bylaws, designation of the principal office of the corporation, election of officers, issuance of shares, authorization for a corporate banking account, and similar matters.

Form 9.6. Information Letter Following Formation of Corporation

Scott Samuels, Ph.D.
[DATE]
Page 2

Every for-profit corporation must issue shares of stock and receive
consideration in return to adequately capitalize the corporation for its
contemplated business. Failure to issue shares to adequately capitalize
the corporation may enable creditors to disregard the corporate entity
and hold the shareholders personally liable for the corporate debts.
Moreover, there are tax considerations concerning capitalizing the corporation by stock rather than by debt or loans to the corporation.

If the corporation is capitalized with too high a debt-to-equity
ratio, the IRS may characterize any interest paid or repayment of the
debt as a dividend. Such payment would then be subject to double taxation—that is, taxation on corporate earnings at both the corporate and
shareholder levels. Generally speaking, a three-to-one (3:1) debt-equi-
ty ratio will pass IRS scrutiny, although higher ratios have also proven
acceptable.

It is my understanding that [NUMBER] shares of Common Stock of the
corporation (out of [NUMBER] authorized) are to be issued by the corporation to you in exchange for $[AMOUNT] in cash, cancellation of in-
debtedness, or property. The reason for not issuing the entire number
of authorized shares is that it is generally preferable to have a number of shares remain "in treasury" for some future purpose. Otherwise,
the Articles of Incorporation would have to be amended to authorize additional shares if a future need arises. If you desire to capitalize the
corporation in some different way, or for other consideration, please
let me know and I can amend the consent accordingly.

Also enclosed are the following documents that are referenced in Section [SPECIFY]:

(a)   Statement by Domestic Stock Corporation,
(b)   Certified copy of the Articles of Incorporation,
(c)   Copy of Bylaws, and
(d)   Application for Employer Identification Number.

The Statement by Domestic Stock Corporation should be completed and
filed with the Secretary of State's office. This document informs the
Secretary of State about the directors and officers of the corporation.
Please sign and date this document where marked by the tab.

The Bylaws provide for the internal governance of the corporation.
Please note that the date listed for the annual meeting of shareholders
will not be binding on the corporation. The board may, by resolution of
the board, declare a different date for the annual meeting. Nonetheless,
it is required that an annual meeting date be stated in the Bylaws.

All businesses must have a Federal Employer Identification Number. We
have completed the application with the information you have previously submitted. After reviewing this document to ensure the accuracy of
the information contained therein, please sign and date it where marked
by the tab.

Form 9.6. Information Letter Following Formation of Corporation *(Continued)*

Scott Samuels, Ph.D.
[DATE]
Page 3

After each of the enclosed documents has been completed and executed, <u>please return the following documents to me</u>, and I will mail them to the appropriate places:

- Statement by Domestic Stock Corporation, and
- Application for Employer Identification Number.

You may return all the original signed documents to me for safekeeping, or you may maintain the documents yourself.

A certified copy of the Articles of Incorporation and the Bylaws should be inserted in the [NAME] Corporation's Minute Book. After we have received the executed copies of the enclosed documents, we will organize your Minute Book and forward the completed Book to you, if you desire.

(3) <u>Corporate Formalities</u>

It is essential to maintain the formal integrity of your new corporation. The corporation is a separate and distinct entity from you and its shareholders. To obtain the tax advantages and liability protection inherent in a corporate business form, all contracts, including employment contracts, loans, and leases, should be made in the name of—and on behalf of—the corporation. It is necessary to conduct all corporate business in the corporate name only and not in the individual name of any director, officer, or shareholder. Furthermore, all important transactions affecting your business should be memorialized in corporate minutes and kept in the corporate Minute Book.

When signing contracts on behalf of the corporation, not only should the corporate name appear, but the respective title of the officer signing on behalf of the corporation (for example, "By: [NAME], President"), should also appear. Any loans made to the corporation should be made in the name of the corporation, even though you may be required to endorse or guarantee such loans personally. The Board of Directors should approve all loans, and the appropriate resolutions should be prepared and inserted in the Minute Book.

With all that in mind, the following initial steps should be taken:

(a) All letterheads, bills, invoices, and other business forms used by the corporation should state the full legal name, as well as the current address and telephone number of the corporation.

(b) All your professional cards with respect to the corporation should reflect the corporation's name.

(c) A new bank account in the name of the corporation should be opened. The opening of this account is authorized in the enclosed documents.

(d) The telephone listing of the corporation, and the listing in all business directories, should be in the corporate name.

(e) The name on the corporation's place of business and the building's directory should show the new corporate name.

(f) All insurance policies relating to the corporation's business should be obtained by the corporation.

Form 9.6. Information Letter Following Formation of Corporation *(Continued)*

Scott Samuels, Ph.D.
[DATE]
Page 4

   (4) <u>Tax and Accounting Matters</u>

   You need to consult with your accountant concerning the taxes that
the corporation must pay on its own behalf and for its employees, if
any. The corporation must file California Income Tax Returns for each
of its tax years whether or not it has any income.

   The corporation will be responsible for certain employer taxes, such
as federal and state wage withholding taxes, social security taxes, and
unemployment taxes for all employees. Depending on whether the corporation sells personal property at the retail level or owns any real property, the corporation may also be responsible for California sales and
use taxes and real property taxes, respectively. Your accountant can assist you with all these taxes.

   If you have any questions or need any additional information, please
do not hesitate to contact me.

                    Sincerely,

                    Paul Ernst, Esq.

[AUTHOR/TYPIST]
Enclosures: [LIST]
[DOCUMENT LOCATOR CODE]

Form 9.6. Information Letter Following Formation of Corporation *(Continued)*

DeLost, Ernst, Meissner, Powell & Wilcox
Attorneys at Law
1257 Main Street, Suite 900
Los Angeles, CA 90066
(310) 555-6000

[DATE]

Scott Samuels, Ph.D.
Senior Engineering Advocate
The High Sierra Telephone Company
8490 Lower Lakeside Road
Los Angeles, CA 90066

Re: [NAME OF CORPORATION]

Dear Dr. Samuels:

Enclosed is (a) the Written Consent of ABC Corporation dated [DATE]
and (b) the Notice of Transaction dated [DATE].

Please review the Written Consent of Directors to ensure it is correct and complete. If so, it should be signed by [NAMES OF SIGNORS] and
placed in the corporate Minute Book.

The Notice of Transaction should be signed by you as President and
mailed to the Department of Corporations at [ADDRESS] (together with a
check payable to the Department of Corporations in the amount of
$[AMOUNT] representing the filing fee for the Notice of Transaction)
within fifteen (15) calendar days after the sale of the [NUMBER] shares
of common stock to [NAME] (see instructions 2 and 3 on the reverse side
of the Notice of Transaction). Please be certain to date the Notice of
Transaction when you send it to the Department of Corporations.

As always, should you have any questions or difficulties regarding the
foregoing request, please don't hesitate to contact me.

Sincerely,

Cara Simons
Paralegal

[AUTHOR/TYPIST]
Enclosures: [LIST]
[DOCUMENT LOCATOR CODE]

Form 9.7. Stock Transaction Information Letter

DeLost, Ernst, Meissner, Powell & Wilcox
Attorneys at Law
1257 Main Street, Suite 900
Los Angeles, CA 90066
(310) 555-6000

[DATE]

[NAME OF BUSINESS ENTITY]
[ADDRESS]

Re: [PURCHASE OF COMPANY]

Dear Sir or Madam:

This letter is furnished to [NAME OF CORPORATION] ("Company"), a California corporation, in connection with the purchase by the undersigned ("Purchaser") from you of [AMOUNT] shares of the Company's stock ("Securities").

The Purchaser hereby represents to the Company that the Purchaser is acquiring the Securities for its own account for investment, and not with a view to, or for resale in connection with, any distribution of the Securities within the meaning of the Securities Action of 1933 (the "Act"). No other person or entity has any interest in or right with respect to the Securities, nor has the undersigned agreed to give any person or entity any such interest or right in the future.

The Purchaser understands that:

- the Securities have not been registered under the Act or qualified under the California Corporate Securities Law of 1968,
- any disposition of the Securities is subject to restrictions imposed by federal and state law, and
- the certificates representing the Securities will bear a restrictive legend.

The Purchaser also understands that because the Securities were issued without registration, the Purchaser must hold them indefinitely unless they are subsequently registered (which the Company is not obligated to do and has no present intention of doing), or an exemption permitting the Purchaser's resale of the Securities is available. The Purchaser understands that the Company is not obligated to register the Securities or to comply with any exemption, and that the Company has no present intention of so doing.

The Purchaser recognizes that no public market exists with respect to the Securities and no representation has been made that such a public market will exist at a future date.

The Purchaser hereby represents that it has not received any advertisement or general solicitation with respect to the sale of the Securities.

Form 9.8. Restricted Stock Letter

[RECIPIENT'S NAME]
[DATE]
Page 2

The Purchaser agrees that it will not sell, transfer or otherwise dispose of the Securities, or any of them, without first having presented to the Company a written opinion of counsel satisfactory to the Company indicating that the proposed transfer will not be in violation of the Act or the rules and regulations promulgated under the Act. The undersigned agrees that a legend to this effect may be placed on the certificate(s) representing the Securities, or any substitutes for the Securities. The Purchaser hereby authorizes the Company to instruct the transfer agent for the Securities to enter a "stop order" with respect to the Securities.

The Purchaser agrees that the Purchaser will indemnify the Company against any and all liabilities, losses, costs, damages, fees, including reasonable attorneys' fees, and other expenses that the Company may sustain or incur in consequence of a sale or sales by the Purchaser of the Securities in violation of the Act.

The Purchaser acknowledges that the Purchaser has a preexisting personal or business relationship with the Company or any of its officers, directors, or principal shareholders, or, by reason of the Purchaser's business or financial experience or the business or financial experience of the Purchaser's financial advisor (who is not affiliated with the Company), could be reasonably assumed to have the capacity to protect the Purchaser's own interest in connection with the purchase of the Securities.

The Purchaser further acknowledges that the Purchaser is familiar with the financial condition and prospects of the Company's business, and has discussed with its officers the current corporate activities of the Company. The Purchaser believes that the Securities are securities of the kind the Purchaser wishes to purchase and hold for investment, and that the nature and amount of the Securities are consistent with the Purchaser's investment program.

Sincerely,

Paul Ernst, Esq.

[AUTHOR/TYPIST]
Enclosures: [LIST]
[DOCUMENT LOCATOR CODE]

Form 9.8. Restricted Stock Letter (*Continued*)

DeLost, Ernst, Meissner, Powell & Wilcox
Attorneys at Law
1257 Main Street, Suite 900
Los Angeles, CA 90066
(310) 555-6000

[DATE]

Scott Samuels, Ph.D.
Senior Engineering Advocate
The High Sierra Telephone Company
8490 Lower Lakeside Road
Los Angeles, CA 90066

Re: [NAME OF CORPORATION]

Dear Dr. Samuels:

This letter acknowledges your desire to dissolve the corporate structure of [NAME OF CORPORATION]. I will begin preparation of the appropriate documents immediately. Please note that a Certificate of Election to Dissolve will need to be signed by all officers and directors
of the corporation and will need to be filed with the Secretary of State.
I will also need a Tax Exemption Certificate for which I will apply to
the Franchise Tax Board.

Please verify your availability during the next week. I will attempt
to deliver the documents to you before week's end.

As always, should you have any questions, please feel free to contact
me at my office.

Sincerely,

Mark C. Williams
Legal Assistant

[AUTHOR/TYPIST]
Enclosures: [LIST]
[DOCUMENT LOCATOR CODE]

Form 9.9. Dissolution Acknowledgment and Information to Client

MEMORANDUM

TO: Anthony Wilcox, Esq./Contract Litigation Department

FROM: Karen Forbes, Contract Analyst

DATE: [DATE]

RE: <u>Findings on Lease Contracts for FYI Leasing Corp.</u>

I have completed analysis on the FYI Leasing Corp. contracts and have located the following problems:

(1) Exemption clause: missing

(2) Default clause: Although the clause is identified, there is no provision for costs or attorneys fees to the prevailing party.

(3) Options: Vague. There is mention and direct reference made regarding options, but they are not set forth anywhere in the document.

Please let me know if you would like me to draft the appropriate clauses for your review.

Form 9.10. Memorandum Re: Findings

End Notes

[1]David Lee Goodrich, *The Basics of Paralegal Studies,* p.7 (1991).

[2]Excerpted from "Paralegal Job Descriptions by Practice Area," compiled by the National Federation of Paralegal Associations. While not intended to be all inclusive, this list does provide examples of the differing types of assignments that can (and should) be delegated to paralegals.

Ten

LABOR LAW AND
EMPLOYEE BENEFITS

10.1 / The Paralegal Role

Form 10.1. EEOC Information Letter

Form 10.2. EEOC Acknowledgment Letter

Form 10.3. Application for Benefit Plan

Form 10.4. Termination Letter

Form 10.5. Letter Agreement Re: Binding Arbitration

Form 10.6. Answer to Request for Information from Union

Form 10.7. Freedom of Information Act Request

Form 10.8. Employee Access to Medical Records

Form 10.9. Certification and Demonstrations Under Rev. Proc. 91-66.

10.1 / The Paralegal Role

The labor and employment law practice can encompass a wide variety of subject matter areas. After all, the laws governing this practice include both federal and state statutes (and numerous administrative regulations), all adopted to "govern such matters as hours of work, minimum wages, unemployment insurance, safety and collective bargaining."[1] As outlined in *Paralegals in American Law,* the labor and employment paralegal's duties may include:

(1)   Interviewing clients.

(2)   Researching and compiling data for collective bargaining negotiations.

(3)   Attending bargaining negotiations between labor and management.

179

(4)   Preparing for hearings before administrative agencies such as the National Labor Relations Board.

(5)   Interviewing witnesses in employment discrimination matters.

(6)   Assisting with litigation involving labor law matters.[2]

The work product in this field often involves compiling large amounts of information to determine if a company has complied with the relevant labor, tax, and other applicable codes. Paralegals may be involved in submitting this information to relevant government agencies. Because of their expertise, employment law paralegals may also be called upon to draft policies and procedures manuals for the law firm or for a client's business.

Much of the labor and employment law practice for paralegals includes filing, organization, and maintenance of important records. Such employment-related records might encompass those used in union-organizing efforts, the outcome of arbitrations and grievances, and tracking employee benefits and pension funds. For example, for paralegals working in the Employee Benefits area, the National Federation of Paralegal Associations has compiled the following task list:

- Draft qualified plan documents, trust agreements, custodial agreements, money purchase, 401(k), stock bonus, defined benefit plans, and IRA plans.

- Draft amendments and restatements to plans to bring into compliance with new law and regulations.

- Draft Summary Plan Descriptions.

- Draft deferred compensation plans, including nonqualified executive compensation, stock option, and medical reimbursement plans.

- Draft Affiliate Adoption Statement.

- Draft Notification of Participation, Election to Participate, Beneficiary Designation, Election Out of Qualified Joint and Survivor Annuity, Application for Benefits, and Election to Contribute.

- Draft Summary Annual Report.

- Draft Benefit Statement.

- Draft promissory note and salary assignment for participant loans.

- Draft Board of Directors resolutions for plan adoption, adoption of amendments, and fixing contributions.

- Prepare and file application for IRS Determination Letter.

- Prepare and file annual report (5500 series and related schedules).

- Prepare PMGC premium forms.

- Monitor progress of implementation of new plans and amendments to verify required actions occur on schedule.

- Coordinate general notice mailings to clients about potential impact of new legal developments on plans.

- Develop and maintain checklists, sets of model plans, administrative documents, and letters, and update as new material is developed.

- Research interpretive questions on prohibited transactions and qualified and nonqualified plans.

- Calculate employer contributions and forfeitures and allocate to participant accounts.

- Determine valuation adjustments and allocate to participant accounts.

- Calculate participants' Years of Service for eligibility and vesting.

- Calculate benefit for terminated participant.

- Test plan for discrimination, top-heaviness, or §415 limits.

- Maintain plan as follows:
  —Pay termination benefits to terminated or retiring employees.
  —Pay loan proceeds, track loan repayments.
  —Deposit employee and employer contributions to accounts.
  —File IRS 1099's for payments made.
  —Pay hardship withdrawals.
  —Set up pension payroll (utilize outside vendor for this).
  —Track accounts to be certain investments are in accordance with investment elections.
  —Review account for updating and revisions to conform with new tax laws.

Labor and employment paralegals may further specialize in ERISA law, which involves the application of the Employee Retirement Income Security Act of 1974. Paralegals specializing in this practice area draft benefit plans such as trust agreements and 401(k) plans, among other important documents.

- summary plan descriptions,

- notes and salary assignments for participant loans,

- employee benefit plans, and

- calculating benefits for termination of participants.

This practice area also involves litigation over employment discrimination claims, such as racial discrimination, sexual harassment, age discrimination, and violations of the Americans with Disabilities Act. Such claims will involve the paralegal in tracking applicant flow documentation, hiring decisions, and promotion records, among other key pieces of information. For general letters used in litigation practices, *see* Chapter 8.

DeLost, Ernst, Miessner, Powell & Wilcox
Attorneys at Law
1257 Main Street, Suite 900
Los Angeles, CA 90066
(310) 555-6000

[DATE]

[NAME]
Equal Employment Opportunity Commission
[ADDRESS]

        Re: [NAME OF COMPLAINANT AND EEOC FILE NO.]

Dear [NAME]:

   This letter is to inform you that the charging party in the above-
referenced Charge has filed a lawsuit in the United States District
court, [DIVISION/BRANCH AND CASE NUMBER].

   I have been requested to inform you that due to this action it is in
the best interest of our client, [NAME], that we cease any future correspondence with you.

                        Sincerely,

                        Mark C. Williams
                        Legal Assistant
[AUTHOR/TYPIST]
[DOCUMENT LOCATOR CODE]

Form 10.1. EEOC Information Letter

DeLost, Ernst, Miessner, Powell & Wilcox
Attorneys at Law
1257 Main Street, Suite 900
Los Angeles, CA 90066
(310) 555-6000

[DATE]

[NAME]
Equal Employment Opportunity Commission
[ADDRESS]

        Re: [NAME OF COMPLAINANT AND EEOC FILE NO.]

Dear [NAME]:

   This letter acknowledges receipt by [COMPANY/CLIENT] of the above-referenced Charge of Discrimination on [DATE]. This law firm represents
[COMPANY] and will be assisting them in preparing a response. Please direct all future correspondence regarding this matter to [NAME], who is
the attorney handling this matter.

                          Sincerely,

                          Angela Shapiro
                          Senior Paralegal

[AUTHOR/TYPIST]
[DOCUMENT LOCATOR CODE]

Form 10.2. EEOC Acknowledgment Letter

DeLost, Ernst, Miessner, Powell & Wilcox
Attorneys at Law
1257 Main Street, Suite 900
Los Angeles, CA 90066
(310) 555-6000

[DATE]

[NAME]
[ADDRESS]

         Re: [IDENTIFY MATTER]

Dear [NAME]:

   The following items for your review:

   • a completed Application for Determination for Employee Benefit
     Plan,
   • [FORM NUMBER] for the above-referenced Plan, and
   • [FORM NUMBER] and the required User Fee.

[FORM NUMBER] Power of Attorney appoints [ATTORNEY OR DESIGNEE] as the
representative handling this matter for the Plan. Please send all inquiries concerning this Application to [HIM/HER].

                    Sincerely,

                    Marjorie Miessner, Esq.
[AUTHOR/TYPIST]
Enclosures: [LIST]
[DOCUMENT LOCATOR CODE]

Form 10.3. Application for Benefit Plan

DeLost, Ernst, Miessner, Powell & Wilcox
Attorneys at Law
1257 Main Street, Suite 900
Los Angeles, CA 90066
(310) 555-6000

[DATE]

John Berkin
23 Ardmore Avenue, Apt. 8
Los Angeles, CA 90099

        Re: <u>Termination of Employment and Remaining Benefits</u>

Dear Mr. Berkin:

   The purpose of this correspondence is to acknowledge that your employment with [COMPANY] officially terminated, effective 5:00 P.M. on
[DATE], and to outline the terms of your separation.

   As a result of the termination, you are entitled to the following benefits:

        [LIST BENEFITS REMAINING]

   You may wish to seek expert advice with respect to your 401(k) plan
or you may contact the plan administrator directly at [PHONE].

                    Sincerely,

                    Angela Shapiro
                    Senior Paralegal
[AUTHOR/TYPIST]
[DOCUMENT LOCATOR CODE]

Form 10.4. Termination Letter

DeLost, Ernst, Miessner, Powell & Wilcox
Attorneys at Law
1257 Main Street, Suite 900
Los Angeles, CA 90066
(310) 555-6000

[DATE]

John Berkin
23 Ardmore Avenue, Apt. 8
Los Angeles, CA 90099

Re: <u>Binding Arbitration Agreement</u>

Dear Mr. Berkin:

You should be receiving a package from the human resources department outlining the terms of your employment. Please note a full copy of the Binding Arbitration Agreement is included for your review.

In accepting employment with our company, you agree that any dispute of any form, nature, or kind between our company, its agents, employees, and assigns and you shall, at our election which can be made at any time prior to the commencement of a company proceeding, be submitted to arbitration before the American Arbitration Association in accordance with the rules.

In addition to the return of documentation required to complete the employment process, please sign this notice and return it to me.

Please call me if you have any questions.

Sincerely,

Patricia Powell, Esq.

[AUTHOR/TYPIST]
Enclosures: [LIST]
[DOCUMENT LOCATOR CODE]

Form 10.5. Letter Agreement Re: Binding Arbitration

DeLost, Ernst, Miessner, Powell & Wilcox
Attorneys at Law
1257 Main Street, Suite 900
Los Angeles, CA 90066
(310) 555-6000

[DATE]

[NAME]
[TITLE]
[UNION NAME AND LOCAL]
[ADDRESS]

Re: Information Requested

Dear [NAME]:

The [INFORMATION] you requested is enclosed. We believe our compliance to your request for information is complete and relevant. If you require additional information regarding your duty as our employees' collective bargaining representative, please contact me to discuss additional documentation.

It is our intention to fully cooperate in providing you with any and all information required to enable you to carry out your duties.

Sincerely,

Angela Shapiro
Paralegal

[AUTHOR/TYPIST]
Enclosures: [LIST]
[DOCUMENT LOCATOR CODE]

Form 10.6. Answer to Request for Information from Union

DeLost, Ernst, Miessner, Powell & Wilcox
Attorneys at Law
1257 Main Street, Suite 900
Los Angeles, CA 90066
(310) 555-6000

[DATE]

[NAME OF FOIA OFFICER]
[ADDRESS]

        Re: [IDENTIFY MATTER]

Dear [NAME]:

   This is a request under the Freedom of Information Act ("FOIA"), 5
U.S.C. § 522, as amended. We write to request a copy of all affidavits,
pleadings, records, documentation, letters, memoranda, and information
referring or pertaining to any and all published or unpublished cases
that qualify [TYPE OF EMPLOYEE] for the [TYPE OF STATUS] status under
the provisions of the [REGULATION NAME AND NUMBER] of the Fair Labor
Standards Act.

   Documentation available refers to the unpublished case, [NAME OF CASE
AND CASE NUMBER], which was heard and decided by a Labor Commissioner
from the Standards Office in [CITY, COUNTY, AND STATE]. We specifically request copies of all affidavits, records, and documentation referring or pertaining to this matter in which [NAME OF EMPLOYEE] was employed by a [TYPE OF EMPLOYER], [NAME OF EMPLOYER] in [ADDRESS OF
EMPLOYER].

   FOIA provides that if only portions of a record are exempt from release, the remainder must be released. We request that we be provided
with all nonexempt portions of the requested information that are reasonably segregable. Of course, we reserve the right to appeal the withholding of any information.

   We are prepared to pay for reasonable costs for locating and repro-
ducing the requested documents. FOIA provides, however, that you may reduce or waive the fees if it "is in the public interest because fur-
nishing the information can be considered as primarily benefitting the
public." See 5 U.S.C. §522(a)4(4)(A).

   We are making this request for [REQUESTOR]. If you have any questions
regarding this request, please telephone me at [PHONE]. As provided in
the FOIA, we will expect to receive a reply within ten (10) working days.
Thank you for your assistance.

                  Sincerely,

                  Anthony Wilcox, Esq.

[AUTHOR/TYPIST
Enclosures: [LIST]
[DOCUMENT LOCATOR CODE]

Form 10.7. Freedom of Information Act Request

DeLost, Ernst, Miessner, Powell & Wilcox
Attorneys at Law
1257 Main Street, Suite 900
Los Angeles, CA 90066
(310) 555-6000

[DATE]

[NAME AND ADDRESS
OF MEDICAL PRACTITIONER]

     Re: [NAME OF EMPLOYEE]

Dear [NAME]:

   [CODE] provides employees and their designated representatives a right
of access to relevant occupational exposure and medical records, while
at the same time affording appropriate privacy and confidentiality protection.

   Each employer is responsible for assuring compliance with this section, but the activities involved in complying with the access to medical records provisions can be carried out, on behalf of the employer,
by the physician or other health care personnel in charge of employee
medical records.

   Attached is a sample authorization letter for the release of employee medical record information to a designated representative.

                         Sincerely,

                         Mark C. Williams
                         Legal Assistant

[AUTHOR/TYPIST]
Enclosures: [LIST]
[DOCUMENT LOCATOR CODE]

Form 10.8. Employee Access to Medical Records

DeLost, Ernst, Miessner, Powell & Wilcox
Attorneys at Law
1257 Main Street, Suite 900
Los Angeles, CA 90066
(310) 555-6000

[DATE]

[CLIENT NAME]
[ADDRESS]

    Re: [PLAN NAME]

Dear [NAME]:

In order to complete the information required pursuant to certifications and demonstrations under Rev. Proc. 91-66, please enter a check mark on the appropriate line if this plan:

_____ (a)   benefits collectively bargained employees only. If so, do not complete the rest of this certification. *See* §6.03(1).

_____ (b)   benefits *both* collectively bargained employees *and* noncollectively bargained employees. If so, answer all the questions below, but answer questions 3 through 8 *only* with respect to the noncollectively bargained part of the plan. *See* §6.03(2).

_____ (c)   benefits the noncollectively bargained employees of more than one employer. If so, enter the number of employers (_____), and complete only one certification for the "plan." However, you may need to provide separate demonstrations for each employer that has noncollectively bargained employees under the plan. *See* §6.03(3).

With respect to the following questions, please mark "Y" for yes or "N" for no in the space provided:

_____ (1)   Does the plan—and, if applicable, each employer maintaining the plan—meet the requirements of §§3.02 and 3.03 of Rev. Proc. 91-66?

_____ (2)   Does this plan automatically satisfy the requirements of §401(a)(26)?

                If "no," attach Demonstration 1 to show that the plan satisfies the requirements of §401(a)(26).

                If "yes," attach Schedule A in lieu of Demonstration 1.

_____ (2a)   Are you required, or do you choose, to disaggregate the plan for purposes of §401(a)(26) under the disaggregation rules of the proposed regulations?

Form 10.9. Certification and Demonstrations Under Rev. Proc. 91-66

[RECIPIENT]
[DATE]
Page 2

If "yes," attach a separate Schedule B as part of Demonstration 1.

_____ (2b)   Is this a defined benefit plan that is providing additional benefit accruals to former employees of any employer maintaining the plan (e.g., ad hoc cost of living increases)?

If yes, attach Schedule C as part of Demonstration 1 and also attach Demonstration 2 showing that the plan meets the ratio percentage minimum coverage test.

_____ (3)   Is the plan a defined benefit plan that includes employee contributions not allocated to a separate account for plan years beginning after 1991?

If "yes," specify the locations of provisions intended to satisfy §1.401(a)(4)-6(b)(3)(ii) of the regulations:

_____

_____

_____ (4)   Does the plan either.

(a)   include a definition of compensation for the purpose of computing benefits or allocations (other than elective, employee, or matching contributions), that FAILS TO SATISFY the requirements of both §1.414(s)-1(c)(2) and §1.414(s)-1(c)(3) of the regulations or that includes imputed compensation credited for periods of absence from service that fails to satisfy §1.414(s)-1(e)(3);

or

(b)   incorporate ADP or ACP test that uses a definition of compensation that fails to meet the requirements of both §1.414(s)-1(c)(2) and §1.414(s)-1(c)(3)?

If "yes" attach Demonstration 3 to show that the definition satisfies §1.414(s)-1(d) of the regulations. *See* §5.07(3).

_____ (5)   Does the plan provide for past service credit that fails to meet the requirements of the safe harbor described in §1.401(a)(4)-5(a)(5) of the regulations?

Form 10.9. Certification and Demonstrations Under Rev. Proc. 91–66 *(Continued)*

If "yes," attach Demonstration 4 to show that such grant of past service does not have the effect of discriminating significantly in favor of highly compensated employees.

_____ (6)   Is the employer requesting a determination that each optional form of benefit, right, and feature under the plan that is not available to all participants on a uniform basis satisfies the current availability requirement of §1.401(a)(4)-4 of the regulations?

If "yes," attach Demonstration 5 to show that the availability of each optional form of benefit, right, or feature under the plan that is not uniformly available meets the requirements of §1.401(a)(4)-4(b) of the regulations, or that each such optional form of benefit, right or feature under the plan, other than ancillary benefits, meets the requirements of §1.401(a)(4)-4(d)(1) of the regulations.

(7)   From the list below, indicate (by check mark) the applicable section of the regulations intended to be satisfied by the design of the plan.

If the plan includes contributions tested exclusively under §1.401(a)(4)-2(d) of the regulations (relating to §401(k) and §401(m) plans), as well as other contributions intended to satisfy a design based safe harbor, check each applicable section:

_____ §401(a)(4)-2(b)(3) defined contribution plan with uniform allocation formula

_____ §401(a)(4)-8(b)(3) target benefit plan

_____ §401(a)(4)-2(d) exclusive tests for §401(k) and §401(m) plans

_____ §401(a)(4)-3(b)(3) unit credit defined benefit plan

_____ §401(a)(4)-3(b)(4) unit credit fractional rule plan

_____ §401(a)(4)-3(b)(5) flat benefit defined benefit plan

_____ §401(a)(4)-3(b)(7) insurance contract plan.

(8)   List the location of plan provisions satisfying the safe harbor indicated in item 7:

_____

Form 10.9. Certification and Demonstrations Under Rev. Proc. 91–66 *(Continued)*

```
[RECIPIENT]
[DATE]
Page 4


        (9)      If the plan received a favorable determination letter
                 in the past, but a copy of the latest determination
                 letter is not attached, explain the reason here:


                 _____


    An original and one copy of this correspondence has been forwarded to
you for your convenience. Please do not hesitate to contact me if you
have any questions about your responses.

                 Sincerely,



                 Mark C. Williams
                 Legal Assistant

[AUTHOR/TYPIST]
Enclosures: [LIST]
[DOCUMENT LOCATOR CODE]
```

Form 10.9. Certification and Demonstrations Under Rev. Proc. 91–66 *(Continued)*

End Notes

[1]Angela Schneeman, *Paralegals in American Law: Introduction To Paralegalism*, p. 16 (1995).
[2]Id. at 16.

Eleven

ENVIRONMENTAL LAW

11.1 / The Paralegal Role
    Form 11.1. Confidentiality Agreement
    Form 11.2. Transmittal of Assessment Statements
    Form 11.3. FOIA (Freedom of Information Act) Request for a Specific Item
    Form 11.4. Assignment of FOIA Request for Identification Number
    Form 11.5. FOIA Request for Documents
    Form 11.6. Typical FOIA Request to Federal Agency
    Form 11.7. Typical FOIA Request to State Agency
    Form 11.8. Public Records Act Request for Specific Information
    Form 11.9. Public Records Act Request for Documents and Records

11.1 / The Paralegal Role

Environmental laws, enacted by both states and the federal government, continue to multiply and grow in complexity and in their application to aspects of both life and work. This is particularly true in states like California, where extreme environmental problems, and public adoption of a strong ecological ethic, have resulted in as many as 80 environmental bills being passed into law each year. Environmental laws govern:

- the pesticides and herbicides used to grow food;

- the air pollution created to generate electricity;

- the waste water created to make clothing, cars, and paper; and

- the disposal of the toxic substances used to make computers and communications networks.

Each new statute results in new regulations and policies, hiring of attorneys and engineers to interpret those policies, and costs for training personnel in the new requirements. The overlapping jurisdiction of federal, state, and local governments can be confusing and require that businesses follow two or three paths to the same result in order to satisfy all these competing agencies. Driving compliance is the threat of penalties, administrative, civil, and criminal, often as much as $25,000 per day for each continuing violation. In the core areas of environmental practice, law firms

- negotiate environmental financial liability,

- work with regulators to obtain the essential pollution permits needed,

- provide legal advice to companies for redesigning their processes to meet pollution reduction requirements,

- help engineering consultants conduct compliance audits of operations,

- prepare reports required by environmental regulators,

- provide legal representation to clients in administrative hearings, civil court proceedings, or criminal courts, and

- conduct litigation to recover environmental cleanup and penalty costs from other liable parties.

The U.S. Environmental Protection Agency offices, Department of Health Services, and the Agricultural Commission are a few of the many government entities with which you will communicate in the practice of environmental law. Some general guidelines should be followed when drafting environmental practice correspondence.

- Segregate public records as state or federal documents and cite the appropriate authority for each.

- Telephone for requirements and include all the information necessary to process the request.

- Include the appropriate fees and return envelope, if necessary.

The agency's response time is often determined by the applicable laws, although most writers also include the deadline as a closing to their letters.

Because of the nature of this practice, almost all the sample letters in this chapter specify and cite specific state and federal statutes, and rights to information under those laws. The Freedom of Information Act (FOIA) (also mentioned in Chapter 10) contains many provisions and guidelines and is often listed as the primary authority for acquisition of information. The Public Records Act is also frequently cited.

DeLost, Ernst, Meissner, Powell & Wilcox
Attorneys at Law
1257 Main Street, Suite 900
Los Angeles, CA 90066
(310) 555-6000

[DATE]

John Douglas
Jergensen, Smith & Ross
2678 Dickens Street
Los Angeles, CA 90066

Re: Recycling Site of [NAME] Corporation

Dear Mr. Douglas:

In your capacity as counsel for [NAME] Insurance company, you requested access to documents in the [NAME] Corporation recycling site document depository. Access to the document depository will be granted for the sole purpose of assisting your client in evaluating whether it has any obligation to defend or indemnify [NAME].

By execution of this letter agreement, [NAME] Insurance company recognizes and acknowledges that such documents are currently subject to a confidentiality agreement between the members of the [NAME] committee. [NAME] Insurance company recognizes and agrees that the documents constitute valuable, special, and unique property of the [NAME] committee and its member companies, and that the [NAME] committee and its member companies wish to maintain and ensure the security and confidentiality of the documents.

Accordingly, your client, [NAME] Insurance company, agrees:

(1)   [NAME] Insurance company will not provide, discuss, allude to, or otherwise disclose the existence of any of the documents to any third party without the prior written consent of the undersigned chairman of the [NAME] committee, except to counsel, employees, agents, or advisors (collectively, "representatives") of [NAME] Insurance company who need to know of such documents for the sole purpose of assisting [NAME] Insurance company in evaluating whether it has any obligation to defend or indemnify [NAME]. [NAME] Insurance company will make all efforts to prevent the disclosure of any such documents by anyone other than as permitted under the conditions set forth in this letter agreement.

(2)   In the event [NAME] Insurance company or any of its representatives are requested or required (by oral question or request for information or documents in legal proceedings, interrogatories, subpoena, civil investigative demand, or similar process) to disclose any such documents, [NAME] Insurance company will provide prompt notice to the chairman of the [NAME] committee of such request(s) or requirement(s) so that an appropriate protective order may be sought and/or a waiver of compliance with the provisions of this letter agreement granted.

Form 11.1. Confidentiality Agreement

John Douglas
[DATE]
Page 2

    (3)   [NAME] Insurance company understands and agrees that:

         (a)   the documents disclosed to it under this agreement are of a confidential or proprietary nature or both,

         (b)   the documents disclosed to [NAME] Insurance company are special and unique, and

         (c)   the [NAME] committee and its member companies could be irreparably harmed by violation of this agreement.

        In the event that [NAME] Insurance company becomes aware of any breach of the confidentiality of, or misappropriation of, any of the documents, it will promptly give notice to the chairman of the [NAME] COMMITTEE.

    (4)   This agreement shall be governed by and construed in accordance with the laws of the state of [NAME].

                Sincerely,

                Paul Ernst, Esq.

[AUTHOR/TYPIST]
Enclosures: [LIST]
[DOCUMENT LOCATOR CODE]

_____

Recognition and Acknowledgment of Confidentiality Agreement:

                _____
                          Signature Line

Form 11.1. Confidentiality Agreement *(Continued)*

DeLost, Ernst, Meissner, Powell & Wilcox
Attorneys at Law

MEMORANDUM

To:

From:

Date:

Re: [NAME] Recycling

This memo transmits the fifth assessment for the [NAME] recycling cleanup project. The assessment was approved by the [NAME] committee at its [DATE] meeting.

In addition, a review of your assessment payment history has been completed. The attached assessment statement sets forth the fifth assessment, outstanding assessments, if any, and the total sum due now. If you are not able to pay the assessed sum in a timely manner, please contact [NAME AND PHONE NUMBER] to discuss a schedule for payment.

Please call the case attorney or [NAME] with any questions or comments.

Form 11.2. Transmittal of Assessment Statements

DeLost, Ernst, Meissner, Powell & Wilcox
Attorneys at Law
1257 Main Street, Suite 900
Los Angeles, CA 90066
(310) 555-6000

[DATE]

[NAME]
FOIA Officer
U.S. Environmental Protection Agency
[ADDRESS]

        Re: <u>FOIA Request for List of [STATE] NPDES Permittees</u>

Dear [NAME]:

  Pursuant to the Freedom of Information Act (FOIA), 5 U.S.C. Section
552, this is a request for a list of the names and addresses (owners'
address) for all National Pollutant Discharge Elimination System (NPDES)
Permittees in the state of [SPECIFY].

  We are prepared to pay the cost for producing the list. As required
by law, we anticipate your reply within ten working days.

  Should you have any questions regarding this request, please do not
hesitate to call me at the above telephone number.

                        Sincerely,

                        Angela Shapiro
                        Senior Paralegal

[AUTHOR/TYPIST]
[DOCUMENT LOCATOR CODE]

Form 11.3. FOIA (Freedom of Information Act) Request for a Specific Item

DeLost, Ernst, Meissner, Powell & Wilcox
Attorneys at Law
1257 Main Street, Suite 900
Los Angeles, CA 90066
(310) 555-6000

[DATE]

George Barker
Finance Administrator
Century Legal Insurance Company
One Embarcadero Center
Tenth Floor
San Francisco, CA 92456

     Re: <u>Assignment of RIN</u>

Dear Mr. Barker:

  Attached please find a copy of the reverse side of the postcard sent by the Environmental Protection Agency confirming your FOIA request. The Agency has ten (10) working days to respond to your request. As each request is assigned an "RIN" or Request for Identification Number, it is important that all subsequent references to this matter contain the number.

  Please feel free to contact our office should you have any questions.

       Sincerely,

       Mark C. Williams
       Legal Assistant

[AUTHOR/TYPIST]
Enclosures: [LIST]
[DOCUMENT LOCATOR CODE]

Form 11.4. Assignment of FOIA Request for Identification Number

DeLost, Ernst, Meissner, Powell & Wilcox
Attorneys at Law
1257 Main Street, Suite 900
Los Angeles, CA 90066
(310) 555-6000

[DATE]

[NAME AND ADDRESS OF EPA OFFICER]

    Re: <u>FOIA Request for documents concerning [SPECIFY]</u>

Dear [NAME]:

    This is a request under the Freedom of Information Act (FOIA), 5 U.S.C. Section 552, for all publicly available documents relating to [SPECIFY BRIEFLY] as described in Attachment A of this letter. As authorized by FOIA, we request one copy of all books, records, papers, files, and other writings maintained by the Agency that comprise final opinions in adjudicated cases, statements of EPA policy, and interpretations of such policies adopted by the Agency, and staff manuals and instructions to Agency personnel concerning the matter described above and on Attachment A. Please note that this request has also been sent to the Washington, D.C., office of the Agency.

    If you claim that any portion of the requested information is exempt from release, we respectfully request you provide us immediately with a copy of the remainder of the records. Please advise us of the specific exemption that you claim covers the information you did not release.

    We are prepared to pay the cost specified in your regulations for locating and reproducing the requested records. As required by law, however, we anticipate your reply within ten working days.

    If you have any questions concerning this request, we would be happy to discuss it by telephone.

                    Sincerely,

                    Mark C. Williams
                    Legal Assistant

[AUTHOR/TYPIST]
Enclosures: [LIST]
[DOCUMENT LOCATOR CODE]

DeLost, Ernst, Meissner, Powell & Wilcox
Attorneys at Law
1257 Main Street, Suite 900
Los Angeles, CA 90066
(310) 555-6000

[DATE]

Freedom of Information Officer
U.S. Environmental Protection Agency
Region V
230 S. Dearborn Street
Chicago, IL 60604

     Re: <u>Northwest Territory Superfund Site</u>

Dear Sir or Madam:

This request is made pursuant to the Freedom of Information Act, 5 U.S.C. §552, and 40 C.F.R. §2, as amended.

This is to request copies of the following documents related to the Northwest Capiscapo Superfund Site, which is located in Capiscapo, Ohio:

- Preliminary Assessment, August 19XX;

- Site Inspection Report, August 19XX; and

- Workplan for RI/FS, September 19XX.

I ask that the person(s) to whom this request is assigned call me at the above telephone number upon receipt to discuss the fastest mode of response. Also, please contact me before gathering documents if charges will total more than $100.

Thank you for your assistance.

     Sincerely,

     Angela Shapiro
     Senior Paralegal

[AUTHOR/TYPIST]
[DOCUMENT LOCATOR CODE]

Form 11.6. Typical FOIA Request to Federal Agency

DeLost, Ernst, Meissner, Powell & Wilcox
Attorneys at Law
1257 Main Street, Suite 900
Los Angeles, CA 90066
(310) 555-6000

[DATE]

Public Information Office
Office of State Fire Marshall
Petroleum and Chemical Safety Division
1035 Stevenson Drive
Springfield, IL 62703-4259

Re: <u>Underground Storage Tank Registrations</u>

Dear Sir or Madam:

This Freedom of Information Act request is made pursuant to the Illinois Freedom of Information Act, Ill. Rev. Stat. ch. 116, §§201, et seq., as amended.

This is a request for a copy of all underground tank registrations and related documents for the following site:

543 Certain Street
Chicago, Illinois 60606

I ask that the person(s) to whom this request is assigned call me at the above telephone number upon receipt of this request to discuss the most expeditious method of response. Also, please contact me before gathering documents if charges will total more than $[AMOUNT].

Thank you for your assistance in this matter.

Sincerely,

Angela Shapiro
Senior Paralegal

[AUTHOR/TYPIST]
[DOCUMENT LOCATOR CODE]

Form 11.7. Typical FOIA Request to State Agency

DeLost, Ernst, Meissner, Powell & Wilcox
Attorneys at Law
1257 Main Street, Suite 900
Los Angeles, CA 90066
(310) 555-6000

[DATE]

[NAME AND ADDRESS OF AGENCY]

  Re: <u>Public Records Act Request</u>

Dear [NAME]:

 This is a request under the Public Records Act, California Government
Code Section 6252, for a copy of the Medical Waste Treatment Facilities
package, no. [THE NUMBER]. I understand these are documents relating to
the Medical Waste Management Act, specifically, the Public Notice, Determination of Finding of Emergency Regulations (22 CCR Sections
65600-65628).

 Enclosed is a check in the amount of $[AMOUNT] payable to [STATE] to
cover the cost for a copy of these documents. Please call me at the
above telephone number should you have any questions. Thank you for your
assistance.

   Sincerely,

   Mark C. Williams
   Legal Assistant

[AUTHOR/TYPIST]
Enclosures: [LIST]
[DOCUMENT LOCATOR CODE]

Form 11.8. Public Records Act Request for Specific Information

DeLost, Ernst, Meissner, Powell & Wilcox
Attorneys at Law
1257 Main Street, Suite 900
Los Angeles, CA 90066
(310) 555-6000

[DATE]

[NAME AND ADDRESS OF AGENCY]

Re: <u>Public Records Act Request for Documents and Records</u>

Dear [NAME]:

This is a request under the California Public Records Act ("Act"), California Government code Section 6256, for copies of all permits, licenses, certifications, notices of intent, use reports, violation notices, and all other documents and records for the period [DATES], pertaining to the following company: [SPECIFY].

We will pay the costs for preparing the documents and records. As specified under the Act, you will notify us within ten days. Should you have any questions, please do not hesitate to call me at the above telephone number.

Sincerely,

Mark C. Williams
Legal Assistant

[AUTHOR/TYPIST]
[DOCUMENT LOCATOR CODE]

Form 11.9. Public Records Act Request for Documents and Records

Twelve

ESTATE PLANNING AND PROBATE

12.1 / The Paralegal Role
    Form 12.1. Hearing Advisement Letter
    Form 12.2. Signature Documents Transmittal
    Form 12.3. Information Letter to Client/Attorney
    Form 12.4. Outline of Information—Duties and Re
    sponsibilities
    Form 12.5. Transmittal of Will Draft to Client for
    Review
    Form 12.6. Publication Request to Newspaper

12.1 / The Paralegal Role

In practice, attorneys and paralegals working in probate and estate planning meet with the client to complete detailed checklists of necessary information. This information is required for later completion of appropriate documents, such as trusts and will for estate planning clients, and petitions and orders for distribution in probate matters. But gathering important information is just the first of many paralegal responsibilities in this practice area, as outlined by the National Federation of Paralegal Associations:

- Meet with client and attorney at initial interview.

- Prepare and maintain a calendar system.

- Notify heirs and devisees of probate proceeding.

- Publish notice to interested persons.

- Collect information and/or assets for preparation of inventory and tax returns.

- Accompany fiduciary and court representative to bank for removal of will from safety deposit box.

- Evaluate assets (date of death and alternate valuation date).
- Draft inventory.
- Maintain financial records of estate.
- Prepare and file probate documents in administration of estate or to relieve estate from administration.
- Surrender insurance policies.
- File life insurance claims and other death benefit claims.
- Verify bank balances.
- Interpret will provisions.
- Prepare preliminary tax and cash estimate.
- Obtain tax releases.
- Prepare income projection.
- Draft state inheritance tax and federal estate tax returns.
- Draft decedent's final federal and state individual income tax returns.
- Draft state and federal fiduciary income tax returns.
- Draft petitions and orders for partial distribution.
- Draft accountings.
- Assist in audit of tax returns.
- Draft distribution schedule.
- Draft closing documents.
- Draft federal and state gift tax returns.
- Review documents and tax returns in connection with ancillary proceedings.
- Draft tax returns for nonprobate estate.
- Collect data for estate planning.
- Draft wills and trusts.
- Draft court documents for conservatorship.
- Draft accountings for conservatorship.
- Draft federal and state tax returns for conservatorship.
- Draft court documents for guardianships.
- Make post-mortem planning calculations.[1]

Separating the tasks involved in the two distinct areas, *Paralegals in American Law* describes the duties of paralegals working in *estate planning* and then *probate* practices as follows:

(1)   Interviewing clients to determine facts relating to their potential estates.

(2)   Reviewing financial information submitted by clients and preparing checklists for attorney review.

(3)   Preparing drafts of wills, trusts, and related documents.

(4)   Obtaining information regarding insurance policies and ensuring that the proper beneficiaries are designated to complement the estate plan.

(5)   Overseeing the proper execution of wills by clients and witnesses.

(6)   Preparing summaries of wills and other documents for clients.

(7)   Drafting petitions, guardianships, conservatorships, and federal and state tax documents.[2]

The paralegal duties involved in handling *probate* matters include the following:

(1)   Attending client conferences to explain proper procedures following the death of a client or family member.

(2)   Preparing and filing (when necessary) probate forms.

(3)   Assisting with collection and inventory of the assets of the deceased, including contents of safety boxes, bank accounts, and all real and personal property.

(4)   Assisting with the clerical, bookkeeping, and accounting functions relating to estates.

(5)   Preparing estate returns.

(6)   Reviewing claims against estates.

(7)   Assisting with the liquidation of assets.

(8)   Maintaining communications with clients to advise them of the progress of settling the estate.[3]

The most informative piece of correspondence dealing with probate matters can be found in Form 12.4. This letter outlines key information, the duties, and responsibilities for probate clients. This comprehensive letter explains each element of the procedures and requirements involved in probating a will in great detail. Other letters included in this chapter are used for other purposes.

- for imparting information about a hearing,
- to transmit a document requiring review and signature, and
- to provide detailed information for clients, outlining the process of probate along with requirements and expectations.

Many legal assistants in this field work on a contract basis with attorneys, as opposed to working as an employee of a firm. For those thinking about working as an independent contractor, this may be an appropriate field to contemplate.

DeLost, Ernst, Meissner, Powell & Wilcox
Attorneys at Law
1257 Main Street, Suite 900
Los Angeles, CA 90066
(310) 555-6000

[DATE]

Cecilia Colbalt, Esq.
Klein, Smith & Jefferson
5689 West Shore Boulevard
Los Angeles, CA 90025

          Re: Estate of:
              Case no.:
              Our file number:

Dear Ms. Colbalt:

  Enclosed is a conformed copy of the Petition for Probate in the above-
captioned estate. The hearing on this matter has been calendared for
[DATE] at [TIME] in [DEPARTMENT] of the [SPECIFY] court. This probate
estate has been assigned case number [SPECIFY].

  Your appearance should not be required at this hearing. I will contact you a couple of days before the hearing to let you know the status of this matter as per the calendar notes.

  Please inform your client about this hearing date and that his/her
appearance should not be required.

              Sincerely,

              Mark C. Williams
              Legal Assistant

[AUTHOR/TYPIST]
Enclosures: [LIST]
[DOCUMENT LOCATOR CODE]

Form 12.1. Hearing Advisement Letter

DeLost, Ernst, Meissner, Powell & Wilcox
Attorneys at Law
1257 Main Street, Suite 900
Los Angeles, CA 90066
(310) 555-6000

[DATE]

Cecilia Colbalt, Esq.
Klein, Smith & Jefferson
5689 West Shore Boulevard
Los Angeles, CA 90025

     Re: Estate of:
       Case no.:
       <u>Our file number: 1234.56</u>

Dear Ms. Colbalt:

I have prepared the following probate documents for signature by you
and your client:

(1)   Petition for Probate for Letters Testamentary. Please sign the
        face page where indicated. Your client needs to date and sign
        the reverse side in two places where indicated.

(2)   Duties and Liabilities of Personal Representative. Your client
        needs to sign the reverse side of this form. Please do not date
        at this time.

(3)   Letters Testamentary. Your client needs to sign the face page.
        Please do not date at this time.

(4)   Application for Probate Referee. You need to sign the face
        page. Please let me know the approximate value of decedent's
        cash and personal property. This confirms my conversation with
        you that there is no real property in this estate.

(5)   Proof of Subscribing Witness to Will. I prepared this document
        because the will you prepared is not self-proving. In order
        for the will to be self-proving, you need to draft the will so
        the beginning of the attestation clause contains the follow-
        ing language:

           "The foregoing instrument, consisting of [NUMBER] pages,
           including the page signed by the Testator and the page
           signed by the witnesses ...".

        Please sign in two places where indicated. Please don't date
        the bottom half of this form. I need to date it after the will
        has been filed for probate.

(6)   Copy of order for probate for your file, which is not completed
        yet. I will mail you a copy of the original once it has been
        signed.

Form 12.2. Signature Documents Transmittal

Cecilia Colbalt, Esq.
[DATE]
Page 2

    (7)   Certificate of assignment form. Please date and sign and re-
             turn to me for filing with the petition for probate.

    (8)   Form SS-4, application for employer identification number.
             Please have your client enter his daytime telephone number on
             the bottom right side and date and sign this form where indi-
             cated.

Please tell your client I will obtain the tax identification number
for the probate estate upon his appointment. [HE/SHE] is to utilize this
number when [HE/SHE] opens the probate estate bank accounts. [HE/SHE]
is not to use [HIS/HER] social security number or that of the decedent.
[HE/SHE] must transfer all accounts in the decedent's name into an interest—bearing savings/checking account in [HIS/HER] name as the Executor of the decedent's estate.

The client's accountant needs to file fiduciary income tax returns for
the probate estate. I have selected a fiscal year for the probate estate. If the accountant wants a calendar year, please let me know, and
I will change the SS-4 form to reflect the calendar year.

Finally, please return the originals to my office for filing with
the court. I also need your check in the sum of $[AMOUNT] made payable
to [PAYEE]. This check represents the filing fee of $[AMOUNT] and the
fax fee of $[AMOUNT]. Please don't hesitate to call me if you have any
questions.

                    Sincerely,

                    Angela Shapiro
                    Senior Paralegal

[AUTHOR/TYPIST]
Enclosures: [LIST]
[DOCUMENT LOCATOR CODE]

Form 12.2. Signature Documents Transmittal *(Continued)*

DeLost, Ernst, Meissner, Powell & Wilcox
Attorneys at Law
1257 Main Street, Suite 900
Los Angeles, CA 90066
(310) 555-6000

[DATE]

Andrew Evans
1936 Tamarack Lane
Genoa, NV 89999

> Re: Estate of [NAME]

Dear Mr. Evans:

I have reviewed decedent's Last Will and Testament and your letter of [DATE]. I have prepared and enclosed the following probate documents for review and signature:

(1)   Petition for Probate: Please sign the fact page authorizing publication with [NAME OF PAPER]. Your client needs to sign the reverse side in two places where indicated. Please have your client verify the names and addresses on Attachment 8.

(2)   Certificate of Assignment: Please sign the bottom where indicated.

(3)   Duties and Liabilities: Please have your client sign the reverse side, but do not date.

(4)   Letters Testamentary: Please have your client sign the face page, but do not date.

(5)   Application and Order Appointing Probate Referee: Please sign the face page.

(6)   Order for Probate: This is a copy and is enclosed for your reference.

Please return the above documents to my office for filing with the court. I will also need your check in the sum of $[AMOUNT] payable to [PAYEE] representing the filing and fax fee.

Once I file the petition for probate with the court, the court will calendar the hearing for one month later. We do not need to send notice of hearing, since the newspaper will publish notice and send notice to all parties named on Attachment 8, including notice to [NAME]. You will receive a bill directly from the newspaper for publication, which should be paid by your client from the probate estate account, once this account has been opened.

Your appearance at the hearing in Department [NUMBER] of the [NAME] court should not be required. I will receive the probate calendar notes a week before the hearing and call you regarding the calendar notes.

I will submit the letters, duties, and liabilities, order for probate and application appointing probate referee on the date of the hearing.

This confirms that I need copies of all deeds and real estate tax bills for the real properties in decedent's probate estate.

Form 12.3. Information Letter to Client/Attorney

Andrew Evans
[DATE]
Page 2

Revenue and Taxation Code section 63.1 requires a change in ownership statement prepared for each parcel of real property held in a decedent's estate within 45 days from the date of death. Since no one really enforces this law, the reasonable period to file these changes in ownership statements is shortly after a personal representative is appointed. I need to prepare and file these forms as soon as possible.

For those properties that are transferred or inherited between parents and children, an application must be filed for exclusion from reassessment for parent-child transfers. I will need to prepare a claim for exemption for reassessment exclusion between parent and child for each parcel of real property transferred to the decedent's child.

Probate Code section 9202 requires that notice be mailed to Medi-Cal enclosing a certified copy of decedent's certificate of death. Said notice needs to be sent to Medi-Cal after your client is appointed as Executor. I will prepare this pleading after [HIS/HER] appointment and mail it to you for signature and filing with the court.

I need to send formal notice to all of decedent's creditors, which your client believes decedent may have owed monies. Your client can pay all small creditor's bills [HE/SHE] believes are valid bills after [HE/SHE] has been appointed and establishes the probate estate checking account. To any creditors of which [HE/SHE] is uncertain, we should probably send written notice. Please have your client provide me the names and addresses of the possible creditors. Before [HE/SHE] pays any medical bills, please inform [HIM/HER] to make sure the medical insurance has made the appropriate payments.

I also need to prepare an inventory and appraisement describing in detail all assets to be inventoried in decedent's estate on his/her date of death. These assets include:

- Bank accounts, including the balance on the date of death, including accrued interest on each account. I need to have:
  - the name of the bank,
  - the account number, and
  - branch and account balance on this date.
- The addresses and legal descriptions of all real properties, including tax assessor parcel number.
- Any checks payable to the decedent, monies due, stocks, bonds, and any other assets in decedent's name alone.

Once the inventory has been submitted to the probate referee for appraisal of the assets, filed with the court, and all creditors paid, we can proceed to close decedent's estate. We cannot close this estate until four months after letters have been issued to your client.

Please call me with any questions you may have regarding the information set forth in this letter.

Sincerely,

Anthony Wilcox, Esq.

[AUTHOR/TYPIST]
Enclosures: [LIST]
[DOCUMENT LOCATOR CODE]

Form 12.3. Information Letter to Client/Attorney (Continued)

DeLost, Ernst, Meissner, Powell & Wilcox
Attorneys at Law
1257 Main Street, Suite 900
Los Angeles, CA 90066
(310) 555-6000

[DATE]

Alena Reynolds
7368 West Falls Road
Albany, NY 12345

Re: Estate of [NAME]

Dear Ms. Reynolds:

As you know, we have prepared a petition for you to be appointed as the Executor of the Will of decedent (Administrator of the Estate of [NAME]). In that petition, we asked the court to grant you authority to administer the estate under The Independent Administration of Estates Act. That authority will enable you to take various actions regarding the administration of the estate without first obtaining court approval. Simply give notice, which we will prepare as required, of your proposed actions to persons having an interest in the estate.

We believe it is helpful for you to have this letter, setting forth your duties and responsibilities as the legal representative of the estate. The following comments relate to the administration of the probate estate only and do not relate to the administration of a trust.

It is our responsibilities, as attorneys for the estate, to see that all steps in the administration of the estate are taken, including preparation and filing of all of the necessary documents. From time to time, we will be communicating with you concerning various aspects of the administration of the estate. However, if at any time you have any questions, please do not hesitate to call.

In general, all steps in the administration of the probate estate will be directed toward three goals:

The collection and management of estate assets;

The payment of debts, expenses, and taxes; and

The distribution of the balance of the assets as provided in the Will and in accordance with the laws of California.

The following paragraphs outline the sequence of events that are applicable to the decedent's estate:

1. Duties of Personal Representatives

In general, your duties are:

- to collect, conserve, manage, and control the assets of the estate,
- pay the debts of the decedent,
- pay all taxes due from the decedent and the estate, and
- distribute the balance of the estate according to the Will or, if there is no such Will, in accordance with the laws of intestate succession.

Form 12.4. Outline of Information—Duties and Responsibilities

Alena Reynolds
[DATE]
Page 2

The law expects you to use care and diligence in carrying out these duties. California law also provides an orderly procedure to accomplish
all these steps.

> As a personal representative, you should do the following:

(a)   Take possession of all the estate's property insofar as prac-
      ticable. Joint tenancy property, life insurance proceeds, and
      retirement plan benefits (unless payable to the estate) are
      not included in the property under the jurisdiction of the pro-
      bate court;

(b)   Collect all dividends, interest, and other income, and deposit
      all such items in an interest-earning estate bank account (or
      accounts) until the estate is closed;

(c)   Keep a detailed account of all your receipts and disbursements
      for the estate: List the date, source, and amount of each re-
      ceipt and the date, nature of payment, and amount of each dis-
      bursement;

(d)   File all tax returns and pay all taxes—we will advise you re-
      garding the tax returns required and when they must be filed;
      and

(e)   Keep estate property adequately insured (we recommend early
      review of all casualty, property, and liability insurance
      policies and of the general need for insurance).

Without consulting us in advance, YOU SHOULD NOT DO ANY OF THE
FOLLOWING:

(a)   Sell any property of the estate;

(b)   Give away any estate property;

(c)   Lease estate property;

(d)   Pay or compromise any debts or claims against the estate (in-
      cluding funeral bills and/or expenses of the decedent's last
      illness);

(e)   Sell stock, exercise subscription rights, or buy stocks or
      bonds for the estate;

(f)   Distribute estate property to any devisee or heir;

(g)   Deposit estate funds in your personal account or otherwise com-
      mingle estate property with your own;

(h)   Act without the concurrence of the other personal representa-
      tive(s) if two or more have been appointed by the probate
      court.

2. Before Formal Administration Begins

Technically, the administration of a decedent's estate does not begin
until the will, if any, has been admitted to probate by the court and
Letters Testamentary or Letters of Administration have been issued.
However, prior to the appointment of a personal representative, the
decedent's family, the nominated executor, and/or other concerned persons should take the necessary steps to:

Form 12.4. Outline of Information—Duties and Responsibilities *(Continued)*

Alena Reynolds
[DATE]
Page 3

    (a)   Determine and carry out the decedent's wishes with respect to funeral, burial, cremation, etc.;

    (b)   Locate the original will;

    (c)   Maintain the decedent's home;

    (d)   Protect the decedent's property;

    (e)   Provide for support of the decedent's dependents; and

    (f)   Notify the state director of health services (if the decedent was receiving Medi-Cal benefits.

The circumstances of each decedent vary widely, and temporary needs will be met differently in each case. There are usually alternative solutions for special problems and temporary difficulties that may exist during the period between death and the court's appointment of a personal representative. We are available to discuss any such problems or difficulties that may arise and will be happy to provide assistance and guidance.

3. Issuance of Letters Testamentary or Letters of Administration

Within thirty (30) days after a decedent's death, the person who has custody of his or her will must file it with the county clerk in the county of the decedent's residence and send a copy to the named executor. The person named as executor and some other interested person must then file a petition with the court asking that the will and any codicils (amendments) to the will be admitted to probate as the decedent's will. The petition also asks that the court appoint the person named in the will as executor. When the appointment is made, Letters Testamentary are issued.

If there is no will, the petition for probate asks that the court appoint the petitioner or some other person as administrator of the estate. When the appointment is made, Letters of Administration are issued.

We will prepare the petition for probate for your signature as soon as we have the necessary information.

The document called "Letters Testamentary" or "Letters of Administration" is a certificate issued by the county clerk evidencing your appointment and authority as personal representative. During the administration of the estate, certified copies of the Letters may be required by banks, title companies, transfer agents, tax authorities, and others. We will obtain certified copies of the Letters for use when they are needed.

4. Notice to Creditors

The law requires publication of a Notice of Petition to Administer Estate. We will arrange for publication in the appropriate newspaper. This Notice also constitutes notice to all creditors of the decedent to file their claims against the estate. Creditors have four months following your appointment and the issuance of your Letters within which to file their claims. If a claim is not properly filed within that time, it is ordinarily barred. If you believe you may have a claim against the estate, please advise us. If a claim is required, we will prepare a claim for your execution.

Form 12.4. Outline of Information—Duties and Responsibilities *(Continued)*

Alena Reynolds
[DATE]
Page 4

        YOU SHOULD THOROUGHLY CHECK THE DECEDENT'S RECORDS AND PER-
SONAL EFFECTS FOR EVIDENCE OF CREDITORS' CLAIMS. ADVISE US IMMEDIATE-
LY so we can send all known or reasonably ascertainable creditors personal notice to file their claims. This is now required by law; known
or reasonably ascertainable creditors of the decedent who do not receive personal notice to file their claims do not face the time bar
mentioned above. In this regard, please provide us with a list of
decedent's creditors, including the creditor's address, account number, and balance owing on the date of death.

5. Payment of Claims

Ordinarily, you may pay a properly approved claim with estate funds
without incurring any personal liability. You may also pay any proper bill of the decedent without requiring a formal claim, but you
will remain personally liable for such payment until it is approved
by the court upon settlement of your accounts. YOU SHOULD CONSULT US
BEFORE PAYING ANY CLAIM OR BILL. Please also send us copies of any
creditor's claims you receive during this administration—this is very
important.

6. Inventories and Appraisal

A personal representative is required to prepare a complete inventory of all assets owned by the decedent at the time of his or her death.
The inventory is a very important document in the administration of
an estate: It is the starting point for almost all the tax returns
and for the accounting that must eventually be filed with the court.
The assets listed in the inventory plus certain other nonprobate assets (such as life insurance, joint tenancy property, and trust assets) comprise the decedent's estate for tax purposes.

        After all of the estate's assets are listed on the inventory,
the personal representative places a value on case and some other similar items. The inventory is then submitted to the court—appointed
probate referee. We will discuss with you whether an independent appraisal of any real property or other estate assets should be made.
The fees paid to appraisers are proper expenses of the estate and can
be claimed as estate or income tax deductions. Ordinarily, the independent appraisers' reports are submitted to the probate referee with
the inventory and are also filed as part of the federal estate tax
return.

        Please make certain that insurance coverages on insurable as-
sets are kept up to date and the insurance amounts are adequate in
light of the assets' appraised values.

        We will prepare the estate inventory as soon as sufficient in-
formation is available.

7. Estate Bank Accounts

An estate checking account should be opened. Cash and uncashed checks
in the possession of the decedent at the time of his or her death,
except for cash in savings accounts, should be deposited in the estate checking account. All subsequent receipts should be deposited in
the estate checking account and all disbursements should be made by
check. Personal representatives should not commingle their own funds
with estate funds. Substantial amounts of estate funds should not be
kept for any appreciable period in the estate checking account. In-

Form 12.4. Outline of Information—Duties and Responsibilities *(Continued)*

Alena Reynolds
[DATE]
Page 5

stead, funds not required for current expenditures and distributions
should be kept in an interest-earning estate savings account.

        The decedent's savings account, if any, should be transferred
into the estate's name. Since all estate receipts and disbursements
should be recorded in the estate checking account, all deposits to a
savings account should be by estate check and all withdrawals from a
savings account should be deposited in the estate checking account.

8. Records and Accountings

Keeping careful records is an essential part of a personal representative's duties. You must either keep detailed records of all estate
transactions yourself, or, as discussed later, have someone else keep
them for you. The record of estate receipts and disbursements will be
needed in preparing the accounting required by the probate court. In
addition, records will be needed for the preparation of estate and
income tax returns. Checking and savings account records and statements supplied by stock brokers, trust company agents, mutual funds,
and others provide much of the information needed to prepare accounting and tax returns.

9. Notices of Fiduciary Relationship

The federal and California tax laws require that personal representatives notify the respective taxing authorities of their appointment
and of their discharge. The effect of these notices is to establish
the place where the taxing authorities must send communications. For
example, your filing of notices of fiduciary relationship will require
the taxing authorities to send any notice of a proposed deficiency in
the decedent's or the estate's income tax to your address rather than
to a beneficiary.

        We will prepare Notices of Fiduciary Relationship addressed to
the Internal Revenue Service and the Franchise Tax Board for your signature.

10. Taxpayer Account Numbers

The use of electronic data processing for federal income tax returns
has resulted in the enactment of laws and regulations requiring the
use of identifying numbers on tax returns. Every estate that is required to file any federal tax returns must apply for an employer
identification number, which is the estate's tax account number. We
will obtain such a number for you.

        When you are asked by a payor of income for a tax number for
the estate, you should furnish the estate's employer identification
number.

11. Federal Estate Tax

The United States government levies an estate tax based on the decedent's right to transmit property at death. The estate tax is normally paid by the estate, but may be allocated and charged to the beneficiaries of the estate under certain circumstances.

        A return must be filed for the estate of a decedent if the es-
tate has a "gross value" of $600,000 or more. "Gross Value" includes
the assets in the probate estate (listed on the inventory) and may

Form 12.4. Outline of Information—Duties and Responsibilities *(Continued)*

Alena Reynolds
[DATE]
Page 6

also include certain assets that are not distributed by the decedent's will, such as life insurance proceeds, jointly owned property, and assets previously transferred by the decedent in trust or otherwise.

The federal estate tax is based upon the value of the assets included in the estate for tax purposes as of the date of death or, at the estate's option, as of the date six months after the date of death. The latter date is called the "alternate valuation date." The federal rule for calculating the value of an estate's assets on the alternate valuation date has exceptions, however. If the alternate valuation date is elected and any assets are sold or distributed during the first six months following the date of death, the estate's assets are valued as follows:

All assets not sold or distributed are valued as of the alternate valuation date, but any assets sold or distributed within the first six months are valued as of the date of sale or distribution. Therefore, if alternate valuation is elected, the sale or distribution of estate assets can affect the federal estate tax due.

Because of the opportunity of electing the alternate valuation date, the administration of the estate usually continues for at least one year. The federal estate tax return is due and the estate tax must be paid nine months after the date of death. You must sign the return as the personal representative.

Certain United States Treasury Bonds may be redeemed in satisfaction of the estate tax, even if the market value is less. If the estate holds any of these eligible bonds, they should not be sold until the federal estate taxes have been finally determined by audit and paid.

12. California Estate Tax

California no longer imposes an inheritance tax. However, there is still a California estate tax, which is equal to the amount of the state death tax credit allowable with respect to property situated in California included on the federal estate tax return. The California estate tax return is due and must be paid nine months after the date of death. You must sign the return as the personal representative.

If the estate is not large enough to require a federal estate tax return, no California estate tax will be due either, and no California estate tax return will be required.

13. Gift Taxes

If the decedent made any gifts in the year prior to his or her death, it may be necessary to file federal and state gift tax returns. California no longer imposes a gift tax, but some other states still do. Please supply us with copies of any gift tax returns for unreported gifts made by the decedent in prior years.

Gift taxes paid after death are deductible on the estate tax return, but any federal gift tax paid or payable with respect to gifts made within three years of the decedent's death must be included as an asset on the federal estate tax return.

Form 12.4. Outline of Information—Duties and Responsibilities (*Continued*)

Alena Reynolds
[DATE]
Page 7

14. Income Taxes

Final income tax returns must be filed for the portion of the year
prior to the decedent's death and are due by April 15th of the following year. Extensions of time to prepare such returns can be obtained, if necessary.

An estate is a separate taxpayer for federal and state income
tax purposes. Personal representatives are responsible for filing estate fiduciary income tax returns. A federal fiduciary income tax return (Form 1041) must be filed for any tax year in which the estate
earns gross income of $600. or more or if any beneficiary is a non-
resident alien. A California fiduciary income tax return (Form 541)
must be filed for any tax year in which the estate earns $1,000. or
more of net (taxable) income, adjusted gross income of $12,000 or
$8,000 of gross income or has any alternative minimum tax.

You may select a fiscal year for the estate. Selection of a
fiscal year may permit some reduction of total tax liability or at
least a deferral of some tax liability. We can recommend the choice
of a fiscal year for the estate when we have more information.

Unlike an individual, an estate is entitled to an income tax
deduction for amounts of income or principal paid or distributed to
certain beneficiaries during the year, who must in turn include those
amounts in their income tax returns for that year. Significant income
tax savings may be possible by proper planning.

15. Real Property Taxes

You must plan to pay all real property taxes when due. The installment of taxes on California real property is delinquent on December
19th, and the second installment is delinquent on April 10th.

The county assessor of each county in which the decedent held
real property must be notified first of the change of ownership from
the decedent to the estate; then upon distribution of the real property from the estate to the beneficiary. The change of ownership may
result in a reassessment for property tax purposes, depending on the
relationship of the transferee. We will prepare the necessary change
of ownership forms.

16. Expenses of Administration and Compensation of Personal Representative and Attorneys

The expenses of administering estates vary depending on many factors,
only one of which is the size of the estate. The expenses of administration may include court fees, certification fees, surety bond premiums, the California probate referee's fees, agency fees, insurance
premiums, expenses of selling assets, and the personal representative's, accountants', and attorneys' compensation. The largest costs
are usually the compensation of the personal representative and the
attorneys.

Form 12.4. Outline of Information—Duties and Responsibilities *(Continued)*

Alena Reynolds
[DATE]
Page 8

a.   <u>Compensation for Ordinary Services of Personal Representatives and Attorneys</u>
As a personal representative, you are allowed compensation for your services. Unless the will makes a special provision for your compensation, the amount of compensation for your "ordinary" services is fixed by California statute and is based on the value of the estate accounted for. The value generally includes the inventory value of the probate estate and income received during the period of administration. Compensation can be paid only after the court orders payment. Fees for ordinary services are calculated based on the amount of the estate accounted for as follows:

4% on the first $15,000 or fraction thereof;
3% on the next $85,000 or fraction thereof;
2% on the next $900,000 or fraction thereof;
1% on the next $9,000,000;
1/2% on the next $15,000,000; and
a reasonable fee on the excess over $25,000,000.

Thus, the fees for an estate of $1,050,000 would be calculated as follows:

4% on $ 15,000	$ 600
3% on $ 85,000	$ 2,550
2% on $ 900,000	$ 18,000
1% on $ 50,000	$ 500
TOTAL	$ 21,650

The same schedule is used to determine the compensation paid to attorneys for their "ordinary" services.

b.   <u>Compensation for Extraordinary Services of Personal Representative and Attorneys</u>
In addition to the statutory commissions and fees discussed above, the probate court may, in proper instances, authorize payment of additional compensation to the personal representative and/or to the estate's attorneys for extraordinary services rendered in the administration of the estate. There is no prescribed schedule of compensation for such services. The amount in each instance is fixed by the court on the basis of a declaration by the applicant as to the nature and extent of the extraordinary services rendered to the estate.

For example, if it were necessary for you to carry on the decedent's business under court order or to participate in litigation involving the estate, such services would be regarded as in addition to the ordinary services you are expected to render in administering the estate, and you would be entitled to apply for and receive additional compensation for such services.

Form 12.4. Outline of Information—Duties and Responsibilities *(Continued)*

Alena Reynolds
[DATE]
Page 9

Similarly, we as attorneys (and our paralegal assistants)
are frequently called upon to perform legal services in connection with the administration of an estate that is regarded
as extraordinary in nature and is not covered by the statutory fees provided for by the Probate Code. Such services may
include the following, fairly common situations:

- handling sales or mortgages of real or personal property;
- contesting or defending litigated claims against the estate;
- preparing the federal and/or state estate, inheritance,
  gift, income, sales, property, or other tax returns;
- representing the estate in an audit or litigation concerning any of those taxes;
- handling litigation relating to property of the estate;
- arranging for the conduct of ancillary administration in
  other states where the decedent owned property; and
- preparing petitions for instructions, to determine heir-
  ship, and for preliminary distribution.

Our fees for extraordinary services are based primarily upon
our hourly rates from time-to-time prevailing, taking into account the size and complexity of the matter at issue, the results achieved, and the benefit ultimately conferred upon the
estate.

Our hourly rates vary from $150-$200 per hour for partners, $90-$140 for associates, and $40-$75 for paralegals. (A
schedule of miscellaneous expected disbursements [filing fees,
copying charges, and the like] is also enclosed with this letter for your reference.)

We will periodically consult with you regarding the prob-
able fees to be incurred as matters calling for such "extraordinary services" arise. Of course, all extraordinary fees
must ultimately be approved by the court after a noticed hearing.

(c)   Agents for Personal Representatives
An individual who is not an experienced fiduciary is entitled
to receive the statutory compensation for serving as a personal representative, even though he or she does not have the
training or experience required to perform all the personal
representative's duties.

Form 12.4. Outline of Information—Duties and Responsibilities (Continued)

Alena Reynolds
[DATE]
Page 10

     We have found that many estates can be more efficiently administered if a nonprofessional personal representative hires others to perform some or all of the services that he or she is expected to perform. The most common examples are examining records of the decedent for information as receiving income and making disbursements, maintaining the accounting records, and preparing periodic accounting reports. However, a personal representative is generally not entitled to reimbursement from the estate for the expenses incurred for such services. Most courts consider such expenses to be expenses of the personal representative, which must be paid from his or her compensation.

     If you wish to engage an agent to perform ministerial functions, there are several alternatives available. Banks and some accountants serve as probate agents. Our firm is also equipped to perform such services. If you wish us to do so, we will arrange fees for such services that will be billed to you individually and will be separate from our fees as attorneys for the estate. Our total fees for the agency services will not exceed the statutory compensation to which you are entitled.

(d)   <u>Waiver of Commissions</u>
Compensation paid to a personal representative is taxable income to him or her. Under some circumstances, a personal representative who is also a beneficiary may benefit by waiving his or her right to receive compensation. We will discuss this option with you at any early stage in the estate administration proceedings.

17. <u>Family Allowance</u>

During the probate of an estate, a surviving spouse and minor children are entitled to a family allowance for their support, commencing with the date of death and continuing until further order of the court. The family allowance is obtained through a petition to the court, which sets the amount to be allowed. If a family allowance is considered advisable, we will take the necessary steps to obtain it. A family allowance will be taxable as income to the recipient.

18. <u>Preliminary Distributions</u>

It is not necessary to wait until the estate is ready to be closed before making distributions. The Probate Code specifically provides for preliminary distributions. However, a preliminary distribution may not be made before two months after the Letters Testamentary or of Administration are issued. If a distribution is made between two and four months after Letters are issued, a bond may be required to protect the rights of creditors. If a distribution is made more than four months after the Letters are issued, that is, after creditors' claims are barred, a bond is not usually required.

Form 12.4. Outline of Information—Duties and Responsibilities *(Continued)*

Alena Reynolds
[DATE]
Page 11

　　　You may want to make a preliminary distribution of any cash or
other specific bequests provided for in the will. You may also want
to make a preliminary distribution of income or principal to establish a trust created by the decedent's will. However, as indicated in
paragraph 14, above, income tax considerations may affect the proper
timing of distributions other than those to specific, demonstrative,
and general legatees.

　　　Of course, an appropriate court order is required before you
make any preliminary distribution.

19. Final Distribution

When all debts and taxes have been paid and the estate is ready for
final distribution, we will prepare for your signature a final account, report, and petition for final distribution, based on your
records of receipts, disbursements, and assets on hand. If all is in
order, the court will enter an order approving your account and report and ordering distribution of the remaining estate assets. This
normally takes approximately three weeks after the petition is filed.
We will then help you distribute the assets and obtain the necessary
receipts from the beneficiaries.

The foregoing is only a general outline of the more important aspects
of the administration of an estate. There will no doubt be additional
matters in your decedent's estate, but we can discuss those as they
arise. We will attempt to keep you fully informed about each significant setup in administration of the estate.

We hope that administration of the estate can be completed as quickly and efficiently as possible and with a minimum of inconvenience to
you. We are looking forward to assisting you.

　　　　　　Sincerely,

　　　　　　Mark C. Williams
　　　　　　Legal Assistant to
　　　　　　Paul Ernst, Esq.

[AUTHOR/TYPIST]
Enclosures: [LIST]
[DOCUMENT LOCATOR CODE]

Form 12.4. Outline of Information—Duties and Responsibilities *(Continued)*

Delost, Ernst, Miessner, Powell & Wilcox
Attorneys at Law
1257 Main Street, Suite 900
Los Angeles, California 90066

[DATE]

Alec Sutherland
1936 Papermill Road
Mission Springs, CO 80301

        Re: <u>Last Will and Testament</u>

Dear Mr. Sutherland:

   Enclosed please find the draft will for you and your wife, Laura.
Please go over each page, paying special attention to paragraph five,
entitled "Bequests." Make sure that each and every item is entirely correct.

   After you have had a chance to review the enclosed, please call me to
set up a meeting date. You and your wife will need to initial each page
and sign the last two before witnesses. We have many people in our office available to witness your will, at your convenience.

   I look forward to meeting with you again.

                        Sincerely,

                        Elisia Llanes
                        Paralegal
[AUTHOR/TYPIST]
[DOCUMENT LOCATOR FILE]

Form 12.5. Transmittal of Will Draft to Client for Review

DeLost, Ernst, Miessner, Powell & Wilcox
Attorneys at Law
1257 Main Street, Suite 900
Los Angeles, CA 90066
(310) 555-6000

[DATE]

[NAME]
[ADDRESS OF PUBLICATION]
Attention: Legal Notices Department

    Re: Estate of [NAME OF DECEDENT]

Dear Classified Officer:

  Please take immediate action to prepare the notice to relatives of
the decedent. You may submit the appropriate forms to me by facsimile
at (310) 555-6011. Please make sure that you include a return fax number, so we can begin publication on the next available issue.

  Thank you for your immediate attention to the enclosed.

        Sincerely,

        Danielle Miller, Esq.

[AUTHOR/TYPIST]
[DOCUMENT LOCATOR CODE]

Form 12.6. Publication Request to Newspaper

End Notes

[1]Excerpted from "Paralegal Job Descriptions by Practice Area," compiled by the National Federation of Paralegal Associations. While not intended to be all inclusive, this list does provide examples of the differing types of assignments that can (and should) be delegated to paralegals.

[2]Angela Schneeman, *Paralegals in American Law: Introduction to Paralegalism,* p. 18 (1995).

[3]Id. at 18.

Thirteen

FAMILY LAW

13.1 / The Paralegal Role
    Form 13.1. Request for Copies of Court Documents
    Form 13.2. Sample Information Request Letter
    Form 13.3. Attorney–Client Agreement
    Form 13.4. Preliminary Disclosure and Asset/Debt Checklist
    Form 13.5. Claim of Community Property Interest in Employee Benefits
    Form 13.6. Claim of Interest to Employee Benefits
    Form 13.7. Outline of Dissolution Agreement
    Form 13.8. Notification of Attorney Unavailability
    Form 13.9. Notice of Continued Health Coverage Entitlements
    Form 13.10. Transmittal of Final Dissolution

13.1 / The Paralegal Role

Many years ago, I worked for a firm that specialized in family law. I recall seeing many urgent phone messages always requiring immediate attention by the attorneys. Very seldom will you find the aspect of family law involving dissolution of marriages an attractive process, although adoptions and name changes can be rather lighthearted.

Paralegals in a family law practice ordinarily attend initial interviews with clients to gather key information. Following an attorney's acceptance of a case, paralegals:

- collect background client information; and

- participate in discussions of remedies, such as:

- reconciliation,
- mediation,
- separation, and
- counseling.

Because of the nature of the practice, paralegals tend to establish close relationships with the firm's clients.

The job description compiled by the National Federation of Paralegal Associations describes paralegal duties for this practice area as follows:

- Attend initial interview with attorney and client; identify legal problems that can be referred to other entities.

- Collect background information on client, including marriage certificates, sources of support, residence, assets, number of children, etc.

- Determine if grounds for divorce or dissolution exist.

- Participate in discussion of other remedies, including counseling, separation, reconciliation, mediation, etc.

- Draft petition for dissolution or response.

- Complete domestic relations questionnaire form.

- Draft temporary motions, affidavits, and orders.

- Draft notice to produce.

- Draft property settlement agreement.

- Determine support needs and calculate child support.

- Draft decree of dissolution, accompanying motions, and affidavits.

- Draft motion and affidavit for modification.

- Serve notice on opposing counsel.

- Arrange for service of documents.

- Obtain settings for court hearings.

- Maintain contact with client and handle calls when legal advice is not needed.

- Assist client in preparation of monthly income and expense sheet.

- Arrange for appraisers for real property and personal property.

- Draft subpoenas and arrange for service.

- Schedule expert witness interviews and availability at trial.

- Obtain information for discovery; organize, categorize, and determine completeness of discovery.

- Draft proposed stipulations.
- Draft petition for adoption and consent for adoption, decree of adoption.
- Draft petition for name change.[1]

This practice area utlilizes standardized court forms a great deal. As a result, it is not difficult to set up correspondence formats that can be used again and again from case to case. Most sample letters in this chapter gather or convey information. An example of this is Form 13.3, "Attorney–Client Agreement," which is a retainer agreement and fee schedule outlining the scope of the attorney-client relationship.

Avoid writing anything that may be construed as a settlement or that would give up any important client rights. All letters relating or referring to outcome, involving property or support, should be reviewed and executed by the attorney. Remember that negotiations for property division, spousal support, and child support are continual.

DeLost, Ernst, Meissner, Powell & Wilcox
Attorneys at Law
1257 Main Street, Suite 900
Los Angeles, CA 90066
(310) 555-6000

[DATE]

Clerk of the Court
New York County Family Court
60 Lafayette Street
New York, NY 10013

Re: <u>Smith v. Jones; Docket No. 1234567</u>

Dear Clerk of the Court:

On [DATE], an order of child support was entered in your court under
Docket no.: [NUMBER]. This order awarded our client, [NAME], child support in the amount of $[AMOUNT] per week. The order was modified in 1987
to $[AMOUNT] per month, and was made payable through the Child Support
Enforcement Agency.

We are seeking to register the order in the state of Maine. This requires three certified copies (each reflecting the raised seal), of the
order of support and all modifications. As required by statute, the orders should be certified by the clerk of the court.

We are also requesting a certified arrears statement and a copy of
your state's Uniform Reciprocal Enforcement of Support Act.

If there is a charge for any of these documents, or if there will be
a delay of more than thirty days, please notify me as soon as possible.
I am enclosing a copy of the orders for your reference, along with a
self-addressed, stamped envelope. If you have any questions, please contact me at the above number. Thank you in advance for your cooperation.

Sincerely,

John B. Watson
Legal Assistant

[AUTHOR/TYPIST]
Enclosures: [LIST]
[DOCUMENT LOCATOR CODE]

Form 13.1. Request for Copies of Court Documents

DeLost, Ernst, Meissner, Powell & Wilcox
Attorneys at Law
1257 Main Street, Suite 900
Los Angeles, CA 90066
(310) 555-6000

                                    [DATE]

Driver Licensing and Information
P.O. Box 1234
Richmond, VA 23269

      Re: [NAME OF INDIVIDUAL]

Dear Director:

  Our firm is attempting to locate [NAME] for the purpose of collecting past due child support payments:

        [NAME AND RACE]
        Date of Birth: [SPECIFY]
        Driver's license number: [SPECIFY]

  Please send our firm a copy of [MR./MRS.] [NAME]'s driver's license
and driving record, and bill us for this service. If you cannot release
the entire abstract of the driving record, I would appreciate receiving
the identification information that contains [HIS/HER] address.

  If you require a prepaid request, please send a list of your current
fees and a requisition form, if applicable. I have enclosed a self-addressed, stamped envelope for your use.

  If you need further information or verification, please call me collect at [PHONE]. You may also reach me at the above address. Thank you
very much for your assistance.

                        Sincerely,

                        Angela Shapiro
                        Senior Paralegal

[AUTHOR/TYPIST]
Enclosures: [LIST]
[DOCUMENT LOCATOR CODE]

Form 13.2. Sample Information Request Letter

DeLost, Ernst, Meissner, Powell & Wilcox
Attorneys at Law
1257 Main Street, Suite 900
Los Angeles, CA 90066
(310) 555-6000

[DATE]

[CLIENT NAME]
[CLIENT ADDRESS]

Re: <u>Dissolution of Marriage</u>

Dear [NAME]:

It was a pleasure to meet with you on [DATE]. The purpose of this letter is to set forth the terms under which our office will agree to represent you in connection with the above-captioned matter.

As I mentioned to you, our services are provided on an hourly basis:

- My billing rate is $[AMOUNT] per hour and $[AMOUNT] per hour for
  my partner, [NAME].
- Other lawyers in our office are billed at the rate of $[AMOUNT]
  per hour.
- Some services may be provided by paralegals or legal assistants
  and their billing rates range from $[AMOUNT] to $[AMOUNT] per
  hour.

In addition to this, you will be charged for costs advanced and incurred
on your behalf, including but not limited to:

- filing fees,
- deposition costs,
- photocopies, long—distance telephone charges,
- messengers, and
- process serving fees.

Our office will charge a minimum fee of one-quarter hour for any service performed on your behalf, including but not limited to:

- telephone conferences,
- correspondence, and
- preparation of documents.

If the service takes longer than one-quarter of an hour, time shall be
charged at increments of .05 of an hour. [FIRM NAME] reserves the right
to change its hourly rates by giving you not less than thirty days written notice of the proposed change.

Form 13.3. Attorney–Client Agreement

[CLIENT NAME]
[DATE]
Page 2

We require a retainer for these services in the amount of $[AMOUNT],
which I have agreed will be a refundable retainer. This means that time
will be billed against the retainer until it is exhausted and should the
matter be concluded prior to exhausting the retainer, any amount remaining will be refunded to you. You will receive monthly statements and
once the retainer is exhausted it is expected that you will keep your
bill current on a twenty-day basis. Should any bill not be paid in a
timely manner, it shall bear interest at the rate of ten percent per
year.

In the event you fail to pay any amount when due, it will be deemed
a material breach of our agreement and constitute grounds for our firm
moving to be relieved as your attorney of record. In this event, should
you fail to execute a Substitution of Attorneys and it becomes necessary for us to bring a motion to be relieved as your attorneys, we will
be paid our usual hourly rate for time expended in such motion. Should
it be necessary to institute legal proceedings to enforce this agreement, the prevailing party will be entitled to recover reasonable attorneys fees and costs in such proceedings.

Disputes arise between clients and firms with regard to:

• the payment for services performed by the firm,
• costs incurred on the client's behalf, or
• any claim of legal malpractice, error, or omission on the part of
  the firm.

In the event a dispute arises between you and our firm in excess of the
jurisdictional limit of Small Claims Court, the dispute will be resolved
by binding arbitration in accordance with the Commercial Arbitration
Rules of the American Arbitration Association, and any judgment on the
award rendered by the arbitrator(s) may be entered in any court having
jurisdiction.

AS A RESULT OF THIS PROVISION, NEITHER PARTY WILL BE ENTITLED TO HAVE
A JUDGE OR A JURY DECIDE THE DISPUTE AND EACH PARTY HEREBY EXPRESSLY
WAIVES ANY RIGHT TO TRIAL BY JURY ON SUCH CLAIM.

However, if the dispute involves our attorney fees, under California
Law, you have the right to request the dispute, be determined first by
nonbinding or binding arbitration administered by local bar associations, such as the Los Angeles County Bar Association. If nonbinding arbitration is selected and either of us is unhappy with the result, the
dispute will then be determined by binding arbitration under the rules
of the American Arbitration Association referred to above.

A recent change in the Business and Professions Code requires that I
include in any retainer agreement a statement as to whether or not our
firm maintains Errors and Omissions Insurance coverage. This is to advise you that I presently maintain Errors and Omissions Insurance coverage that will apply to your case. Nothing in this paragraph should be
construed to require our firm to maintain such coverage or notify you
in the event that we no longer choose to maintain it. Should you wish
to inquire as to our insurance coverage in the future and do so in writing, we will respond to your request for that information.

Form 13.3. Attorney–Client Agreement *(Continued)*

[CLIENT NAME]
[DATE]
Page 3

We have made no promises or representations to you concerning the
final outcome of this case, with the exception that our firm will use
its best efforts in furthering the purposes of this agreement and in
protecting your interests in this matter. I have made no estimate of the
total costs that will be involved in this proceeding, and the retainer
is in no way intended to be an estimate of the total cost. The reason
I cannot give you an estimate is that I do not know how much resistance
and/or cooperation we will receive from the opposing party.

If the foregoing terms are agreeable to you, please sign the enclosed
copy of this letter and return it to me. This letter acknowledges receipt of your retainer check in the amount of $[AMOUNT]. Please be ad-
vised this letter is an agreement that creates legal obligations. You
have the right to have this letter-agreement reviewed by an attorney of
your choosing prior to executing it.

Sincerely,

Marjorie Meissner, Esq.

[AUTHOR/TYPIST]
Enclosures: [LIST]
[DOCUMENT LOCATOR CODE]

THE ABOVE IS AGREED TO AND UNDERSTOOD

_____

Form 13.3. Attorney–Client Agreement (Continued)

DeLost, Ernst, Meissner, Powell & Wilcox
Attorneys at Law
1257 Main Street, Suite 900
Los Angeles, CA 90066
(310) 555-6000

[DATE]

[CLIENT NAME]
[ADDRESS]

Re: <u>Marriage of [NAME]</u>

Dear [NAME]:

I prepared an initial draft of the Preliminary Declaration of Disclosure and Schedule of Assets and Debts based upon the preliminary information you recently sent me.

These documents are required to be served upon the [RESPONDENT/PETITIONER], [NAME], according to Civil Code Section 4800.10. Failure to accurately disclose the information requested can result in a judgment of dissolution of marriage being set aside at a later date. A copy of the initial draft is enclosed for you to complete and return to me.

In addition, I need you to provide me with copies of the required documents to be attached to the Schedule of Assets and Debts.

- Grant Deed to the family residence and any other real estate owned by you and your [HUSBAND/WIFE] as well as the lender's statement for each property;
- Pink slip for each automobile;
- Title document to any boat or trailer;
- Latest statement for each savings account;
- Latest statement for each checking account;
- Latest statement for each credit union account;
- Declaration page for each whole life insurance policy owned by you and your [HUSBAND/WIFE];
- Stock certificates or latest brokerage statement;
- Latest summary plan and benefit statement for each pension or retirement plan;
- Latest statement for each profit-sharing plan in which either of you is a participant, annuity, IRA, or other deferred compensation plan;
- Accounts receivable and unsecured notes;
- Current Schedule K-1 for each partnership;
- Schedule C for any business interest;
- Latest statement for any unsecured loans, including the bank name, address, and loan number; and
- Latest statement from any creditor, including the name, address, and account number.

Form 13.4. Preliminary Disclosure and Asset/Debt Checklist

[CLIENT NAME]
[DATE]
Page 2

    As soon as I receive the above information, I will complete and fi-
nalize the Preliminary Declaration of Disclosure and Schedule of Assets
and Debts and return the forms to you for your signature. The forms must
be signed by you under penalty of perjury. When I receive the final
signed documents, they will be served upon [PETITIONER/RESPONDENT] along
with your Income and Expense Declaration. The Preliminary Declaration
of Disclosure and Schedule of Assets is not filed with the court.

    A Final Declaration of Disclosure and Schedule of Assets must be filed
with the court prior to entry of judgment. Amendments and revisions to
the Preliminary Declaration of Disclosure may become necessary before
it is filed with the court prior to entry of judgment.

    If you have any questions, please do not hesitate to call.

    Thank you.

                Sincerely,

                Clark Laird
                Litigation Assistant

[AUTHOR/TYPIST]
Enclosures: [LIST]
[DOCUMENT LOCATOR CODE]

Form 13.4. Preliminary Disclosure and Asset/Debt Checklist

DeLost, Ernst, Meissner, Powell & Wilcox
Attorneys at Law
1257 Main Street, Suite 900
Los Angeles, CA 90066
(310) 555-6000

[DATE]

[PLAN ADMINISTRATOR]
[ADDRESS]

        Re: Marriage of [SPECIFY]
            Employee [NAME AND SOCIAL SECURITY NUMBER]

Dear Plan Administrator:

   [ATTORNEY NAME] is representing [CLIENT NAME] in a dissolution of marriage proceeding involving your employee [NAME]. Pursuant to California
civil Code Section 5106 (Family Code Section 755), [CLIENT NAME] claims
a community property interest in the retirement plan, profit sharing
plan, 401(k) plan, accumulated vacation benefits, and any other employee benefit plan or savings plan in the name of or accrued for the benefit of [EMPLOYEE NAME] through your company.

   Please do not make any disbursement of monies held for the benefit of
[EMPLOYEE NAME] without the prior written consent of [CLIENT NAME] or
pursuant to a court order.

   I enclose an authorization signed by [NAME OF EMPLOYEE] for you to
release the information. If you provide the information requested within thirty (30) days, it will not be necessary to subpoena you for a deposition.

   I am providing you with the following information identifying the parties to assist you in locating the information requested.

                    PLAN PARTICIPANT INFORMATION

Valuation date:
Name: [NAME OF EMPLOYEE]
Social Security number:
Employer:
Name of plan:

                     ALTERNATE PAYEE INFORMATION

Name:
Social Security Number:

   The participant's authorization for written and telephone release allows you to release information regarding the participant's interest in
all plans you administer to our office and to our valuation consultant.
Please forward the information as soon as possible. If you anticipate
any delay in supplying any item, you may send the information you have
been able to gather and notify me when you can send the balance.

Form 13.5. Claim of Community Property Interest in Employee Benefits

[PLAN ADMINISTRATOR]
[DATE]
Page 2

. For each employee benefit plan, the following information is requested.

- Date of birth, plan participant
- Date of birth, alternate payee
- Minimum retirement age, or "N/A"
- Minimum years of service for retirement or "N/A"
- Service years at which benefits reach maximum value, or "N/A"
- Begin creditable service date, or "N/A"
- Defined benefit at retirement (Vested and nonvested accrued month-
  ly benefit as of the date of valuation shown above [including
  method of calculation] for age/date of earliest eligibility for
  retirement)
- Defined benefit at valuation (Vested and nonvested accrued month-
  ly benefit as of date of valuation shown above [including method
  of calculation] for age/date of normal retirement [if retired, any
  loan and show monthly amount now received])
- Interest or discount rate
- Actuarial table
- Postretirement COLA, or "none"

Also, please provide documentation relating to the following:

- Dates of military, parental, or other leaves;
- Plan summary plus any changes effective after publication;
- If salary affects the accrued monthly benefit, your record of the
  annual salary for the most recent five years;
- The current contributions account balance; and
- Name, title, address, and telephone number of the person we may
  contact for additional information.

If you have any questions, please do not hesitate to call.

Thank you.

                         Sincerely,

                         James B. Watson
                         Legal Assistant

[AUTHOR/TYPIST]
Enclosures: [LIST]
[DOCUMENT LOCATOR CODE]

Form 13.5. Claim of Community Property Interest in Employee Benefits *(Continued)*

```
[PLAN ADMINISTRATOR]
[DATE]
Page 3
```

_____[PAGE BREAK]_____

INSTRUCTIONS AND AUTHORIZATION FOR RELEASE OF INFORMATION

Please release by telephone or letter any and all information regarding my participation in plans you administer to [PETITIONER/RESPON-
DENT]'s attorney, [NAME OF ATTORNEY], their staff, and their valuation
consultant.

This authorization shall expire 180 days from the date signed below.

Dated: _____   Signed: _____

Form 13.5. Claim of Community Property Interest in Employee Benefits *(Continued)*

DeLost, Ernst, Meissner, Powell & Wilcox
Attorneys at Law
1257 Main Street, Suite 900
Los Angeles, CA 90066
(310) 555-6000

[DATE]

[EMPLOYER/DIRECTOR OF BENEFITS AND COMPENSATION]
[ADDRESS]

        Re: Marriage of [NAME]
            Your employee [NAME]

Dear [EMPLOYER/DIRECTOR OF BENEFITS AND COMPENSATION]:

   [ATTORNEY NAME] is representing [NAME OF CLIENT] in a dissolution of marriage proceeding involving your employee [NAME]. [NAME OF CLIENT] claims a community property interest in the retirement plan, profit sharing plan, 401(k) plan, accumulated vacation benefits, and any other employee benefit plan or savings plan, in the name of or accrued for the benefit of [EMPLOYEE NAME] through your company.

   Please do not make any disbursement of monies held for the benefit of [EMPLOYEE NAME] without the prior written consent of [CLIENT NAME] or pursuant to a court order. In addition, please furnish me with the information requested below. I have enclosed an authorization signed by [EMPLOYEE] for you to release the information. If you provide the information requested within thirty (30) days, it will not be necessary to subpoena you for a deposition.

   Please provide, for each employee benefit or plan, the following information and documentation:

- The name and description of the plan;
- The name, address, and telephone number of the trustee, administrator, or custodian of the plan;
- A copy of the summary plan description and other written materials furnished to employees describing their rights, privileges, and benefits;
- The date [EMPLOYEE] commenced employment with the employer providing the plan;
- The date [EMPLOYEE] became a participant in the plan;
- The number of years of plan-covered employment to date;
- Is the retirement plan a defined benefit plan or a defined contribution plan?
- The date of earliest permitted retirement;
- The date of normal retirement;
- The vesting schedule of the plan, and date of 100% vesting;
- The monthly benefit at employee's earliest retirement date if employment continues until then;
- The monthly benefit at employee's normal retirement date if employment continues until then;
- The current account balance of a defined contribution plan, if one exists;
- If employee's interest in the plan has matured;

Form 13.6. Claim of Interest to Employee Benefits

[EMPLOYER/DIRECTOR]
[DATE]
Page 2

- If employee retired today, when would employee begin receiving monthly benefits under the plan, and what amount would those benefits be;
- Is there a survivor benefit or survivor election provision? And if so, describe or provide relevant plan documents;
- Are any benefits of the plan subject to forfeiture? And, if so, describe the events that involve forfeiture under the plan;
- List the beneficiaries under the plan and indicate if there have been any change of beneficiaries in the last 12 months;
- Does the plan allow the employee to select from any options that may affect the monthly benefits payable on retirement or the survivor benefits? And, if so, describe the option and how each change affects the benefits;
- Is social security included in the total monthly benefits the employee will receive from the plan at retirement, and, if so, what portion of the total monthly benefit is attributable to social security; and
- Does the plan have a provision for segregation of the benefits of the alternate payee and does the plan permit alternate payees to make elections with their interest free from interference from the employee?

Also, send me a current booklet for each plan in which employee is enrolled and a statement showing the employee's accrued vacation benefits, and any other benefits, to date. If the Plan in which the employee is enrolled has prepared a form or suggested Domestic Relations Order, I would appreciate a copy.

Thank you for your cooperation. If you have any questions or wish to discuss these requests, please do not hesitate to call. Thank you.

Sincerely,

Mark C. Williams
Paralegal

[AUTHOR/TYPIST]
Enclosures: [LIST]
[DOCUMENT LOCATOR CODE]

Form 13.6. Claim of Interest to Employee Benefits (Continued)

DeLost, Ernst, Meissner, Powell & Wilcox
Attorneys at Law
1257 Main Street, Suite 900
Los Angeles, CA 90066
(310) 555-6000

[DATE]

[CLIENT NAME]
[AND ADDRESS]

Re: <u>Dissolution of [LAST NAME]</u>

Dear [CLIENT]:

As you know, the Judgment in your dissolution matter was entered on [DATE]. As of that date, your marriage was terminated. You were restored at that time to the status of an unmarried person. I have enclosed copies of the Notice of Entry of Judgment and the Judgment.

I trust you have reviewed your Will, insurance policies, and retirement benefit plans in order to make any changes in beneficiaries you deem appropriate. Because of the dissolution of your marriage, I would encourage you to do so as soon as possible.

You are currently covered under the health care plan provided to you by [NAME], and you may wish to continue those benefits under your own name. This is now possible, and most medical coverage is transferrable. You have only 60 days from Entry of Judgment to convert this insurance, and must do so by [DATE].

It is my understanding all property has been divided between you and [NAME]. The only remaining obligations pursuant to the Judgment are as follows:

(1) [NAME] shall pay your spousal support payments in the amount of $[AMOUNT] per month until [DATE], at which spousal support will absolutely terminate.

(2) [NAME] must also continue to maintain you as beneficiary on [HIS/HER] life insurance policy until [HIS/HER] spousal support obligation terminates.

(3) As and for [HIS/HER] contributive share of attorneys fees and costs, [NAME] is to pay directly to [FIRM] the sum of $[AMOUNT].

Form 13.7. Outline of Dissolution Agreement

```
[CLIENT NAME]
[DATE]
Page 2
```

It is customary after Entry of Final Judgment of Dissolution of Marriage for us to formally withdraw as your attorney of record. Enclosed you will find a copy of a Notice of Withdrawal of Attorney that we filed and served on [DATE]. We customarily withdraw from matters after entry of the Final Judgment because otherwise, we remain your attorney of record for all postjudgment proceedings. This leaves the opposing side to believe that service upon your attorney is effective service upon the client. By filing and service of a Notice of Withdrawal, the attorney of record puts the court and parties on notice that the relationship with the client has been formally terminated. I will, of course, be available to consult with you with respect to any problems that may occur.

I believe this brings the matter for which we were retained to a close, and I will be closing your file on this matter. If in the future we can be of service to you, please do not hesitate to contact us. It was a pleasure working with you. Best of luck to you in the future.

Sincerely,

Paul Ernst, Esq.

```
[AUTHOR/TYPIST]
Enclosures: [LIST]
[DOCUMENT LOCATOR CODE]
```

Form 13.7. Outline of Dissolution Agreement *(Continued)*

DeLost, Ernst, Meissner, Powell & Wilcox
Attorneys at Law
1257 Main Street, Suite 900
Los Angeles, CA 90066
(310) 555-6000

[DATE]

[NAME OF OPPOSING COUNSEL]
[ADDRESS]

Re: [NAME AND IDENTIFICATION OF MATTER]

Dear [NAME]:

This is to inform you that I will be on vacation, out of the country, from [DATES], and will be unavailable during that time period for any court appearances, depositions, ex parte applications, etc. Other than in emergency situations, I am asking you hold any matters in abeyance until I return. Please allow me at least five days after my return to file any documents in response or opposition to any of your pleadings or discovery.

During my absence, if you have any questions or problems, please feel free to contact my secretary [NAME], or one of my partners [NAME].

Sincerely,

Scott Powell, Esq.

[AUTHOR/TYPIST]
Enclosures: [LIST]
[DOCUMENT LOCATOR CODE]

Form 13.8. Notification of Attorney Unavailability

DeLost, Ernst, Meissner, Powell & Wilcox
Attorneys at Law
1257 Main Street, Suite 900
Los Angeles, CA 90066
(310) 555-6000

[DATE]

Leslie Morris
717 Parr Drive
Orlando, OH 45678

           Re: [CASE TITLE]
           <u>DISSOLUTION</u>

Dear Ms. Morris:

I am writing to let you know that you and your dependents are entitled to continued health coverage through [NAME]'s insurance plan, if
you have been covered by the plan in the past.

Under Title X of the Consolidated Omnibus Budget Reconciliation Action of 1985 (COBRA), if your spouse's employer provided group health
plans and has a minimum of twenty employees, your divorce entitles you
to continued insurance coverage through [NAME]'s company plan.

You have sixty (60) days after your divorce (date of final judgment)
to give <u>written</u> notification to the administrator of the insurance plan
that your divorce has occurred, and then you may be entitled to continued coverage. <u>You are directly responsible for notifying the insurance
carrier.</u> We can only advise you of your right to continued benefits.
Without your written notification to the insurance carrier within the
sixty-day limit, you will lose your entitlement to these benefits. You
should make a copy of the letter you send to the insurance carrier.

COBRA says continued insurance coverage must be offered for a maximum period of three years if the qualifying event is a divorce or legal
separation. Continued coverage may terminate earlier under certain circumstances. For instance, if you obtain coverage through another plan
or if you remarry and become covered under your new spouse's insurance
plan, COBRA will terminate.

To qualify for continued coverage, you must have been covered under
the group health plan on the date before the qualifying event. In your
case, the qualifying event is your divorce. If you are eligible, you are
considered a qualified beneficiary. But, the three years' coverage is
<u>not</u> available if, at the time marital status is terminated, the health
insurance for the employee spouse is not in effect.

In several local cases, the nonemployee spouses have lost their three
years' health insurance benefits under this new legislation because they
did not realize that at the time their marital status was terminated
(judgment was entered), their health insurance was not in effect, due to
nonpayment of premiums or a cancellation of coverage by the employee
spouse.

Form 13.9. Notice of Continued Health Coverage Entitlements

Leslie Morris
[DATE]
Page 2

It is very important for you to independently confirm through your spouse's employer or the employer's insurance company that you continue to be covered by your spouse's health insurance plan.

Some insurance policies allow you to enroll new defendants or spouses under your insurance coverage if you are a qualified beneficiary through COBRA. However, since these family members are added to the policy <u>after</u> the qualifying event, they are not eligible to receive COBRA benefits.

As a COBRA beneficiary, you will pay the same premiums as any other group plan member and receive the same coverage. When the continued coverage under COBRA expires, the plan must offer a <u>conversion</u> option that is generally available to active employees under the plan.

To find out further details about COBRA benefits and whether you qualify, you should contact your spouse's employer and/or health insurance carrier as soon as possible.

To summarize then, there are two important functions that you must perform with regard to your continued COBRA benefits.

(1)   You must confirm your continued coverage under your spouse's group plan.
(2)   You must notify the insurance company of the termination of your marital status (entry of judgment) within sixty (60) days of the entry of such judgment.

If you have any questions, please do not hesitate to call.

                    Sincerely,

                    Scott Powell, Esq.

[AUTHOR/TYPIST]
Enclosures: [LIST]
[DOCUMENT LOCATOR CODE]

Form 13.9. Notice of Continued Health Coverage Entitlements *(Continued)*

DeLost, Ernst, Meissner, Powell & Wilcox
Attorneys at Law
1257 Main Street, Suite 900
Los Angeles, CA 90066
(310) 555-6000

[DATE]

Lisa Campanella
123 Norris Street
Minneapolis, MN 12345

Re: Dissolution
[CASE TITLE]

Dear Ms. Campanella:

The final judgment document in regard to your dissolution to Dominick Campanella is enclosed. Please keep this document in a safe place. I will also keep a copy in your office file should you need it.

Please feel free to call me if you have any questions or run into any documentation problems with your stockbroker. He may contact me directly if he needs more informaton about the appropriate distribution of assets.

Sincerely,

Scott Powell, Esq.

[AUTHOR/TYPIST]
Enclosures: [LIST]
[DOCUMENT LOCATOR CODE]

Form 13.10. Transmittal of Final Dissolution

End Note

[1]Excerpted from "Paralegal Job Descriptions by Practice Area," compiled by the National Federation of Paralegal Associations. While not intended to be all inclusive, this list does provide examples of the differing types of assignments that can (and should) be delegated to paralegals.

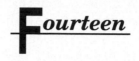ourteen

INSURANCE DEFENSE

14.1 / The Paralegal Role
   Form 14.1. Indemnification Demand/Notification of Lawsuit
   Form 14.2. Corresponding with the Client-Subrogation Matter
   Form 14.3. Corresponding with Opposing Party
   Form 14.4. Information Transmittal to Client
   Form 14.5. Letter Re: Discovery and Request for Execution of Verification
   Form 14.6. Request for Corporate Information

14.1 / The Paralegal Role

Insurance defense work is simply litigation on the defense side, in matters involving insurance claims. Once coverage is established, the scope of liability (if any), must be identified. Some of the legal issues involved in insurance coverage and policy limits include:

- who can be sued and when
- duty to defend and exclusion clauses
- "occurrences" and the trigger of coverage
- single vs. multiple occurrences
- broker liability
- defenses and the burden of proof
- reimbursement rights
- significance of the forum and choice of law analysis

- special issues involved in "mega" cases
- litigation vs. settlement

Discovery and trial tasks constitute the major part of the workload in this area, just as in a general litigation practice. However, insurance defense cases can involve some difficult discovery issues:

- joint defense privilege
- work product doctrine
- insurer-reinsurer privilege
- conflicts involving primary and excess insurers
- problems in complex coverage cases

Particular paralegal tasks involved in insurance defense practices include the following:

- process claims with carriers for liability, uninsured motorists, comprehensive general liability, and other basic policies
- coordinate negotiations with the insurance carrier and participate in such negotiations when appropriate
- attend initial intake meetings for cases which failed to settle at the claims stage between the plaintiffs' law office and the carrier's claims office
- draft cross-complaints for comparative indemnity, implied equitable indemnity, and for declaratory relief
- handle logistics involved in lawsuits removed to federal court, when subsequent/pending insurance bad faith actions are filed, or when class action joinder occurs

In addition, according to *Paralegals in American Law,* paralegals specializing in insurance defense may

- Interview clients and witnesses to determine the facts of cases.
- Schedule medical examinations of plaintiffs by doctors chosen by the defendants' attorneys.
- Review insurance policies to determine the extent of coverage.
- Review medical information and information concerning a plaintiff's expenses stemming from the accident.
- Review police reports and witness statements.[1]

Many of the forms found in Chapter 8, "Litigation," can also be used in an insurance defense practice. This is especially true for Forms 8.1 through 8.4. See also §8.11, which discusses preparing for trial.

DeLost, Ernst, Meissner, Powell & Wilcox
Attorneys at Law
1257 Main Street, Suite 900
Los Angeles, CA 90066
(310) 555-6000

[DATE]

Eleanor Sedgewick
Chief Operating Officer
Donaldson Pen Company
243 Admiral Road, Suite 1020
Los Angeles, CA 90099

            Re: [IDENTIFY MATTER]

Dear Ms. Sedgewick:

Enclosed you will find a copy of the summons and complaint that were
served upon [NAME] on [DATE], which we tender to you pursuant to the
indemnification clause of our contract relating to construction of the
nuclear plant at [PLACE]. Further pursuant to such contract, we ask that
you indemnify and save harmless [NAME] from and against any and all liability arising from injury or death to plaintiffs and/or damage to
property occasioned by any negligent act or omission alleged in the complaint and that you defend [NAME] against all such claims.

Please advise in writing to the undersigned as soon as possible that
you have accepted such tender. Also, please let us know which legal firm
will be assigned this matter.

Thank you for your cooperation.

                    Sincerely,

                    Angela Shapiro
                    Senior Paralegal

[AUTHOR/TYPIST]
Enclosures: [LIST]
[DOCUMENT LOCATOR CODE]

Form 14.1. Indemnification Demand/Notification of Lawsuit

DeLost, Ernst, Meissner, Powell & Wilcox
Attorneys at Law
1257 Main Street, Suite 900
Los Angeles, CA 90066
(310) 555-6000

[DATE]

George Martinson
Finance Administrator
Century Legal Insurance Company
Tenth Floor
San Francisco, CA 92456

          Re: [CASE TITLE, CASE NUMBER]

Dear Mr. Martinson:

   [COMPANY NAME] retained this law firm to represent it in the subrogation claim relating to your insurance loss. This loss occurred on
[DATE] located at your rental residence between [STREET NAME] and
[STREET NAME] in the city of [IDENTIFY LOCATION]. At that time, the at-
fault driver, [NAME OF PARTY]'s vehicle went out of control causing damages in the amount of $[AMOUNT].

   Our efforts have led us to commence suit on behalf of [COMPANY NAME]
and against [NAME OF PARTIES]. The suit will be commenced in your name
pursuant to the subrogation rights of [COMPANY NAME]. As set forth in
the relevant insurance policy provisions, we require your cooperation
in the prosecution of this case.

   Enclosed is a copy of the complaint we intend to file in the [NAME OF
COURT] involving this accident. Please review this complaint and contact his/her office within the next ten days to confirm that everything
stated in this pleading is accurate. Once we hear from you, we will serve
and file the complaint.

   It is my understanding [NAME] has paid for your entire loss sustained
in the above-referenced incident including your deductible, which was
absorbed due to excess loss. If any uninsured loss exists from this incident or if any uninsured claims arise in the future, please notify us
immediately. All claims arising out of this incident must be brought in
the present action. Should you fail to advise us and fail to bring any
uninsured loss claim relating to this incident, you may lose your right
to these amounts, as you will be barred from bringing them in any future lawsuit.

   If any uninsured loss or future claim related to this incident arises, you will need to obtain separate counsel to pursue that claim. Our
office will cooperate with any attorneys you hire to pursue an unin-
sured-related claim. Our firm would not be able to represent you on such
a claim because a conflict of interest may arise. This conflict of interest is based on the fact that should a settlement offer be made by
the defendants, a controversy may arise over whose claim should be com-
promised, the insurer's or your uninsured claim. Therefore, separate
counsel will be needed to pursue these related claims.

Form 14.2. Corresponding with the Client-Subrogation Matter

Mr. Martinson
[DATE]
Page 2

We request that you do not talk with anybody at any time regarding
this matter unless it is someone from this office. If anyone calls to
discuss this matter, please ask them to contact me directly. Should you
have any questions or comments concerning any of the matters discussed
in this letter, please do not hesitate to give me or [NAME], paralegal,
at [PHONE NUMBER], a call.

Once again we ask that you contact this office directly to confirm
the accuracy of the enclosed complaint. Thank you.

Sincerely,

Sandra Wilson
Litigation Manager

[AUTHOR/TYPIST]
Enclosures: [LIST]
[DOCUMENT LOCATOR CODE]

Form 14.2. Corresponding with the Client-Subrogation Matter *(Continued)*

DeLost, Ernst, Meissner, Powell & Wilcox
Attorneys at Law
1257 Main Street, Suite 900
Los Angeles, CA 90066
(310) 555-6000

[DATE]

Lauren Tambor
1234 Highway Two
Localy, AZ 12345.

Re: [CASE TITLE, CASE NUMBER]

Dear Ms. Tambor:

This office has been retained by [NAME] and his insurer, [NAME], to pursue a claim against [NAME]'s insurance company for the damages caused in the accident referred to above. This letter is being submitted for settlement purposes only. Neither this letter nor its contents will be admissible at trial in this case.

FACTS

On [DATE], a moving van owned by [NAME], and driven by an employee of that company named [NAME], damaged [NAME]'s driveway located at [ADDRESS]. Due to this employee's actions, the residence was damaged in an amount at least equal to $[AMOUNT]. Based on the testimony of the parties involved, there is no question the driver of this van was liable for the accident that caused this property loss.

LIABILITY

Due to the above, [NAME]'s insurance company will provide coverage for this accident. Therefore, we are making demand that you release information stating its insurer on [DATE] so a claim may be filed to settle this matter.

We ask that you take steps to finalize this incident within ten days of the date of this letter or collection action will be necessary with no additional notice. Enclosed is a copy of a complaint that will be filed with the [LOCATION] court after that time. Call me or [NAME], paralegal, at [PHONE NUMBER] to discuss settlement of this claim.
Lauren Tambor

Because these matters involve your legal interests, you should consider consulting an attorney. Thank you for your prompt assistance in handling this matter.

Sincerely,

Marjorie Meissner, Esq.

[AUTHOR/TYPIST]
Enclosures: [LIST]
[DOCUMENT LOCATOR CODE]

Form 14.3. Corresponding with Opposing Party

DeLost, Ernst, Meissner, Powell & Wilcox
Attorneys at Law
1257 Main Street, Suite 900
Los Angeles, CA 90066
(310) 555-6000

[DATE]

George Martinson
Finance Administrator
Century Legal Insurance Company
One Embarcadero Center
Tenth Floor
San Francisco, CA 92456

     Re: Insured:
       Policy No.
       Claim No.:
       Date of Loss:
       Our file No.: _____

Dear Mr. Martinson:

Enclosed for your files are the following documents:

(1)   Petition for order compelling arbitration and for order compelling appointment of neutral umpire/arbitrator;

(2)   Notice of hearing on petition for order compelling arbitration and for order compelling appointment of neutral umpire/arbitrator; memorandum of points and authorities; declaration in support.

These documents have been filed and served. The hearing will be held on [DATE, TIME, AND PLACE]

If you have any questions, please call at any time. We will continue to keep you advised of relevant developments as they occur.

      Sincerely,

      David Wesley
      Legal Assistant

[AUTHOR/TYPIST]
Enclosures
[DOCUMENT LOCATOR CODE]

Form 14.4. Information Transmittal to Client

DeLost, Ernst, Meissner, Powell & Wilcox
Attorneys at Law
1257 Main Street, Suite 900
Los Angeles, CA 90066
(310) 555-6000

[DATE]

Lauren Tambor
1234 Highway Two
Localy, AZ 12345

Re: [CASE TITLE, CASE NUMBER]

Dear Ms. Tambor:

Draft copies of our responses to defendant's request for identification and production of documents and special interrogatories are enclosed for your approval. We will be producing the inspection report from the Underwriting file and most of the documents in the Claims files, excluding documents that fall within the attorney-client privilege and work product protection.

Also enclosed is the original verification for the responses to the special interrogatories. Please review and note any changes. If there are any changes, we will make the corrections and provide another form. If approved, please sign and return it to us in the enclosed envelope.

Thank you for your assistance. If you have any questions, please call at any time.

Sincerely,

Sandra Wilson
Litigation Manager

[AUTHOR/TYPIST]
Enclosures: [LIST]
[DOCUMENT LOCATOR CODE]

Form 14.5. Letter Re: Discovery and Request for Execution of Verification

DeLost, Ernst, Meissner, Powell & Wilcox
Attorneys at Law
1257 Main Street, Suite 900
Los Angeles, CA 90066
(310) 555-6000

[DATE]

TO SECRETARY OF STATE
[ADDRESS]

        Re: _____

Dear Secretary of State:

  Please provide this office with a certified copy of the most recent
filing of the statement of officers and directors for [NAME OF CORPORA-
TION]. Please advise us as to whether or not this corporation is in good
standing.

  We enclose our check in the amount of $[AMOUNT] for your services,
together with a self-addressed, stamped return envelope. If you need additional fees, please contact us immediately.

  Thank you for your assistance.

                            Sincerely,

                            Mark C. Williams
                            Paralegal

[AUTHOR/TYPIST]
Enclosures: [LIST]
[DOCUMENT LOCATOR CODE]

Form 14.6. Request for Corporate Information

End Note

[1]Angela Schneeman, *Paralegals in American Law: Introduction to Paralegalism*, p. 14 (1995).

Fifteen

REAL ESTATE

15.1 / The Paralegal Role

  Form 15.1. Transmittal to Client for Review and Exe
  cution

  Form 15.2. Demand for Beneficiary Statements

  Form 15.3. Demand for Payoff of Subordinate Liens

  Form 15.4. Letter to Title Company to Modify Terms
  of Loan

  Form 15.5. Closing Documents; Instructions to
  Escrow

  Form 15.6. Letter of Advice Re: Eviction

  Form 15.7. Letter of Advice Re: Eviction

15.1 / The Paralegal Role

Real estate paralegals are responsible for a wide variety of tasks specific to this practice area. Generally, such tasks include the following:

- researching zoning ordinances and other laws relating to the transfer and use of real estate,

- drafting contracts and financing agreements,

- ordering title research from title companies,

- reviewing abstracts or certificates of title,

- preparing maps of property based on the legal description of property,

- preparing drafts of title opinions,

- preparing deeds, notes, and mortgages,

- providing lenders with necessary documentation,
- following up on necessary closing items and scheduling closings,
- attending closings to assist with document review and execution and the transfer of funds, and
- filing the necessary documentation after closings.

In addition, the detailed job description compiled by the National Federation of Paralegal Associations lists the following responsibilities:

- Draft subdivision, condominium, and timeshare registrations for in-state and out-of-state registrations.
- Draft registrations of recreational subdivisions for federal registration.
- Organize recording procedures for large-scale recording and prepare draft of opinion letters.
- Perform financial calculations (amortization, net present value, discounting, APR).
- Conduct a title search in the records office or order title search and updates.
- Prepare a preliminary abstract of title and opinion on the title.
- Negotiate title insurance coverage.
- Arrange for the purchase of title insurance.
- Assist client in obtaining mortgage financing.
- Review mortgage applications for clients that sell mortgages.
- Assist in recording mortgages.
- Assemble tax receipts.
- Adjust property taxes for closing.
- Record capital gains or losses in clients' income tax returns.
- Prepare appropriate capital gains tax affidavit.
- Draft Truth-in-Lending Disclosure Statements.
- Draft and review permits and easements.
- Draft, review, and plot legal descriptions.
- Draft grant, warranty, and other deeds.
- Draft Deeds of Trust and other loan documentation.
- Draft leases, assignments, extensions, amendments.
- Draft contracts, assignments, modifications.
- Blackline changes in documents as each is revised.

- Draft and arrange for filing of UCC filings, amendments, extensions, terminations.

- Prepare closing checklist for acquisition and loan transactions.

- Draft escrow instructions.

- Analyze and digest leases, assignments, extensions, amendments, and deeds.

- Review and determine validity of mineral claims through search of BLM (Bureau of Land Management) records.

- Check and review zoning, Subdivision Map Act, and comprehensive plan designations; obtain letters on designation as closing requirements.

- Review land surveys, Parcel Maps, and condominium plats.

- Draft closing statements and arrange closing date.

- Notify all parties involved of closing date.

- Order amortization table.

- Prepare equalization form.

- Arrange for discharge of mortgage.

- Obtain closing figures from bank, and prorate all closing figures.

- Appear or assist attorney at closing.

- Notarize documents at closing.

- Follow up on post-closing items, including preparation of closing index and binder.

- Assist client in obtaining liability insurance (e.g., homeowner's policy).

- Coordinate office handling of insurance claims of client.

- Prorate real and personal property taxes.[1]

DeLost, Ernst, Meissner, Powell & Wilcox
Attorneys at Law
1257 Main Street, Suite 900
Los Angeles, CA 90066
(310) 555-6000

[DATE]

Leslie Morris
717 Parr Drive
Orlando, OH 45678

    Re: [IDENTIFY MATTER]

Dear Ms. Morris:

Confirming our telephone conversation of [DATE], we agreed that this office would draft a deed of trust securing all amounts due to [NAME] by former resident [NAME] in the amount of $[AMOUNT], plus interest.

Please review the attached deed of trust. If it meets with your approval, please ask [NAME] to sign the document before a notary public. Kindly return it directly to my attention so it may be recorded with the county auditor's office.

If you have any questions, please call me directly at [PHONE NUMBER].

    Sincerely,

    Angela Shapiro
    Senior Paralegal

[AUTHOR/TYPIST]
Enclosures: [LIST]
[DOCUMENT LOCATOR CODE]

Form 15.1. Transmittal to Client for Review and Execution

DeLost, Ernst, Meissner, Powell & Wilcox
Attorneys at Law
1257 Main Street, Suite 900
Los Angeles, CA 90066
(310) 555-6000

[DATE]

Joseph R. Martin
Eastern Bank
1945 Berks Boulevard
Suite Three
Shillington, PA 19613

         Re: [IDENTIFY MATTER]

Dear Mr. Martin:

    IN ACCORDANCE with Civil Code Section [CITE], demand is hereby made
for a Beneficiary Statement pertaining to the obligation described as
follows:

    Face Amount:
    Trustor:
    Beneficiary:
    Dated:
    Recorded:

affecting the property described as follows:

    [LEGAL DESCRIPTION]

more commonly described as:

    [STREET ADDRESS]

    Please include a complete copy of the note/deed or other evidence of
indebtedness and any subsequent modification. If there is a charge for
this service, please let me know immediately. The code section cited
above indicates that a beneficiary may not charge in excess of $[AMOUNT]
for the statement.

    Please be advised that if you fail to provide the completed Benefi-
ciary Statement within twenty-one (21) days after receipt of this demand, you may be liable for damages pursuant to Civil Code Section
[CITE].

    Mail the Beneficiary Statement and accompanying documents to:

    [PARALEGAL NAME AND ADDRESS]

Form 15.2. Demand for Beneficiary Statements

Joseph R. Martin
[DATE]
Page 2

   Please feel free to contact my paralegal, [NAME], directly with any
questions you have. The undersigned is entitled to such information in
the capacity of attorney for plaintiff and judgment creditor.

                          Sincerely,

                          Anthony Wilcox, Esq.
[AUTHOR/TYPIST]
Enclosures: none
[DOCUMENT LOCATOR CODE]

Form 15.2. Demand for Beneficiary Statements *(Continued)*

DeLost, Ernst, Meissner, Powell & Wilcox
Attorneys at Law
1257 Main Street, Suite 900
Los Angeles, CA 90066
(310) 555-6000

[DATE]

Joseph R. Martin
Eastern Bank
1945 Berks Boulevard
Suite Three
Shillington, PA 19613

Re: [IDENTIFY MATTER]

Dear Mr. Martin:

IN ACCORDANCE with Civil Code Section [CITE], demand is hereby made for a Payoff Demand Statement pertaining to the obligation identified as follows:

Face amount:
Trustor:
Beneficiary:
Dated:
Recorded:

affecting the property described as follows:

[LEGAL DESCRIPTION]

more commonly described as:

[STREET ADDRESS]

Please include a complete copy of the documents evidencing the indebtedness and any subsequent modification. If there is a charge for this service, please let me know immediately.

Please be advised that if you fail to provide the completed Payoff Demand Statement within twenty-one (21) days after receipt of this demand, you may be liable for damages pursuant to Civil Code Section [CITE].

Mail the Beneficiary Statement and accompanying documents to:

[PARALEGAL NAME AND ADDRESS]

Form 15.3. Demand for Payoff of Subordinate Liens

Joseph R. Martin
[DATE]
Page 2

   Please feel free to contact my paralegal, [NAME], directly with any
questions you may have. The undersigned is entitled to such information
in the capacity of attorney for plaintiff and judgment creditor.

                 Sincerely,

                 Anthony Wilcox, Esq.

[AUTHOR/TYPIST]
Enclosures: none
[DOCUMENT LOCATOR CODE]

Form 15.3. Demand for Payoff of Subordinate Liens *(Continued)*

DeLost, Ernst, Meissner, Powell & Wilcox
Attorneys at Law
1257 Main Street, Suite 900
Los Angeles, CA 90066
(310) 555-6000

[DATE]

Mr. Alec Sutherland
1936 Papermill Road
Mission Springs, CA 90067

     Re: [IDENTIFY MATTER]

Dear Mr. Sutherland:

   On [DATE], [NAME OF COMPANY] issued ALTA loan policies for the benefit of our client, [NAME]. [NAME] purchased the subject loans from
[NAME]. The insured loans were secured by certain real property located in [NAME OF COUNTIES] counties held in fee by [HOLDER]. For your convenience, copies of these policies are enclosed.

   [NAME] now desires to modify these loans upon the terms and conditions in the enclosed (draft) Loan Modification Agreements. It would be
timely for your office to commence a datedown of title to be prepared
to issue a Modification Endorsement to each of the original policies.

   In addition, [NAME] anticipates selling both of these loans in the
near future, possibly to [NAME] (or a subsidiary or affiliate), but not
until the loans have been modified. Enclosed are copies of the title reports issued on [DATE] when [NAME] previously anticipated sale of these
loans to [NAME]. These title reports may be of assistance to you in down-
dating title.

   We expect to record the Loan Modifications within three to four weeks,
once [NAME] agrees on the terms of the modified loans. Please let me
know if you need further information from me to commence a datedown of
the original policies. Of course, if you have any questions regarding
the enclosed, do not hesitate to call me.

                         Sincerely,

                         Allison Curtis
                         Legal Assistant

[AUTHOR/TYPIST]
Enclosures:none
[DOCUMENT LOCATOR CODE]

Form 15.4. Letter to Title Company to Modify Terms of Loan

DeLost, Ernst, Meissner, Powell & Wilcox
Attorneys at Law
1257 Main Street, Suite 900
Los Angeles, CA 90066
(310) 555-6000

[DATE]

Joseph R. Martin
1945 Berks Boulevard
Suite Three
Shillington, PA 19613

        Re: [IDENTIFY MATTER]

Dear Mr. Martin:

   (A)   Closing documents. In connection with the $[AMOUNT] cross-col-
          lateralized loan to [NAME with shortened form in quotes and
          parentheses, example: ABC Banking Company ("Bank")] in favor
          of [NAME] and the recording in [LOCATION] counties of the re-
          spective Deeds of Trust and Assignments of the respective ben-
          eficial interests thereunder to [NAME], the following docu-
          ments are hereby delivered to you for the purpose of closing
          the above-described escrow:

          (1)   Deed of Trust encumbering the [SPECIFY] property, for
                 recording in [LOCATION] county;

          (2)   Assignment of Deed of Trust for recording in said Coun-
                 ty; and

          (3)   Copy of Promissory Note in the amount of [AMOUNT], the
                 original of which has been delivered to the bank.

   (B)   Conditions of Closing. You may close the transaction upon ful-
          fillment of the conditions set forth below:

          (1)   You have telephoned and received oral advice from the
                 undersigned that all conditions of closing required by
                 [NAME] or by [NAME] to be fulfilled outside of this es-
                 crow have been fulfilled to their satisfaction;

Form 15.5. Closing Documents; Instructions to Escrow

Joseph R. Martin
[DATE]
Page 2

(2)   You are unconditionally committed to issue your ALTA
Loan Policy of Title Insurance insuring [NAME] in the
amount of $[AMOUNT], showing the Deed of Trust referred
to in Paragraph A.1 above as a valid and existing lien
on the property described therein and subordinate to
the Deed of Trust referenced as Item [NUMBER] of your
preliminary report, and containing: (a) only those exceptions shown in your preliminary title report dated
as of [DATE]; (b) CLTA Endorsements [NUMBERS]; and (c)
a tie-in endorsement that shows that the total liability under your policy and the policy to be issued by
the title company insuring the remaining liability
does not exceed $[AMOUNT]. Any questions you may have
regarding the arrangement among the parties should be
directed to [NAME AND PHONE NUMBER].

(C)   Closing Procedures. In closing you will strictly adhere to the
procedures in the order set forth herein below. All requirements with respect to closing shall be considered as having
been made until all deliveries and closing transactions have
been accomplished. Further, the recordings specified herein
below are to be done concurrently with the respective recordings in [LOCATION] county by [NAME], and you are to contact
[NAME] to coordinate the recordings. Your closing procedures
are as follows:

(1)   Record the Deed of Trust referred to in Paragraph A.1
above in the Official Records of [LOCATION] county; and

(2)   Record (after providing on the face thereof the recording information from the Deed of Trust) the Assignment
referred to in Paragraph A.2 above in the Official
Records of [LOCATION] county.

(D)   General Instructions.

(1)   All costs and expenses for the escrow with respect to
the closing of this transaction shall be paid by
[NAME]. You shall be responsible for collection of all
such costs and expenses, although you may bill us for
same; and

(2)   If you are unable to comply with these instructions and
close this escrow on or before [TIME: usually 5:00
P.M.] of the tenth (10th) business day following the
date of these instructions, or if there are to be any
changes therein, you are not to proceed without further written authorization from the undersigned.

If there are any questions concerning the above, please contact the
undersigned immediately.

Form 15.5. Closing Documents; Instructions to Escrow *(Continued)*

Joseph R. Martin
[DATE]
Page 3

   PLEASE IMMEDIATELY RETURN AN EXECUTED COPY OF THESE INSTRUCTIONS TO
THE UNDERSIGNED.

                      Sincerely,

                      Allison Curtis
                      Paralegal
[AUTHOR/TYPIST]
Enclosures: [LIST]
[DOCUMENT LOCATOR CODE]

   The undersigned acknowledges receipt of the within escrow instructions
and agrees to proceed in strict accordance therewith:

[NAME OF TITLE COMPANY]

By: _____

  Its: _____

Dated: September _____, 19XX

Form 15.5. Closing Documents; Instructions to Escrow *(Continued)*

DeLost, Ernst, Meissner, Powell & Wilcox
Attorneys at Law
1257 Main Street, Suite 900
Los Angeles, CA 90066
(310) 555-6000

[DATE]

George Martinson
Finance Administrator
Century Legal Insurance Company
One Embarcadero Center
Tenth Floor
San Francisco, CA 92456

          Re: PROPERTY LOCATED AT 235 Sear Street
              Lease number 234.56/whal

Dear Mr. Martinson:

   Our client advises us that the lease agreement for the tenants at the
building located at 235 Sear Street has expired. The current tenants
have refused to vacate the premises.

   Our office has prepared a three-day notice to pay rent or quit, to be
posted this afternoon. Since we have always dealt with you in a spirit
of cooperation, it is our hope this matter can be rectified within the
three-day period.

   Please have your sub-tenant representative contact my paralegal,
[NAME], immediately for instructions. I will return to the office on
Friday to execute any releases, as necessary.

   Thank you for your immediate consideration.

                         Sincerely,

                         Scott Powell, Esq.

[AUTHOR/TYPIST]
cc: Mark C. Williams
[DOCUMENT LOCATOR CODE]

Form 15.6. Letter of Advice Re: Eviction

DeLost, Ernst, Meissner, Powell & Wilcox
Attorneys at Law
1257 Main Street, Suite 900
Los Angeles, CA 90066
(310) 555-6000

[DATE]

Janet Jergens
1256 Astoria Lane
Holewood, WI 12345

        Re: <u>COMPLEX 3, 123 NORAL AVENUE</u>

Dear Ms. Jergens:

   As the tenant advocate and president of the association of dwellers,
you are hereby notified that you are in violation of the waste/nuisance
ordinance that governs your building and surrounding areas.

   Any tenant committing waste ... contrary to the conditions or covenants
of his lease, or maintaining, committing, or permitting the maintenance or commission of a nuisance upon the demised premises <u>or using
such premises for an unlawful purpose,</u> thereby terminates the lease,
and the landlord, or his successor in estate, shall upon service of
three days' notice to quit upon the person or persons in possession,
be entitled to restitution of possession.

   Attached is a copy of the police and arrest reports for the tenants
in question. We intend to move forward upon expiration of the notice
that has been posted today.

                        Sincerely,

                        Mark C. Williams
                        Paralegal
[AUTHOR/TYPIST]
[DOCUMENT LOCATOR CODE]

Form 15.7. Letter of Advice Re:Eviction

End Note

[1]Excerpted from "Paralegal Job Descriptions by Practice Area," compiled by the National Federation of Paralegal Associations. While not intended to be all inclusive, this list does provide examples of the differing types of assignments that can (and should) be delegated to paralegals.

PERSONAL INJURY

16.1 / The Paralegal Role
  Form 16.1. Letter to Opposing Counsel Transmitting
  Medical Summary
  Form 16.2. Authorization for Release of Medical
  Information
  Form 16.3. Letter to Potential Client Declining
  Representation
  Form 16.4. Demand Letter to Opposing Counsel
  Form 16.5. Letter to Opposing Counsel Claiming
  Damages
  Form 16.6. Request to Client for Additional
  Information
  Form 16.7. Letter to Opposing Counsel Re: Expert
  Deposition
  Form 16.8. Letter Requesting Medical Charges and
  Records
  Form 16.9. Letter Requesting Copies of Medical
  Records
  Form 16.10. Additional Medical Records Request
  Form 16.11. Request for Records, History, and x-Rays
  Form 16.12. Request for Billing Records
  Form 16.13. Request for Records of Driver
  Form 16.14. Letter to Obtain DMV Collision Reports

16.1 / The Paralegal Role

Personal injury practices deal predominantly with litigation. In offices handling large volumes of personal injury cases, paralegals may be assigned to various "stages" of the litigation, such as commencement, investigation, and settlement. In other offices one or two paralegals may be assigned to their own cases, reporting directly to the supervising attorney and indirectly to the client. Paralegals are also responsible for establishing systems and keeping records.

As with other litigation-based practice areas, personal injury usually involves the initiation of an action, discovery, and then settlement or trial. Since injury is the key issue, medical records and expert witness testimony are relied upon heavily for evidence. In *Paralegals in American Law,* the author lists the following as typical tasks for personal injury paralegals:

- Interviewing clients to ascertain the extent of their injuries and to obtain consents for receiving medical information.

- Obtaining medical reports from doctors, hospitals, and other medical facilities.

- Obtaining reports regarding wage loss.

- Collecting other information concerning a client's out-of-pocket expenses stemming from the accident.

- Researching pertinent state laws concerning negligence and personal injury.

- Obtaining insurance information from opposing counsel.[1]

Some personal injury firms also handle workers' compensation matters. While this type of litigation looks a great deal like other personal injury cases, other steps in the process are required to meet state administrative regulations. For example, the job description compiled by the National Federation of Paralegal Associations includes the following tasks:

- Obtain copy of accident report.

- Organize file and place on case diary/docket.

- Prepare appropriate claim forms and transmit to Department of Labor or other agency.

- Draft Request for Hearing or Response.

- Draft Application to Schedule Date or Reply.

- Attend pretrial conference and obtain hearing dates.

- Draft Response or Motion to Postpone.

- Obtain and organize medical reports, personnel information, and other documents pertinent to hearing.

- Schedule doctor appointments and independent medical evaluations.

- Schedule medical and lay witness testimony for trial or by deposition.
- Obtain personnel information and job description.
- Schedule meetings and interview doctors, rehabilitation experts, and lay witnesses (employees and employer).
- Request employer medical mileage reimbursement.
- Prepare narrative case evaluation.
- Supervise compliance with Demand for Documents.
- Evaluate disability utilizing WCB (Workers' Compensation Board) rules and guidelines.
- Research claim options.
- Check average weekly wage calculations.
- Negotiate settlement.
- Assist attorney at WCB hearings.
- Draft Petition for Judicial Review.
- Draft Statement of Case.
- Draft Motion for Reconsideration.
- Draft affidavit regarding attorneys' fees, witness expenses, and medical expenses.
- Investigate Second Injury Fund and/or Third Party Potential.
- Draft Stipulation and Order for Second Injury Fund cases.[2]

Most sample letters presented in this chapter can be utilized many times over, with only small changes from case to case. This is true primarily because a great deal of the correspondence is transmittal in nature, such as:

- retainer agreements,
- witness letters,
- complaint and answer allegations,
- client statements, and
- medical authorizations.

See also Chapter 14, "Insurance Defense," for additional letters that may be useful in a personal injury practice.

DeLost, Ernst, Meissner, Powell & Wilcox
Attorneys at Law
1257 Main Street, Suite 900
Los Angeles, CA 90066
(310) 555-6000

[DATE]

Paul Holler, Esq.
Vance, Region, Early and Moore
22 Locktree Circle
Tower Two
Atlanta, GA 12345

Re: [CASE TITLE, CASE NUMBER]

Dear Mr. Holler:

Enclosed please find a medical summary regarding the medical care and treatment of [NAME]. This summary has been prepared in accordance with Federal Rule 1006 and is based on and consistent with [NAME]'s medical records.

I plan to offer this summary at the pretrial conference and use it at trial. I am sending it to you at this time in the spirit of cooperation. Please review it and if you have any questions or comments, please notify me in writing.

Thank you for your attention to this matter.

Sincerely,

John B. Watson
Legal Assistant

[AUTHOR/TYPIST]
Enclosures: Summary as noted
[DOCUMENT LOCATOR CODE]

Form 16.1. Letter to Opposing Counsel Transmitting Medical Summary

DeLost, Ernst, Miessner, Powell & Wilcox
Attorneys at Law
1257 Main Street, Suite 900
Los Angeles, CA 90066
(310) 555-6000

[DATE]

Lauren Tambor
1234 Highway Two
Localy, AZ 12345

Re: [CASE TITLE, CASE NUMBER]

Dear Ms. Tambor:

My responsibilities as the paralegal on this case include:

* gathering additional information,
* calendaring important dates,
* processing medical bills received by you, and other medical bills, medical records, and other entities.

Feel free to call me at any time. I will be able to answer many of your questions or you may consult with [ATTORNEY] if necessary. In addition, I will be sending you copies of certain documents we receive as well as copies of paperwork we prepare and send to the other side. This keeps you informed as to how the case is proceeding. If we need you to take some action, we will call or write to let you know what you need to do.

Normally, medical visits and records are confidential under the "physician/patient privilege." We are requesting that you execute the enclosed original Authorization for Release of Information and return it to me in the enclosed, self-addressed, stamped envelope.

I will be requesting all of your medical records needed to prove your claim and records of treatment occurring after the accident to show what injuries were caused. We also may obtain copies of records of treatment received before the accident to explain prior injuries or conditions. If there are matters in these medical records you believe will hurt this case or are so sensitive you do not want them disclosed, please let me know.

In addition, I plan to request additional billings from [NAME OF PROVIDERS]. If there are other health care providers that I have omitted, please advise.

Since we will need to clarify injuries that occurred during the first accident and those occurring during the second accident, please indicate if these health care providers were visited for each separate accident. Also, please explain why you feel there is an overlapping of injuries caused by the first and second accidents. Be sure to point out any previous medical history that would matter to this case and which hospitals provided any previous medical care.

Form 16.2. Authorization for Release of Medical Information

Lauren Tambor
[DATE]
Page 2

I understand you will not be filing a form for Worker's Compensation
with the Department of Labor and Industries since your employer does not
have this insurance.

In general, here are a few suggestions:

(1)   Do not discuss this case with anyone other than members of this
        firm, your spouse, your doctors, or others with whom we au-
        thorize you to discuss your case.

(2)   Please consult us before you do something that might affect
        your case, including changing doctors.

(3)   Sign nothing dealing with your claim until you have received
        our instructions or approval.

(4)   Obtain a receipt for all medications or appliances purchased
        by you and forward them to us.

(5)   Keep a record of any other expenses incurred as a result of
        the accident.

(6)   Make a list identifying how we might best demonstrate your loss
        of income due to this accident.

(7)   Notify us right away of a change of address, or of home or
        business telephone number.

(8)   Please notify us immediately if you hear anything that you feel
        may affect your case.

I look forward to receiving the information as outlined above and discussing this further with you.

                        Sincerely,

                        Meagan O'Keefe
                        Paralegal
[AUTHOR/TYPIST]
Enclosures: [LIST]
[DOCUMENT LOCATOR CODE]

Form 16.2. Authorization for Release of Medical Information (*Continued*)

AUTHORIZATION FOR RELEASE OF MEDICAL INFORMATION

Name of Patient: _____   Date of Birth: _____

Social Security Number: _____

Name of Patient: _____   Date of Birth: _____

Social Security Number: _____

To Whom It May Concern:

This is to authorize [NAME] to furnish to my attorneys, [NAME AND TELEPHONE], any information or opinions regarding myself and/or the person whose name appears above, for whom I have the legal authority to make this authorization relating to car accident injuries. This release of information is to allow my attorneys, or any representative on their behalf authorized by them to obtain any and all information or opinions, and to view or receive any x-rays, hospital records, physician's records, or any other material regarding car accident injuries. With this Authorization, I hereby waive any physician/patient privilege in this regard.

(1)   **Copy in Lieu of Original.** A copy of the original authorization for release of medical information shall have the same force and effect as the signed original.

(2)   **Unlawful Disclosure Prohibited.** YOU ARE HEREBY NOTIFIED THAT STATE LAW PROHIBITS ANY PHYSICIANS, HOSPITAL, OR HEALTH CARE PROVIDER FROM RELEASING ANY INFORMATION ABOUT THE PATIENT TO SOME OTHER PERSON UNLESS THE PATIENT FIRST CONSENTS TO THE RELEASE OF THE SAME. THE UNAUTHORIZED RELEASE OF INFORMATION ABOUT A PATIENT CAN RESULT IN THE LOSS OF THE PATIENT'S LEGAL RIGHTS AND RESULT IN A DAMAGE CLAIM FOR SUCH UNAUTHORIZED RELEASE.

THEREFORE, YOU ARE DIRECTED NOT TO RELEASE ANY INFORMATION OF ANY NATURE WHATSOEVER TO INSURANCE ADJUSTORS, ATTORNEYS OR THEIR REPRESENTATIVES, OR ANY OTHER PERSONS WHO MAY CONTACT YOU OR YOUR OFFICE STAFF ABOUT THIS PATIENT UNLESS WRITTEN CONSENT HAS BEEN GIVEN BY THE PATIENT FOR THE RELEASE OF SUCH INFORMATION.

(3)   **Revocation of Other Waivers.** I hereby revoke any other authorization for release of medical information that may have been provided by you, by any insurance adjustor, or insurance company other than my medical insurance company or the Department of Labor and Industries.

(4)   **Caution.** PLEASE ALERT YOUR STAFF ABOUT THE RESTRICTIONS ON RELEASE OF INFORMATION OF ANY NATURE WHATSOEVER REGARDING THIS PATIENT TO PERSONS UNAUTHORIZED TO RECEIVE THE SAME IN ORDER TO AVOID POSSIBLE LEGAL COMPLICATIONS.

Signature: _____

Typed Name of Patient: _____

Date of Signature: _____

Form 16.2. Authorization for Release of Medical Information (Continued)

DeLost, Ernst, Miessner, Powell & Wilcox
Attorneys at Law
1257 Main Street, Suite 900
Los Angeles, CA 90066
(310) 555-6000

[DATE]

Leslie Morris
717 Parr Drive
Orlando, OH 45678

    Re: [IDENTIFY MATTER]

Dear Ms. Morris:

  We appreciate the opportunity to review the facts regarding your potential medical malpractice claim. This letter confirms that we are declining acceptance at this time.

  The elements of medical negligence and causation are sometimes difficult to prove. This does not mean your case is without merit, but that
we cannot assist you in this matter.

  Please find enclosed a copy of a booklet entitled: "Statute of Limitations and Pre-Suit Notice of Claim in Texas Medical Malpractice Actions under Article 4590i, Texas Revised Civil Statutes," which contains
information regarding potential medical negligence claims. You should
read this information carefully and if you decide to pursue your case,
contact another attorney for advice or to answer any questions you have.

  You are advised that if proper legal action is not commenced within
the applicable time periods, any legal remedies will be forever barred.

  Thank you for the opportunity to review your case. Please contact us
if we may be of assistance in the future with another matter.

      Sincerely,

      Sandra Wilson
      Litigation Manager

[AUTHOR/TYPIST]
Enclosures: [LIST]
[DOCUMENT LOCATOR CODE]

Form 16.3. Letter to Potential Client Declining Representation

DeLost, Ernst, Miessner, Powell & Wilcox
Attorneys at Law
1257 Main Street, Suite 900
Los Angeles, CA 90066
(310) 555-6000

[DATE]

Paul Holler, Esq.
Vance, Region, Early and Moore
22 Locktree Circle
Tower Two
Atlanta, GA 12345

    Re: [CASE TITLE, CASE NUMBER]

Dear Mr. Holler:

[NAME] was referred to our office a few months ago regarding injuries
he received as a result of the accident that occurred on [DATE]. In an
attempt to settle [NAME]'s claim before initiating litigation, I am forwarding a settlement package that sets forth [HIS/HER] biographical
data, a summary of [HIS/HER] damages, and copies of [HIS/HER] medical
records.

Although suit has not been filed on behalf of (client), in all prob-
ability [HE/SHE] will seek recovery for the following damages:

(1)   Physical pain and suffering
(2)   Mental pain and suffering
(3)   Lost wages—past and future
(4)   Medical expenses—past and future
(5)   Punitive damages

Considering all of the above, [NAME] hereby tenders [HIS/HER] settlement demand of [AMOUNT SPELLED OUT AND IN NUMBERS, IN PARENTHESES].

Please review this settlement package and forward it to the defendant's insurance carrier for review and consideration. Also, please fax
your response to me as soon as possible.

                    Sincerely,

                    Mark C. Williams, Esq.

[AUTHOR/TYPIST]
Enclosures: [LIST]
[DOCUMENT LOCATOR CODE]

Form 16.4. Demand Letter to Opposing Counsel

DeLost, Ernst, Miessner, Powell & Wilcox
Attorneys at Law
1257 Main Street, Suite 900
Los Angeles, CA 90066
(310) 555-6000

[DATE]

Paul Holler, Esq.
Vance, Region, Early and Moore
22 Locktree Circle
Tower Two
Atlanta, GA 12345

          Re: [CASE TITLE, CASE NUMBER]

Dear Mr. Holler:

   As you know, this office represents [NAME], who is [AGE] years old.
[NAME] continues to have problems as a result of an automobile collision caused by your insured, [NAME], on [DATE]. For that reason, we are
making a claim on [HIS/HER] behalf.

   Your file will reflect that your insured was cited for [LIST VIOLA-
TIONS]. At that time [NAME]'s vehicle made a [DIRECTION] turn onto [LO-
CATION] and crossed the centerline to collide into the [AREAS OF VEHI-
CLE HIT AND MAKE OF VEHICLE] at a high enough rate of speed to render
[NAME]'s vehicle totally disabled. At the time of the accident, [NAME]
was driving the [VEHICLE YEAR AND MAKE] at approximately [SPEED] miles
per hour ("mph"). [NAME] was wearing [HIS/HER] seatbelt. Attached as Ex-
hibit "1" is a copy of the Police Collision Report.

   After the accident, [NAME] felt dizzy, experienced neck pain, abdom-
inal pain, and lower shoulder pain as well as pain along the clavicle
and the ribline. [NAME] complained of headaches after the accident. Attached as Exhibit "2" are copies of medical records prepared by [NAME]
relating to [NAME]'s medical problems pursuant to this accident. Note
that [DOCTOR'S NAME], M.D., documented all the complaints I have described and detected acute tenderness of musculature and soft tissue
just inferior to the lower clavicle and associated cervical muscle pain.
These findings are, of course, consistent with [NAME]'s history of being
in the accident with your insured.

   Although [NAME] continued treatment by physical therapy, two years
later, [HE/SHE] still experiences difficulties, including headaches in
addition to a tightness in [HIS/HER] neck. This has caused difficulty
for [NAME] at [HIS/HER] part-time employment, with housecleaning, gro-
cery shopping, and miscellaneous clerical duties. The accident has af-
fected [HIS/HER] ability to assist the family and to help {HIS/HER}
grandmother with a totally disabled grandfather, as [HE/SHE] did prior
to the accident.

Form 16.5. Letter to Opposing Counsel Claiming Damages

Paul Holler, Esq.
[DATE]
Page 2

   Our claim for [NAME]'s recoverable damages includes recovery for past
and future medical expenses, including $[AMOUNT] for [NAME OF HOSPI-
TAL]'s medical bills. In addition, jury verdicts and settlements from
the publication "Jury Verdicts" for cases involving similar injuries as
[NAME]'s demonstrate the potential for a case like this one to receive
a verdict in excess of $[AMOUNT]. Therefore, in an effort to settle
[NAME]'s claims at this time, I am authorized to accept $[AMOUNT] in
complete settlement of all the claims for [NAME]'s pain, suffering, and
loss of enjoyment of life, plus [HIS/HER] past uninsured and future damages in exchange for a full and final release of all claims against your
insured. We would prefer to resolve this matter without litigation if a
fair resolution can be obtained promptly.

   I look forward to hearing from you within thirty days and await your
reply.

            Sincerely,

            Scott Powell, Esq.

[AUTHOR/TYPIST]
Enclosures: [LIST]
[DOCUMENT LOCATOR CODE]

Form 16.5. Letter to Opposing Counsel Claiming Damages *(Continued)*

DeLost, Ernst, Miessner, Powell & Wilcox
Attorneys at Law
1257 Main Street, Suite 900
Los Angeles, CA 90066
(310) 555-6000

[DATE]

Leslie Morris
717 Parr Drive
Orlando, OH 45678

    Re: [IDENTIFY MATTER]

Dear Ms. Morris:

As a follow-up to my letter of [DATE], a copy of which is attached, we need the following information faxed to us by [DATE]:

(1)   Current names, addresses, and telephone numbers for anyone on the enclosed list that we do not have information for. We especially need the names and addresses of all your relatives who were at the scene of the accident, including spouses and children. This information is very important to your case.

(2)   Other potential witnesses on your behalf. People who know about the accident and what the family have gone through. We need names of friends and relatives who were not at the accident scene but have been supportive or know of the situation, and your supervisor at work, and people you have worked with.

When you send us your list, please indicate who each person is. We will not necessarily call each person on your list, but we need everyone you can think of to list for the Court. If we do not list them in advance, we cannot use them, so your list needs to be as complete as possible. You may drop your list off or fax it to me. Thank you for your assistance in this matter.

    Sincerely,

    Meagan O'Keefe
    Paralegal

[AUTHOR/TYPIST]
Enclosures: [LIST]
[DOCUMENT LOCATOR CODE]

Form 16.6. Request to Client for Additional Information

DeLost, Ernst, Miessner, Powell & Wilcox
Attorneys at Law
1257 Main Street, Suite 900
Los Angeles, CA 90066
(310) 555-6000

[DATE]

Paul Holler, Esq.
Vance, Region, Early and Moore
22 Locktree Circle
Tower Two
Atlanta, GA 12345

    Re: [CASE TITLE, CASE NUMBER]

Dear Mr. Holler:

This is to advise you that we would like to take the depositions of your expert witnesses, Dr. [NAME] and Dr. [NAME], at your earliest convenience. Please let me know what dates are convenient for you and your witnesses.

We are in the process of scheduling [CLIENT]'s current doctors, Dr. [NAME] and Dr. [NAME], pursuant to your request. We will notify you as soon as we have the dates, times, and places confirmed.

Thank you for your cooperation in this matter.

        Sincerely,

        Robert Rogers
        Paralegal

[AUTHOR/TYPIST]
Enclosures: none
[DOCUMENT LOCATOR CODE]

Form 16.7. Letter to Opposing Counsel Re: Expert Deposition

DeLost, Ernst, Miessner, Powell & Wilcox
Attorneys at Law
1257 Main Street, Suite 900
Los Angeles, CA 90066
(310) 555-6000

[DATE]

Juan Vasquez, M.D.
D.O.T. CENTER
3000 Lorna Lane
Tuskin, ME 34098

     Re: [CASE TITLE, CASE NUMBER]

Dear Custodian of Records:

  Enclosed please find an Affidavit concerning the medical treatment rendered to [NAME], and an Affidavit concerning charges made for the medical treatment of [NAME] on [DATE]. **We request the medical records and medical charges from the initial treatment date to the present.** Please see the attached release for specific medical records requested.

  These Affidavits, when signed and returned to us, will be filed with the Court and used at the time of trial to prove the medical treatment for [NAME]'s injuries and the charges for the treatment.

  Unless we have these Affidavits signed and filed with the Court prior to the time of trial, it <u>may</u> be necessary to subpoena someone from your office to testify concerning medical treatment and charges rendered to [NAME]. Since this would be time consuming and inconvenient, please fill out the Affidavits, attach copies of your medical records and billing records to these Affidavits, sign before a Notary Public, and return them to me.

  Please return the Affidavits to me at your earliest possible convenience.

        Sincerely,

        Allison Curtis
        Paralegal

[AUTHOR/TYPIST]
Enclosures: [LIST]
[DOCUMENT LOCATOR CODE]

Form 16.8. Letter Requesting Medical Charges and Records

DeLost, Ernst, Miessner, Powell & Wilcox
Attorneys at Law
1257 Main Street, Suite 900
Los Angeles, CA 90066
(310) 555-6000

[DATE]

Juan Vasquez, M.D.
Custodian of Records
3000 Lorna Lane
Tuskin, ME 34098

     Re: [NAME OF PERSON, ACCOUNT NUMBER,
       IF ANY, DATE OF BIRTH, DATE OF INJURY]

Dear Dr. Vasquez:

We represent [CLIENT] regarding an automobile accident in which [SHE/HE] was injured on [DATE]. It is our understanding [CLIENT] received treatment at your facility on or after the date of the accident.

Enclosed are two copies of an authorization to release medical information which have been signed by our client. One copy is for your medical records department, the other for your billing department. Please provide us with copies of all medical records and bills as requested on the authorization. Reasonable costs of duplicating your records, as provided in Evidence Code Section [CITE], will be paid upon receipt of your billing.

Also enclosed is a form declaration for the custodian of records. Please have the custodian sign this declaration and return it to us along with the copies of the medical records and bills.

If you have any questions, please do not hesitate to contact the undersigned. Thank you for your prompt attention to this matter.

       Sincerely,

       Mark C. Williams
       Legal Assistant

[AUTHOR/TYPIST]
Enclosures: [LIST]
[DOCUMENT LOCATOR CODE]

Form 16.9. Letter Requesting Copies of Medical Records

DeLost, Ernst, Miessner, Powell & Wilcox
Attorneys at Law
1257 Main Street, Suite 900
Los Angeles, CA 90066
(310) 555-6000

[DATE]

Juan Vasquez, M.D.
D.O.T. CENTER
3000 Lorna Lane
Tuskin, ME 34098

     Re: [CASE TITLE, CASE NUMBER]

Dear Dr. Vasquez:

   Your office previously provided us with copies of office notes and
records on this patient, whom we represent in a third—party injury
claim.

   At this time, please provide us with a copy of all office notes and
records for treatment rendered after [DATE], which is the last date for
which we have this information. An authorization for release of this information is also enclosed.

   Please send your statement for copying expenses and we will promptly
remit payment. Thank you for your assistance.

                    Sincerely,

                    Sandra Wilson
                    Litigation Coordinator

[AUTHOR/TYPIST]
[DOCUMENT LOCATOR CODE]

Form 16.10. Additional Medical Records Request

DeLost, Ernst, Miessner, Powell & Wilcox
Attorneys at Law
1257 Main Street, Suite 900
Los Angeles, CA 90066
(310) 555-6000

[DATE]

Juan Vasquez, M.D.
D.O.T. CENTER
3000 Lorna Lane
Tuskin, ME 34098

Re: [CASE TITLE, CASE NUMBER]

Dear Dr. Vasquez:

We represent [CLIENT'S NAME] in a lawsuit filed by [OPPOSING PARTY'S
NAME]. Enclosed is a copy of a medical release that has been signed by
[NAME].

Please provide this office with any and all medical records contained
in your file for [PATIENT'S NAME], including, but not limited to:

- medical reports,
- histories,
- emergency room reports,
- psychiatric or psychological reports,
- laboratory reports,
- hospital chart information,
- radiology reports,
- correspondence,
- notes, and
- all other documents.

[PATIENT'S NAME] was seen between [BEGIN DATE] and [END DATE].

Additionally, please include a complete billing history from your accounting department for all medical expenses incurred by [PATIENT'S
NAME] for your services.

Also enclosed for your convenience is an original Certificate of Authenticity of Records. I would appreciate it if you would sign the certificate and attach the copies of the records to it. Your attestation to
the authenticity of the records via the enclosed certificate may make it
possible for us to avoid taking your records deposition in the future.

Should your office have possession of actual x-rays, please give me
a call to discuss the cost of duplicating these x-rays. Do not make
copies before we have a chance to discuss this.

Any costs associated with this request will be paid promptly. If you
have any questions, please do not hesitate to give me a call.

Form 16.11. Request for Records, History, and x-Rays

Dr. Vasquez
[DATE]
Page 2

    If your facility has no records pertaining to this patient, please
make a note and return this letter to me. Thank you for your assistance.

              Sincerely,

              Allison Curtis
              Litigation Assistant
[AUTHOR/TYPIST]
Enclosures: [LIST]
[DOCUMENT LOCATOR CODE]

Form 16.11. Request for Records, History, and x-Rays *(Continued)*

DeLost, Ernst, Miessner, Powell & Wilcox
Attorneys at Law
1257 Main Street, Suite 900
Los Angeles, CA 90066
(310) 555-6000

[DATE]

George Martinson
Finance Administrator
Century Legal Insurance Company
One Embarcadero Center
Tenth Floor
San Francisco, CA 92456

Re: [CASE TITLE, CASE NUMBER]

Dear Mr. Martinson:

We represent [NAME] in an insurance injury claim pursuant to an automobile accident dated [DATE]. Please forward all copies of group
health billing records, including co-pay charges, for treatment rendered
to [NAME] as a result of these accidents.

An authorization for release of this information is enclosed. Please
forward your statement for copying expenses and we will promptly remit
payment. Thank you and if you have any questions, please call me directly at [PHONE].

Sincerely,

Avery Simpson, Esq.

[AUTHOR/TYPIST]
[DOCUMENT LOCATOR CODE]

Form 16.12. Request for Billing Records

DeLost, Ernst, Miessner, Powell & Wilcox
Attorneys at Law
1257 Main Street, Suite 900
Los Angeles, CA 90066
(310) 555-6000

[DATE]

[DMV NAME]
[ADDRESS]

        Re: Driver's name:
            License no.:
            Last known address:
            <u>Our client:</u>

Dear Sir or Madam:

Please conduct a search of the driving records of the above-referenced license number and forward a Certified Driving Record to me. We
have enclosed our firm check in the amount of $[AMOUNT] for your
agency's fee for this service.

Thank you for your prompt attention to this request. If you have any
questions, please do not hesitate to call me. Our toll-free number is
800/555-5555.

                Sincerely,

                Mark C. Williams
                Paralegal

[AUTHOR/TYPIST]
Enclosures: [LIST]
[DOCUMENT LOCATOR CODE]

Form 16.13. Request for Records of Driver

DeLost, Ernst, Miessner, Powell & Wilcox
Attorneys at Law
1257 Main Street, Suite 900
Los Angeles, CA 90066
(310) 555-6000

[DATE]

[DMV NAME]
[ADDRESS]

To Whom it May Concern:

This office represents [NAME] in regard to the following accident:

Date:
Driver:
Vehicle:
Accident address:
At-fault driver:

Kindly forward copies of this completed collision report with witness information in regard to the above incident. Enclosed is a check for $[AMOUNT] for your services and a self-addressed, stamped envelope for your reply.

Thank you. If you have any questions, please call me directly at [PHONE NUMBER].

Form 16.14. Letter to Obtain DMV Collision Reports

End Notes

[1]Angela Schneeman, *Paralegals in American Law: Introduction to Paralegalism,* p. 14 (1995).

[2]Excerpted from "Paralegal Job Descriptions by Practice Area," compiled by the National Federation of Paralegal Associations. While not intended to be all inclusive, this list does provide examples of the differing types of assignments that can (and should) be delegated to paralegals.

Seventeen

COLLECTIONS AND
CREDITORS' RIGHTS

17.1 / The Paralegal Role

 Form 17.1. Client Letter Re: Delinquent Account

 Form 17.2. Second Client Letter Re: Delinquent
 Account

 Form 17.3. Demand Letter

 Form 17.4. Settlement Letter, Informal

 Form 17.5. Settlement Letter, Formal

 Form 17.6. Letter Setting Forth Earnings Withholding
 Procedures

 Form 17.7. Instructions to Marshal for Levy of
 Personal Property

 Form 17.8. Letter Advising Equipment Availability
 and Sale

 Form 17.9. Letter After Sale of Equipment

 Form 17.10. Transmittal of Sister State Judgment

 Form 17.11. Notice of Intent to Sell Repossessed
 Equipment

17.1 / The Paralegal Role

Action on delinquent accounts usually begins with a demand letter. And then, if necessary, legal action follows. The best approach is to convince the parties of their obligations without being threatening. Unfortunately, most creditor/debtor issues are not settled amicably.

Frequently, defendants or debtors in commercial litigation matters have extensive financial difficulties . . . . The paralegal can effectively monitor and handle [collection] calls by explaining to the defendants that they must contact an independent attorney to represent their interests. At the same time, the paralegal can obtain additional information from the defendants, if they are willing to provide it, and may have the opportunity to negotiate a settlement. [T]he paralegal can provide defendants with the amounts due and owing, and discuss the possibility of negotiating a settlement, effecting return of the collateral and/or payoff of the account. As a result, the paralegal can draft the appropriate documents, such as the stipulation for settlement.[1]

Efforts to collect past due debts can involve several steps. In smaller firms and firms specializing in collections, the following tasks are frequently assigned to paralegals for handling:

- Initial interview and review of documents provided by client.
- Conduct asset investigation.
- Draft demand letter to debtor.
- Draft summons and complaint.
- Draft motion for, or in opposition to, summary judgment, including memoranda and affidavits in support.
- Draft judgment, cost bill, and other supporting pleadings.
- Maintain judgment account work sheet to record payments, collection costs, and court costs.
- Draft notice of demand to pay.
- Draft, file, and serve documents for judgment debtor examination.
- Appear in court at hearing for initial claim of plaintiff.
- Draft, have issued, and serve writ of garnishment.
- File request for dismissal form.
- Draft, have issued, and serve order to release garnishment.
- Draft, have issued, and serve order of examination.
- Appear in court and conduct examination.
- Draft, have issued, and serve writ of execution.
- Arrange for indemnity bond for sheriff.
- Arrange for posting of notice of sale or publication of notice of sale.
- Maintain communication with sheriff re: levy on personal property.
- Prepare bid and amend sheriff's sale on real property.
- Obtain certified copy of judgment transcript.
- Transfer judgment transcript to a different court.
- Obtain exemplified copy of foreign judgment.

- Prepare affidavit for transfer of a foreign judgment.
- Register judgment in a different state.
- Prepare and file satisfaction of judgment.[2]

Typically, correspondence related to collections involves many demand and settlement letters. If the matter cannot be settled informally, the formal measure must then be taken. Keep in mind that any letters directed to the Marshal or Sheriff's office will probably be considered "instructions" for further action and will not be honored if not signed by an attorney. *See, e.g.,* Form 17.7, "Instructions to Marshal for Levy of Personal Property."

DeLost, Ernst, Meissner, Powell & Wilcox
Attorneys at Law
1257 Main Street, Suite 900
Los Angeles, CA 90066
(310) 555-6000

[DATE]

Scott Samuels, Ph.D.
Senior Engineering Advocate
The High Sierra Telephone Company
8490 Lower Lakeside Road
Los Angeles, CA 90066

        Re: [NAME OF MATTER]

Dear Dr. Samuels:

   The accounting department and our managing partners have reminded me
that you are more than sixty (60) days delinquent in paying our billings
for fees and costs. I have enclosed a summary reconciliation showing the
dates of billings and payments that you have made. As you can see, you
are delinquent to the firm in the amount of $[AMOUNT].

   Please refer to our fee agreement. Paragraph [SPECIFY] provides that
you are obligated to pay our billings "within thirty (30) days of submission of invoices."

   If you are having financial problems or need to discuss the subject
of fees in any way, please call me to arrange an appointment. Otherwise,
the firm will expect prompt payment of the amount currently outstanding.

                    Sincerely,

                    Angela Shapiro
                    Senior Paralegal

[AUTHOR/TYPIST]
Enclosures: [LIST]
[DOCUMENT LOCATOR CODE]

Form 17.1. Client Letter Re: Delinquent Account

DeLost, Ernst, Meissner, Powell & Wilcox
Attorneys at Law
1257 Main Street, Suite 900
Los Angeles, CA 90066
(310) 555-6000

[DATE]

Lauren Tambor
1234 Highway Two
Localy, AZ 12345

        Re: [CASE TITLE, CASE NUMBER]

Dear Ms. Tambor:

   I wrote to you on [DATE] asking that you bring your bill current. At
that time I enclosed a reconciliation statement demonstrating that your
account had been delinquent for at least sixty (60) days. I am now enclosing a second reconciliation statement.

   I do not like sending this letter any more than you probably like receiving it. I want to devote all of my time and energy to solving your
legal problem, and the firm obviously needs the cash flow to meet its
financial obligations. I am reminding you that paragraph [SPECIFY] of
our fee agreement reserves the right to us to "discontinue our legal services if billings are not paid within sixty-one (61) days of their date."

   Again, if you are having financial problems or wish to discuss the
subject of finances with me, please call me for an appointment. Otherwise, please pay your bill promptly.

   If this request for payment is ignored, we may exercise our option
under paragraph [SPECIFY] and cease working on your case. We consider
you to be a valuable client of this office, and we will work with you
in any way we can. However, unless special arrangements or prompt payment is made, you are leaving us very few options.

                        Sincerely,

                        Erik Swanson
                        Paralegal

[AUTHOR/TYPIST]
Enclosures: [LIST]
[DOCUMENT LOCATOR CODE]

Form 17.2. Second Client Letter Re: Delinquent Account

DeLost, Ernst, Meissner, Powell & Wilcox
Attorneys at Law
1257 Main Street, Suite 900
Los Angeles, CA 90066
(310) 555-6000

[DATE]

Leslie Morris
717 Parr Drive
Orlando, OH 45678

        Re: [IDENTIFY MATTER]

Dear Ms. Morris:

   Our office represents [NAME OF CLIENT] with respect to your [TYPE OF CONTRACT] and account with them. We have been advised that your account is seriously delinquent, with an outstanding balance due of $[AMOUNT].

   As a result of this delinquency, our client has chosen to declare this account in default and secure possession of the subject equipment. On behalf of [CLIENT], our office hereby demands immediate payment of the entire sum. If our office is not in receipt of the full amount of $[AMOUNT], in certified funds payable to [PAYEE], within the next ten (10) days and on or before [DATE], we will have no alternative but to proceed with commencement of a legal action against you, thereby adding additional costs and fees to the amount already owing by you

   Do not mistake this correspondence as merely another letter demanding payment. If we do not hear from you on or before the date listed above, our next contact with you will be in the form of a summons and complaint.

   Please feel free to contact the undersigned should you have any questions or wish to discuss this matter further.

                Sincerely,

                Frank Bran
                Legal Assistant

[AUTHOR/TYPIST]
Enclosures: [LIST]
[DOCUMENT LOCATOR CODE]

Form 17.3. Demand Letter

DeLost, Ernst, Meissner, Powell & Wilcox
Attorneys at Law
1257 Main Street, Suite 900
Los Angeles, CA 90066
(310) 555-6000

[DATE]

Leslie Morris
717 Parr Drive
Orlando, OH 45678

        Re: [IDENTIFY MATTER]

Dear Ms. Morris:

   This letter confirms our telephone conversation about your desire to
settle this matter. Commencing [DATE], and continuing on the [DATE] of
each consecutive month, you will remit the sum of $[AMOUNT], payable to
[FIRM or CLIENT], with the envelope marked to my attention. Interest
continues to accrue on the unpaid principal balance of $[AMOUNT] from
the date of entry on [DATE]. Interest will be calculated on the unpaid
balance and any amounts received from you will then be credited to the
remainder.

   As we discussed, our office will hold off on enforcement of this judgment as long as the monthly payments are received in a timely manner.
You also indicated that, since your business is seasonal, the amount of
the payments may increase later this year.

   I look forward to a resolution of this matter in an amicable fashion.
Please feel free to contact me should you have any questions.

                        Sincerely,

                        Sandra Wilson
                        Litigation Manager

[AUTHOR/TYPIST]
Enclosures: none
[DOCUMENT LOCATOR CODE]

Form 17.4. Settlement Letter, Informal

DeLost, Ernst, Meissner, Powell & Wilcox
Attorneys at Law
1257 Main Street, Suite 900
Los Angeles, CA 90066
(310) 555-6000

[DATE]

Mr. Alec Sutherland
1936 Papermill Road
Mission Springs, CA 90067

Re: [IDENTIFY MATTER]

Dear Mr. Sutherland:

   This letter confirms your [DATE] telephone conversation with [NAME],
paralegal regarding settlement of the above-referenced matter. You have
agreed to set up a payment schedule and to make $[AMOUNT] per month pay-
ments until the judgment in the above action is satisfied in full. The
first payment is to be received by this office on or before [DATE].
Please make each check directly payable to [NAME] and forward your payments to this office, Attention: [NAME].

   In addition, on or before [DATE], we request that you return answers
to the enclosed Information Requested and Production of Documents pleading, including all copies of your documentation as required by that
pleading. If we receive each payment due to satisfy the judgment, complete answers, and documentation as agreed, this office will not continue legal efforts to collect the $[AMOUNT], plus postjudgment inter-
est.

   To confirm your acceptance of the foregoing terms, please return a
signed copy of this letter along with your first payment, documentation,
and complete answers to the Information Requested pleading prior to
[DATE]. Please note that the supplemental proceedings hearing set before the [NAME] court has been continued by agreement until [DATE,
PLACE, AND TIME].

   Your continued cooperation to finalize this matter is appreciated.

                         Sincerely,

                         Anthony Wilcox, Esq.

[AUTHOR/TYPIST]
Enclosures: [LIST]
[DOCUMENT LOCATOR CODE]

Form 17.5. Settlement Letter, Formal

DeLost, Ernst, Miessner, Powell & Wilcox
Attorneys at Law
1257 Main Street, Suite 900
Los Angeles, CA 90066
(310) 555-6000

[DATE]

George Moorepark, Finance Administrator
Century Legal Insurance Company
One Embarcadero Center, Tenth Floor
San Francisco, CA 92456

                Re: [CASE TITLE, CASE NUMBER]

Dear Mr. Moorepark:

Enclosed is a check in the amount of $[AMOUNT], which I am returning
to your offices. Pursuant to state statutes, and as set forth in the
pleadings served upon [NAME] as garnishee, the wage garnishment served
on [DATE] is a Continuing Lien on [NAME]'s earnings for a 60-day period. Your office is required to hold 25% of [NAME]'s commissions, earnings, bonuses, and wages from [DATE] to [DATE].

Just prior to [DATE], I will transmit Second Answers to your office,
which are to be completed by setting forth monies captured for the total
60-day garnishment period. All monies captured pursuant to this writ
must be held by your office until a conformed judgment on answer is forwarded to [NAME], confirming amounts it should transmit directly to the
County Superior Court.

In addition to the wage garnishment, a financial institution writ of
garnishment was served upon [NAME] as garnishee on [DATE], to capture
monies in securities or other financial accounts of the debtors. Kindly complete and return the completed answers relating to this second
garnishment action in the attached envelopes prior to [DATE]. Once
again, do not forward any monies until you receive a conformed judgment
on answer, at which time monies will be disbursed directly to the County
Superior Court.

Because these matters involve your legal interest, you should consider consulting an attorney if you have additional questions relating to
these pleadings. Thank you for your assistance.

                Sincerely,

                Allison Curtis
                Paralegal

[AUTHOR/TYPIST]
Enclosures: [LIST]
[DOCUMENT LOCATOR CODE]

Form 17.6. Letter Setting Forth Earnings Withholding Procedures

DeLost, Ernst, Miessner, Powell & Wilcox
Attorneys at Law
1257 Main Street, Suite 900
Los Angeles, CA 90066
(310) 555-6000

[DATE]

Marshal's Office
Civil Bureau
[ADDRESS]

Re: [CASE TITLE, CASE NUMBER, AND DATE OF LEVY]

Dear [NAME OF MARSHAL]:

This office is collecting a judgment that was awarded in [CASE TITLE, CASE NUMBER]. A writ of execution has been issued to the [COUNTY] sheriff for levy upon [SPECIFY PROPERTY] ("personal property"), which is owned by the judgment debtors.

Since we will be effecting service on the judgment debtors by publication, pursuant to [CITE], enclosed is a copy of the Notice to Judgment Debtors of Execution on Personal Property. Once you have scheduled the date of sale, please contact me so the original notice may be filed with the court and a copy published in the local newspaper for six consecutive weeks.

Enclosed are the following documents and pleadings for your office to levy upon this personal property:

(1)   the original and two copies of the issued writ of execution on personal property;

(2)   a check for $[AMOUNT] made payable to the [COUNTY] sheriff;

(3)   an Indemnity to Sheriff's Bond in an amount equal to twice the value of the personal property, $[AMOUNT];

(4)   a copy of an insurance rider extending [SPECIFY TYPE] insurance on the personal property for 60 days or until it is sold;

(5)   an authorization to Appoint Keeper and Keeper's Receipt appointing [NAME], manager of [SPECIFY NAME OF STORAGE FACILITY], as keeper of the personal property.

The personal property is located at [ADDRESS]. I understand that your office will immediately levy upon this personal property and that the sale will be held at [PLACE], allowing six consecutive weeks for service by publication of the Notice to Judgment Debtor of Execution on Personal Property.

Form 17.7. Instructions to Marshal for Levy of Personal Property

Marshal's Office
[DATE]
Page 2

   Once your office sets the date of the sale, it will also serve the
debtors with notices of sale by mailing to the debtors' last-known addresses, which are as follows: [LIST ADDRESSES].

   In addition, pursuant to [CITE], your office will post a copy of the
notice in three public places for a period of not less than four weeks
prior to the date of sale. Please forward a copy of the sheriff's notice to this office and advise of the date of sale. Also, please forward a receipt for payment of your service fees for our records.

   This office will provide the sheriff with a bid for this personal
property approximately one week before the date set for the sale. If you
have any questions, call me or [NAME], who is the paralegal assigned to
this matter, directly at [PHONE]. Thank you for your assistance.

                    Sincerely,

                    Olivia Oldsman, Esq.

[AUTHOR/TYPIST]
Enclosures: [LIST]
[DOCUMENT LOCATOR CODE]

Form 17.7. Instructions to Marshal for Levy of Personal Property (*Continued*)

DeLost, Ernst, Meissner, Powell & Wilcox
Attorneys at Law
1257 Main Street, Suite 900
Los Angeles, CA 90066
(310) 555-6000

[DATE]

Lauren Tambor
1234 Highway Two
Localy, AZ 12345

     Re: <u>Deliquent Account</u>

Dear Ms. Tambor:

  This letter is to inform you that the equipment subject to the lease agreement as identified above has been repossessed as a result of default. The equipment will be made available for sale twenty (20) days from the date of this letter at [ADDRESS OF SALE]. The net proceeds, minus costs and fees incurred as a result of the repossession and sale, will be credited to your account and you will be responsible for any deficiency remaining.

  Should you wish to redeem your equipment prior to sale, please refer to the attached realization for the amounts due.

         Sincerely,

         Regino Stein
         Collections Analyst

[AUTHOR/TYPIST]
Enclosures: [LIST]
[DOCUMENT LOCATOR CODE]

Form 17.8. Letter Advising Equipment Availability and Sale

DeLost, Ernst, Meissner, Powell & Wilcox
Attorneys at Law
1257 Main Street, Suite 900
Los Angeles, CA 90066
(310) 555-6000

[DATE]

Lauren Tambor
1234 Highway Two
Localy, AZ 12345

Re: <u>Sale of Equipment/Deliquent Account</u>

Dear Ms. Tambor:

Please be advised the equipment subject to the lease agreement as identified above has been sold and the amounts realized have been applied to your account, after reducing the amount by costs and fees incurred as a result of the repossession and sale. The attached realization of amounts due show the balance due and owing.

Please contact the undersigned immediately to discuss payment of this account without the necessity of litigation.

Sincerely,

Elizabeth Brown
Portfolio Analyst

[AUTHOR/TYPIST]
Enclosures: [LIST]
[DOCUMENT LOCATOR CODE]

Form 17.9. Letter After Sale of Equipment

DeLost, Ernst, Meissner, Powell & Wilcox
Attorneys at Law
1257 Main Street, Suite 900
Los Angeles, CA 90066
(310) 555-6000

[DATE]

Ronald F. Nicolson, Esq.
Vance, Region, Early and Moore
22 Locktree Circle
Tower Two
Atlanta, GA 12345

    Re: [CASE TITLE, CASE NUMBER]

Dear Mr. Nicholson:

  In regard to our telephone conversation today about the above-referenced defendant, listed below is the address of the attorney domesti-
cating the foreign judgment in [STATE].

  [NAME AND ADDRESS OF ATTORNEY]

  Upon your receipt of the Certified and Exemplified Judgment, please
send me a copy. Thank you.

                    Sincerely,

                    Todd M. Johansen
                    Judgment Coordinator

[AUTHOR/TYPIST]
Enclosures: [LIST]
[DOCUMENT LOCATOR CODE]

Form 17.10. Transmittal of Sister State Judgment

DeLost, Ernst, Miessner, Powell & Wilcox
Attorneys at Law
1257 Main Street, Suite 900
Los Angeles, CA 90066
(310) 555-6000

[DATE]

Joseph R. Martin
1945 Berks Boulevard
Suite Three
Shillington, PA 19613

          Re: [IDENTIFY MATTER]

Dear Mr. Martin:

  Please be advised that because of the default on the contract referenced below, and in accordance with its provisions, [CLIENT] has de-
clared the entire unpaid balance of the contract immediately due and
payable in the sum of $[AMOUNT]. [CLIENT] has already repossessed the
equipment described below. It is stored and available for inspection at
[ADDRESS].

  You may redeem the property for the sum of $[AMOUNT], plus all costs
incurred by [CLIENT] in the repossession of the listed equipment. Any
prospective purchasers for the equipment should be referred to the
undersigned.

    [CONTRACT INFORMATION]
    [DESCRIPTION OF EQUIPMENT]

  On or after [DATE], the above equipment will be disposed of by sale
or lease. You will be credited with the net amount received upon disposition of the equipment after deduction from the gross credit all expenses of disposition, including, but not limited to, the cost of repossession and reconditioning, attorney fees, legal costs, storage,
sales commission, etc.

  You will be responsible for any deficiency remaining after deducting
the net upon resale from all sums due under the contract, including insurance premiums, personal property taxes, late charges, interest, attorney fees, and costs.

                      Sincerely,

                      Mark C. Williams
                      Legal Assistant

[AUTHOR/TYPIST]
Enclosures: [LIST]
[DOCUMENT LOCATOR CODE]

Form 17.11. Notice of Intent to Sell Repossessed Equipment

End Notes

[1]Sonia von Matt Stoddard, "Effectively Using Paralegals in Commercial Litigation and Creditor's Rights Matters," *Legal Assistant Today,* p. 74 (Sept./Oct. 1990) (emphasis added).

[2]Excerpted from "Paralegal Job Descriptions by Practice Area," compiled by the National Federation of Paralegal Associations. While not intended to be all inclusive, this list does provide examples of the differing types of assignments that can (and should) be delegated to paralegals.

Eighteen

INTELLECTUAL PROPERTY

18.1 / The Intellectual Property Practice
18.2 / Trademark Responsibilities
18.3 / Patent Responsibilities
18.4 / Copyright Responsibilities
    Form 18.1. Request for Permission to Reprint
    Form 18.2. Permission Granted to Reprint
    Form 18.3. Unauthorized Use of Copyrighted Material
    Form 18.4. Application to Customs Department to Record Copyright Registration
    Form 18.5. Request for Additional Certificate
    Form 18.6. Transmittal of Copyright Certificate and Registration
    Form 18.7. Notice of Copyright Registration Renewal
    Form 18.8. Request to Copyright Office for Specia Handling of Copyright Application
    Form 18.9. Transmittal of Patent Information to Client
    Form 18.10. Patent Application Transmittal
    Form 18.11. Execution of Assignment
    Form 18.12. Foreign Filing Listing
    Form 18.13. Notice of Patent
    Form 18.14. Transmittal of Patent
    Form 18.15. Registration Notification and Information
    Form 18.16. Registration Information
    Form 18.17. Amendment for Alleged Use
    Form 18.18. Information Re: Notice of Allowance
    Form 18.19. "Intent to Use" Status to Client
    Form 18.20. Transmittal of Filing Receipt
    Form 18.21. Trademark Search Information Letter
    Form 18.22. Transmittal of Application for Trademark

Form 18.23. Service Mark Application

Form 18.24. Request for Extension of Time to File Statement of Use

Form 18.25. Request for Correction to Filing Receipt

18.1 / The Intellectual Property Practice

Intellectual property involves trademarks, patents, copyrights, and the various methods for ensuring protection of such intellectual property. In this chapter, for example, you will find letters regarding registration of copyrights, and correspondence about licensing the use of trademarked products.

The National Federation of Paralegal Associations has developed a detailed listing of tasks performed by paralegals in a wide variety of practice areas. In the Intellectual Property practice, these tasks include:

- Prepare patent and/or trademark status summary reports.

- Docket and/or maintain docket system for due dates for responses, renewals, oppositions, Sections 8 and 15 filings, use affidavits, and working requirements.

- Docket and/or maintain docket system for payment of patent annuities in foreign counties.

- Conduct patent/trademark searches.

- Conduct on-line computer information searches of technical literature for patent/trademarks.

- Draft trademark/servicemark registration applications, renewal applications, Section 8 and 15 affidavits.

- Draft response to trademark examining attorney's official action.

- Draft registered user agreements.

- Draft power of attorney.

- Draft copyright applications.

- Research procedural matters, case law, and unfair competition matters.

- Prior art search, patent/trademark searches.

- Assist in opposition, interference, infringement, and related proceedings.

- Arrange for visual aids/models/mock-ups for trial use.

- Communicate with foreign trademark attorneys and agents about registrations, officials' actions needing response, and trademark services.

- Maintain files of new products and invention development.

- Review patent filings with engineers.

- Draft licenses/agreements regarding proprietary information/technology.[1]

18.2 / Trademark Responsibilities

Registration of a product, name, or service in the trademark practice consists of several concise steps. You can find a quick overview of this area of practice in *Paralegals in American Law*. Paralegals working in the trademark and service mark specialty may be responsible for the following tasks:

(1)   Researching existing trademarks.

(2)   Assisting with the preparation and filing of trademark registration applications.

(3)   Researching pertinent state and federal trademark laws.

(4)   Assisting with all aspects of litigation dealing with trademarks.[2]

18.3 / Patent Responsibilities

In order to obtain a patent, inventors must keep detailed records of the research, prototype development, and finalization of their inventions. Once the invention has been set into final form, the work on obtaining a patent can begin. Paralegal duties typically performed when working with patents include the following:

(1)   Researching existing patents.

(2)   Assisting with the preparation and filing of patent applications.

(3)   Assisting with patent infringement litigation.[3]

18.4 / Copyright Responsibilities

Copyright issues are obviously very germane in the writing and publishing fields. It is necessary to protect the intellectual property developed by the author of a novel, music, software, or other copyrightable product from infringement. Paralegals dealing with copyrights generally

(1)   Assist with the preparation and filing of copyright applications.

(2)   Research pertinent copyright laws.

(3)   Research current copyrights.[4]

You can write to the Library of Congress, Copyright Office, Washington, D.C. 20559, for a complete guide to copyrighting material. This very informative package is free of charge.

DeLost, Ernst, Miessner, Powell & Wilcox
Attorneys at Law
1257 Main Street, Suite 900
Los Angeles, CA 90066
(310) 555-6000

[DATE]

[Name]
[Address]
[City, State and Zip]

Re: Permission to Reprint

Dear [NAME]:

I am writing to seek your permission to reprint the material specified below in a [article/book] I am writing. It is scheduled for publication by [Publishing Company].

The tentative title of my [article/book] is
_____.
The approximate number of manuscript pages is _____. The publication date is expected to be _____.

The rights I desire are for nonexclusive use worldwide. [If a book, include the following language: "I would also like permission to reprint this material in any future revisions and new editions of my book."] Of course, I will give full credit to the author and publisher as the original source of this material. A second copy of this letter is enclosed for your records.

The material I would like permission to reprint is from the following source:

Title of work:

Copyright date:

Edition and/or revision:

Volume and number: [for magazine articles, if applicable]

Author:

Material requesting permission to reprint is attached:

   [Provide appropriate citation of source material here, and attach
   copies of material being requested for permission.]

Form 18.1. Request for Permission to Reprint

[RECIPIENT]
[DATE]
Page 2

From page number _____ to and including page number
_____.

Number of words and/or number of lines:_____

A Release Form is provided below for your convenience. I would appreciate your designating the format you prefer for the credit line.

Please return this completed form to the following address:
                         [Your home address]

Thank you for your assistance in this matter. Please do not hesitate
to call if you have any questions.

                         Sincerely,

                         Your name,
                         [Daytime telephone number]
cc: Editorial Director
    [Publishing Company]

PERMISSION IS HEREBY GRANTED FOR THE USE OF THE MATERIAL AS

DESCRIBED ABOVE IN _____

                              [List tentative title of your book]
Credit line to be used: _____

    _____

Authorized signature: _____

Position: _____

Date: _____

Form 18.1. Request for Permission to Reprint *(Continued)*

DeLost, Ernst, Miessner, Powell & Wilcox
Attorneys at Law
1257 Main Street, Suite 900
Los Angeles, CA 90066
(310) 555-6000

[DATE]

George Martinson
Finance Administrator
Century Legal Insurance Company
One Embarcadero Center
Tenth Floor
San Francisco, CA 92456

Re: <u>Article Reprint Permission</u>

Dear George:

Thank you for your request to reprint Anthony Wilcox's most recent article, "Ways to Find a New Associate." It was originally published in the [DATE] issue of *Legal World* (at pp. 53-57).

I understand the Insurance Group plans to reprint the entire article in its Annual Conference Materials. With this letter, Anthony Wilcox, Esq., grants your request, as long as you also print the following information as the article's credit line:

Anthony Wilcox, Esq., is the managing partner of DeLost, Ernst, Miessner, Powell & Wilcox, founded in 1955. He publishes career and business books for practicing and retired attorneys. He has written ten books relating to the legal field, along with two books directly dealing with insurance issues [LIST TITLES AND PUBLISHER]. This article first appeared in the [DATE] issue of *Legal World* magazine, and is reprinted here by permission.

Also, please send us a copy of the conference materials. Don't hesitate to call me directly if I can be of service in the future.

Sincerely,

Jennifer King
Marketing Director

Form 18.2. Permission Granted to Reprint

DeLost, Ernst, Miessner, Powell & Wilcox
Attorneys at Law
1257 Main Street, Suite 900
Los Angeles, CA 90066
(310) 555-6000

[DATE]

Paul Holler, Esq.
President, Insurance Society
Vance, Region, Early & Moore
22 Locktree Circle, Tower Two
Atlanta, GA 12345

Re: <u>Unauthorized Use of Copyrighted Material</u>

Dear Mr. Holler:

The [DATE] issue of the *Insurance Journal* (Vol. 13, issue 1, p. 16), contains an **unauthorized** reprint of Anthony Wilcox's copyrighted article, "What to Expect in Your First Ten Years as an Attorney." This article, originally printed in the [DATE] issue of *Legal World* magazine (pp. 26-29), is **clearly** copyrighted by the author. (*See* page 29 of the original article, a copy of which is enclosed.)

Not only did the *Insurance Journal* not list Anthony Wilcox as the author, more importantly, your organization failed to obtain his permission to reprint this copyrighted article. This is a clear violation of federal copyright laws. (*See* 17 U.S.C. §106.)

At the end of the reprinted article is a statement that permission to reprint the article was obtained from "Legal World/[DATE]." It is clear from this credit line that your organization intended to acknowledge the article's original source, and such an effort is gratifying.

However, Anthony Wilcox did **not** grant a blanket permission to all legal associations to reprint his articles. Even when a specific permission to reprint is given, that permission is **limited to a one-time reprint,** reserving all remaining copyright rights. Anthony Wilcox is the legal, exclusive owner of the copyright to this and all other articles and columns he writes for *Legal World*.

You are requested to remedy this violation by printing the following acknowledgment in the next edition of the *Insurance Journal*. This statement should be printed in bold type, and placed on the first page of the newsletter:

The article "What to Expect in Your First Ten Years as an Attorney," which was printed in the [DATE] *Insurance Journal,* was in fact written by Anthony Wilcox, and first published in *Legal World* [DATE]. The Insurance Society sincerely regrets not identifying Anthony Wilcox as the author.

Form 18.3. Unauthorized Use of Copyrighted Material

Paul Holler, Esq.
[DATE]
Page 2

   Please feel free to call if you have any questions about this matter.

                       Sincerely,

                       Marlene Hall
                       Assistant to
                       Anthony Wilcox, Esq.
Enclosures: [LIST]

Form 18.3. Unauthorized Use of Copyrighted Material *(Continued)*

DeLost, Ernst, Miessner, Powell & Wilcox
Attorneys at Law
1257 Main Street, Suite 900
Los Angeles, CA 90066
(310) 555-6000

[DATE]

Commissioner of Customs
Attn: Chief of the Entry, Licensing,
  and Restricted Merchandise Branch
130 Constitution Avenue, N.W., Room 2417
Washington, DC 20229

        Re: [SPECIFY ITEM AND DOCKET NO.]

Dear Chief:

  Pursuant to §§133.31 through 133.33 of the Customs Regulations, this
constitutes an application by [NAME OF APPLICANT], an [SPECIFY], having
an address of [STATE ADDRESS], to record the Copyright Registration for
the [NAME OF ITEM], No. [SPECIFY], entitled "[NAME/TITLE OF ITEM]."

  (1)   The name and complete address of the copyright owner:

         [NAME AND ADDRESS]

  (2)   The copyright owner manufactures the goods protected by the
         Copyright Registration in [SPECIFY].

         (a) If the applicant is a person claiming actual or potential
             injury by reason of actual or potential importations of
             the eligible works, a statement explaining the circum-
             stances of such actual or potential injury: [STATEMENT]

         (b) Applicant, [NAME], believes the piratical, infringing
             copies of its copyrighted [NAME OF ITEM] may shortly be
             imported into the United States.

  (3)   The name and principal address of any foreign person or busi-
         ness entity authorized or licensed to use the work protected
         by copyright, and a statement as to the use authorized:

         [NAME AND ADDRESS] [STATEMENT]

  (4)   The foreign title of the work, if different from the U.S.
         title:

         [NAME OF FOREIGN TITLE, IF ANY]

Form 18.4. Application to Customs Department to Record Copyright Registration

[RECIPIENT]
[DATE]
Page 2

Enclosed with this application are the following documents and items:

- An Additional Certificate of Copyright Registration No. [NUMBER], issued by the United States Copyright Office;

- Five photographic likenesses each of two perspective views of the [NAME OF ITEM] and perspective views of the [SPECIFIC PART OF THE ITEM], reproduced on paper approximately [SIZE OR REDUCTION PERCENTAGES], showing the [PART], respectively, as protected by Copyright Registration No. [NUMBER]; and

- A check in the amount of $[AMOUNT], payable to the United States Customs Service.

Due to the possibility of severe, ongoing economic harm, we request that you take the necessary steps to notify the appropriate field offices of our filing and promptly record this registration so that the infringing goods will be denied entry.

Only [NAME] of [COMPANY], whose address is [ADDRESS], and telephone number is [NUMBER], is authorized to approve shipment of the goods covered by Copyright Registration No. [NUMBER] into the United States. Applicant requests the Commissioner of Customs to contact [NAME] at the above address for all questions concerning the importation of genuine materials into the United States as well as the prohibiting of counterfeit and/or piratical copies of the subject work.

Should you have any further questions or comments, or if you require any additional information to process this application for recordation, please do not hesitate to contact me.

                              Sincerely,

                              Allison Curtis
                              Paralegal

[AUTHOR/TYPIST]
Enclosures: [LIST]
[DOCUMENT LOCATOR CODE]

Form 18.4. Application to Customs Department to Record Copyright Registration *(Continued)*

DeLost, Ernst, Miessner, Powell & Wilcox
Attorneys at Law
1257 Main Street, Suite 900
Los Angeles, CA 90066
(310) 555-6000

[DATE]

Register of Copyrights
Library of Congress
Attn: Certification and
Documents Section
Washington, DC 20559

        Re: [SPECIFY]
            Copyright "[NAME OR TITLE"]
            Reg. No.
            Our Docket No.

Dear Chief:

   This letter is a written request for an additional Certificate of Registration for the above Copyright Registration No.[NUMBER]. Please
charge all necessary fees to our Deposit Account No. [NUMBER]. Our check
in the amount of $[AMOUNT] is enclosed.

   We understand the fee for the additional certificate is $[AMOUNT].
Please note the total charge on this letter and return with the additional certificate.

                          Sincerely,

                          Mark C. Williams
                          Paralegal

[AUTHOR/TYPIST]
Enclosures: [LIST]
[DOCUMENT LOCATOR CODE]

Form 18.5. Request for Additional Certificate

DeLost, Ernst, Miessner, Powell & Wilcox
Attorneys at Law
1257 Main Street, Suite 900
Los Angeles, CA 90066
(310) 555-6000

[DATE]

Register of Copyrights
Library of Congress
Attn: Certification and
Documents Section
Washington, DC 20559

      Re: [NAME OF REGISTRANT]
         U.S. Copyright Reg. No.
         Title:
         Registration Date:
         <u>Our Docket No.</u>

Dear [NAME]:

The original Certificate of Copyright Registration [NUMBER] for the
Claim of Copyright for [NAME OF ITEM OR TITLE] is enclosed for your review. The duration of the copyright protection is for a period of either [SPECIFY] years from the date of creation, or [SPECIFY] years from
the date the work was first published, whichever expires first. It is
not renewable.

Please note the effective date of registration is [DATE], the date of
filing the application.

This is a valuable record and should be kept in a secure place. It
provides proof of your rights in the copyright, should you need that at
some future date.

Please sign and return the enclosed copy of this letter to indicate
receipt of the above-identified Certificate of Copyright Registration.

         Sincerely,

         Pat Kearns
         Paralegal

[AUTHOR/TYPIST]
Enclosures: [LIST]
[DOCUMENT LOCATOR CODE]

Receipt of the above-identified Certificate of Copyright Registration
is hereby acknowledged.

Date: _____   By: _____

Form 18.6. Transmittal of Copyright Certificate and Registration

DeLost, Ernst, Miessner, Powell & Wilcox
Attorneys at Law
1257 Main Street, Suite 900
Los Angeles, CA 90066
(310) 555-6000

[DATE]

Register of Copyrights
Library of Congress
Attn: Certification and
Documents Section
Washington, DC 20559

VIA CERTIFIED MAIL
RETURN RECEIPT REQUESTED
Receipt number:

Re: [NAME OF REGISTRANT AND ITEM]
    Copyright Registration No.
    [TITLE OF ITEM]
    Our Docket No.

Dear [NAME]:

   Your original [SPECIFY]-year term for the subject copyright registration expires at the end of calendar year [DATE]. Under the present law, your copyright registration may be renewed and extended for a further term of [NUMBER] years. To renew your copyright registration please fill out the appropriate application for renewal and extension within the one-year period prior to the expiration date of your original [SPECIFY]-year term.

   Please let me know if you want us to prepare the application for renewal and extension so it is filed during calendar year [DATE].

   THIS IS THE ONLY NOTICE WE WILL SEND TO YOU OF THE RENEWAL DATE AND THE NECESSITY FOR FILING AN APPROPRIATE APPLICATION FOR RENEWAL.

                    Sincerely,

                    Pat Kearns
                    Paralegal

[AUTHOR/TYPIST]
Enclosures: [LIST]
[DOCUMENT LOCATOR CODE]

Form 18.7. Notice of Copyright Registration Renewal

DeLost, Ernst, Miessner, Powell & Wilcox
Attorneys at Law
1257 Main Street, Suite 900
Los Angeles, CA 90066
(310) 555-6000

[DATE]

<u>REQUEST FOR SPECIAL HANDLING</u>

Register of Copyrights
United States Copyright Office
Library of Congress
Washington, DC 20559

  Re: [NAME OF APPLICANT]
    Copyright "[IDENTIFY]"
    <u>Our Docket No. [SPECIFY]</u>

Dear Sir or Madam:

 Applicant [NAME], a [SPECIFY] corporation, respectfully requests Special Handling of the above-identified application pursuant to the notice published in the Federal Register of May 4, 1972, Vol. 47, No. 86, on pages 19254-19255.

 Applicant will shortly be importing these goods into the United States and expects that "knock offs," comprising copyright infringements, are now, or shortly will be, imported into the United States by third parties. Consequently, this Special Handling is requested to protect the rights of Applicant by enabling Applicant to record this registration with Customs, and to bring an infringement action against the infringers, should infringing activities occur in the United States.

 Applicant would be the plaintiff in such litigation. It is expected that at least one such action would be filed in the U.S. District Court, Central District of California. Applicant is not aware of the exact identities of the third parties whose infringing activities may give rise to this litigation.

 The following materials are submitted with this letter:

- Application (Form VA) for "[DESCRIBE]."

- Our check in the amount of $[AMOUNT], covering the $[AMOUNT] Special Handling charge and the $[AMOUNT] filing fee specified in 27 U.S.C. §708(a)(1), $[AMOUNT] to cover the cost of two additional Certificates, and $[AMOUNT] for expedited handling of the two additional Certificates. Please forward the original Certificate of Registration and the two additional Certificates as promptly as possible.

Form 18.8. Request to Copyright Office for Special Handling of Copyright Application

```
Register of Copyrights
[DATE]
Page 2


   The Application is accompanied by (two sets of [DESCRIBE] pho-
tographs), and ([NUMBER] specimens of the packaging) of the work for
which copyright is claimed.

   No copyright notice appeared on the packaging.

   Your prompt examination and registration of this Application is
requested.

   I certify that the materials contained in this letter are true and
accurate to the best of my knowledge, information, and belief.

                       Sincerely,



                       John B. Watson
                       Paralegal

[AUTHOR/TYPIST]
Enclosures: [LIST]
[DOCUMENT LOCATOR CODE]
```

Form 18.8. Request to Copyright Office for Special Handling of Copyright Application *(Continued)*

DeLost, Ernst, Miessner, Powell & Wilcox
Attorneys at Law
1257 Main Street, Suite 900
Los Angeles, CA 90066
(310) 555-6000

[DATE]

CLIENT
[ADDRESS]

     Re: [NAME]
        U.S. Patent Application No.
        "[IDENTIFICATION]"
        <u>Our Docket No.</u>

Dear [NAME]:

  Enclosed please find the filing receipt for the application identified above. Details of the filing are as follows:

  Filing Date:
  Serial No.:

  The United States Patent and Trademark Office will take this application up for examination. We will keep you informed of all developments. No action is required from you at this time.

  We strongly recommend the invention be marked with the words "Patent
Pending."

              Sincerely,

              Angela Shapiro
              Senior Paralegal

[AUTHOR/TYPIST]
Enclosures: [LIST]
[DOCUMENT LOCATOR CODE]
Enc.-Filing Receipt

Form 18.9. Transmittal of Patent Information to Client

DeLost, Ernst, Miessner, Powell & Wilcox
Attorneys at Law
1257 Main Street, Suite 900
Los Angeles, CA 90066
(310) 555-6000

                              [DATE]

U.S. PATENT OFFICE
[ADDRESS]

         Re: [NAME OF APPLICATION]
             [SPECIFY] Patent Application for
             "[TITLE]"
             Our Docket No.

Dear Sir or Madam:

   Enclosed for filing in the U.S. Patent Office is a copy of the above-
identified application as filed in the United States. It was filed on
[DATE], consists of [NUMBER] pages of specifications and claims, and
[NUMBER] sheets of informal drawings. Formal drawings are being prepared
and sent to you as soon as we receive them.

   Also enclosed is a copy of the Combined Declaration and Power of Attorney filed in the United States application. It shows the full name
and address of the inventor, and a copy of the Assignment of all rights
in any applications filed and any patents issued, anywhere in the world,
from [SPECIFY] to [SPECIFY].

   Our check in the amount of $[AMOUNT] is enclosed as a retainer in this
case.

   Please let us know the serial number and filing date at your earliest convenience.

                              Sincerely,

                              Allison Curtis
                              Paralegal

[AUTHOR/TYPIST]
Enclosures: [LIST]
[DOCUMENT LOCATOR CODE]

Form 18.10. Patent Application Transmittal

DeLost, Ernst, Miessner, Powell & Wilcox
Attorneys at Law
1257 Main Street, Suite 900
Los Angeles, CA 90066
(310) 555-6000

[DATE]

U.S. PATENT OFFICE
[ADDRESS]

    Re: [NAME OF APPLICANT]
       Patent Application for
       "[TITLE]"
       <u>Our Docket No.</u>

Dear [NAME]:

In accordance with the standard procedure in [SPECIFY], it is necessary for [NAME] to execute a confirmatory assignment document. This document will be filed in the above-identified [SPECIFY] application in
order to show the transfer of interest to you.

I am enclosing the original and two copies of an appropriate assignment. Please have the original signed, notarized, and returned to me.
The copies are for you and [NAME].

            Sincerely,

            Mark C. Williams
            Paralegal

[AUTHOR/TYPIST]
Enclosures: [LIST]
[DOCUMENT LOCATOR CODE]

Form 18.11. Execution of Assignment

DeLost, Ernst, Miessner, Powell & Wilcox
Attorneys at Law
1257 Main Street, Suite 900
Los Angeles, CA 90066
(310) 555-6000

[DATE]

U.S. PATENT OFFICE
[ADDRESS]

        Re: [APPLICANT]
            U.S. Patent Application for
            "[IDENTIFICATION]"
            <u>Our Docket No.</u>

Dear [NAME]:

   As we discussed during our telephone conversation on [DATE], I have
reviewed my files of the subject patent application. I am enclosing a
copy of the foreign filing listing we used when we selected the [SPEC-
IFY] foreign countries to file the counterpart applications.

   Please contact me at your earliest convenience so we can review this
matter to determine which countries from which we are still able to obtain foreign counterparts.

                              Sincerely,

                              Allison Curtis
                              Paralegal

[AUTHOR/TYPIST]
Enclosures: [LIST]
[DOCUMENT LOCATOR CODE]

Form 18.12. Foreign Filing Listing

DeLost, Ernst, Miessner, Powell & Wilcox
Attorneys at Law
1257 Main Street, Suite 900
Los Angeles, CA 90066
(310) 555-6000

[DATE]

U.S. PATENT OFFICE
[ADDRESS]

        Re: [APPLICANT]
             Patent Number
             "[IDENTIFICATION]"
             Our Docket No.

Dear [NAME]:

  Enclosed is the original Patent No. [NUMBER] issued [DATE]. The term
of the patent is for a period of [SPECIFY] years from the date of issue.

  To avoid conflict with the United States' and possibly other countries' laws, the notice "Patented [YEAR] ([COUNTRY])" must be affixed
to patented articles where possible. If this is not practical then the
notice must be used on labels attached to the article or to containers
used in packaging the article. In cases where marking or labeling is not
possible, all relevant literature must include the notice.

  The patentee is liable to a fine not exceeding $[AMOUNT] for failure
to use the notice.

  If the patentee fails to work the invention commercially in [SPECI-
FY] within [NUMBER] years of the date of issue, any interested entity
may apply to the Commissioner of Patents for a compulsory license. The
terms of such license are set by the Commissioner of Patents.

  This is a valuable document and should be kept in a secure place.
Please acknowledge receipt of the original Patent No. [NUMBER] enclosed
by signing and dating the copy of this letter and returning it to me.

                         Sincerely,

                         Mark C. Williams
                         Paralegal

[AUTHOR/TYPIST]
Enclosures: [LIST]
[DOCUMENT LOCATOR CODE]

  Receipt of the original of [SPECIFY] Patent No.[NUMBER] is hereby acknowledged.

Dated: _____   By: _____

Form 18.13. Notice of Patent

DeLost, Ernst, Miessner, Powell & Wilcox
Attorneys at Law
1257 Main Street, Suite 900
Los Angeles, CA 90066
(310) 555-6000

[DATE]

U.S. PATENT OFFICE
[ADDRESS]

    Re: U.S. Patent No.
       for
       Inventor:
       Filed:
       <u>Our Docket No.</u>

Dear [NAME]:

We are pleased to enclose the original U.S. Letters Patent No. [NUM-BER], issued on [DATE], for your "[ITEM IDENTIFICATION]," Soft copies are also enclosed for your use.

The term of the patent is 17 years from the date of issue. In accordance with the Notice on the inside of the front cover, maintenance fees are due:

- 3 years and 6 months,
- 7 years and 6 months,
- 11 years and 6 months after the date of issue, or
- with payment of a surcharge, within a grace period of 6 months.

The amount of the payment is subject to change, as well as when the payment is due. We noted the dates on our calendar. We will notify you to pay the maintenance fees and the patent be kept in good order. However, we suggested you also note the dates on your calendar as a double precaution.

Please sign and return the enclosed copy of this letter to indicate receipt of this document and the soft copies. As always, if you have any questions or concerns, please don't hesitate to call.

    Sincerely,

    Mark C. Williams
    Paralegal

[AUTHOR/TYPIST]
Enclosures: [LIST]
[DOCUMENT LOCATOR CODE]

Receipt of the above-identified original Letters Patent document and soft copies thereof is hereby acknowledged.

Date: _____   By: _____

Form 18.14. Transmittal of Patent

DeLost, Ernst, Miessner, Powell & Wilcox
Attorneys at Law
1257 Main Street, Suite 900
Los Angeles, CA 90066
(310) 555-6000

[DATE]

U.S. PATENT OFFICE
[ADDRESS]

        Re: [NAME OF REGISTRANT]
            U.S. Trademark Reg. No.
            Mark:
            Registration Date:
            Our Docket No.
            Our Order Letter No.

Dear [NAME]:

Enclosed is the original Certificate of Registration for the above-identified trademark in International Class [SPECIFY] for "[NAME]." This Registration is for [NUMBER] years from the date of issuance. It may be renewed at that time if it is still in use.

Please read the notice on the inside of the front cover relating to the filing of Section 8 and 15 Affidavits between the fifth and sixth anniversaries of issuance of this Registration. Unless such affidavit is filed, the Registration will be cancelled in due course by the Patent and Trademark Office. We have entered this date on our calendar and will notify you in a timely manner. We also suggest that you make a note on your calendar as a double safeguard.

This is a valuable record and should be kept in a secure place. It will provide proof of [NAME]'s rights to the mark if it becomes necessary some time in the future.

In order to fully maintain [NAME]'s rights in this mark, it should always be identified as being registered by the use of the letter R:

• within a circle,
• ®, or
• by an asterisk.

Reference the mark in a footnote, "Registered in the U.S. Patent & Trademark Office" or "Reg. U.S. Pat. & TM Off."

I suggest you have your labels and advertising revised accordingly at the earliest convenient time.

Form 18.15. Registration Notification and Information

```
U.S. Patent Office
[DATE]
Page 2


    Please sign and return the enclosed copy of this letter to indicate
receipt of the above-identified Certificate of Registration.

                              Sincerely,



                              Robert Rogers
                              Paralegal
[AUTHOR/TYPIST]
Enclosures: [LIST]
[DOCUMENT LOCATOR CODE]

    Receipt of the above-identified Certificate of Registration is here-
by acknowledged.

Date: _____     By: _____
```

Form 18.15. Registration Notification and Information *(Continued)*

DeLost, Ernst, Miessner, Powell & Wilcox
Attorneys at Law
1257 Main Street, Suite 900
Los Angeles, CA 90066
(310) 555-6000

[DATE]

U.S. PATENT OFFICE
[ADDRESS]

      Re: [Registrant]
          California Trademark Reg.
          Mark:
          Registration Date:
          <u>Our Docket No.</u>

Dear [NAME]:

Enclosed is the original Certificate of Registration for the above-identified California trademark in Class [SPECIFY] for "[IDENTIFICATION]." The goods covered are [DESCRIBE].

The term of this Registration is for a period of [NUMBER] years from the date of issuance, [DATE]. It may be renewed for further periods of [NUMBER] years each, if it is still in use at the expiration of each [NUMBER]-year period.

We have entered this date on our calendar and will notify you in a timely manner. We suggest that you also make note of the dates on your calendar.

This is a valuable record and should be kept in a secure place. It will provide proof of [NAME]'s rights in the mark if it becomes necessary in the future.

Please sign and return the enclosed copy of this letter to indicate receipt of the above-identified Certificate of Registration.

          Sincerely,

          Angela Shapiro
          Senior Paralegal

[AUTHOR/TYPIST]
Enclosures: [LIST]
[DOCUMENT LOCATOR CODE]

Receipt of the above-identified Certificate of Registration is hereby acknowledged.

Date: _____   By: _____

Form 18.16. Registration Information

DeLost, Ernst, Miessner, Powell & Wilcox
Attorneys at Law
1257 Main Street, Suite 900
Los Angeles, CA 90066
(310) 555-6000

[DATE]

[NAME AND ADDRESS]

    Re: [APPLICANT OR ITEM]
        Trademark
        Our Docket No.

Dear [NAME]:

Thank you for the information and specimens you provided regarding the actual use of the above-identified trademark.

We prepared an Amendment to Allege Use that sets forth the dates of actual use. Please sign and date this original Amendment and return it to us for filing with the United States Patent and Trademark Office. We must file the Amendment to Allege Use before the application is accepted for publication.

In the event the status records of the United States Patent and Trademark Office are not up to date and, unbeknownst to us, the application has been accepted for publication, we will have to wait until a Notice of Allowance issues before we can file evidence of use.

If you have any questions or comments, please do not hesitate to contact us.

                          Sincerely,

                          Alex Kelly
                          Legal Assistant

[AUTHOR/TYPIST]
Enclosures: [LIST]
[DOCUMENT LOCATOR CODE]

Form 18.17. Amendment for Alleged Use

DeLost, Ernst, Miessner, Powell & Wilcox
Attorneys at Law
1257 Main Street, Suite 900
Los Angeles, CA 90066
(310) 555-6000

[DATE]

[NAME]
[ADDRESS]

        Re: [IDENTIFY]
            Trademark
            Our Docket No.

Dear [NAME]:

We are pleased to let you know we received the Notice of Allowance in
the subject trademark application. A copy is enclosed for your records.

You have six months from the mailing date of [DATE], shown on the enclosed Notice of Allowance or until [DATE] to commence utilization of
the mark as a trademark in a true commercial manner and to file a Statement of Use.

If you do not utilize the mark you may apply for a first six-month extension of time. This first six-month extension is granted on request. A
total of four additional extensions of time for six months each may be
granted if you explain why you have not yet commercialized the use of the
mark as a trademark. You also need to explain the steps you have taken
to try to use the mark. When you finally use the mark as a trademark, we
may file a Statement of Use and your trademark registration will issue.

You must use the mark as a trademark in interstate commerce before
the end of the last extension of time granted by the United States Patent
and Trademark Office <u>and</u> file the Statement of Use within this time period or your application will become abandoned.

No trademark registration will issue without actual trademark use of
the mark.

There are additional costs and fees associated with preparing and filing the Statement of Use.

If you have any questions concerning the above, please do not hesitate to contact me.

                    Sincerely,

                    Angela Shapiro
                    Senior Paralegal

[AUTHOR/TYPIST]
Enclosures: [LIST]
[DOCUMENT LOCATOR CODE]

Form 18.18. Information Re: Notice of Allowance

DeLost, Ernst, Miessner, Powell & Wilcox
Attorneys at Law
1257 Main Street, Suite 900
Los Angeles, CA 90066
(310) 555-6000

[DATE]

[NAME]
[ADDRESS]

        Re: [NAME]
            Trademark
            Application No.
            In the United States/Class
            <u>Our Docket No.</u>

Dear [NAME]:

   We are pleased to report the above-identified "intent to use" trademark application was accepted and will be published for Opposition purposes by the United States Patent and Trademark Office on [DATE].

   If no Opposition or Extension of Time to File a Notice of Opposition
is filed within the statutory period allowed by law, we will receive a
Notice of Allowance. We then have a 6-month period to effect true commercial use of the mark (not "token" use) or file for a 6-month extension of time to file the declaration.

   Please let us know as soon as you commence use.

                            Sincerely,

                            Pat Sherwood
                            Paralegal

[AUTHOR/TYPIST]
Enclosures: [LIST]
[DOCUMENT LOCATOR CODE]

Form 18.19. "Intent to Use" Status to Client

DeLost, Ernst, Miessner, Powell & Wilcox
Attorneys at Law
1257 Main Street, Suite 900
Los Angeles, CA 90066
(310) 555-6000

[DATE]

[NAME]
[ADDRESS]

  Re: U.S. Trademark Application for
   Trademark "[I.D.]"
   Serial No.
   Filed:
   <u>Our Docket No.</u>

Dear [NAME]:

  Enclosed is a copy of the official filing receipt showing that the subject trademark application was filed in the United States Patent and Trademark Office. It was filed on [DATE] and received the serial number [SPECIFY].

  Applications are taken for examination in the order they are filed with the United States Patent and Trademark Office. Your application must await its turn for action. The filing receipt indicates that it will be approximately five months before we receive any correspondence regarding this mark.

  We will keep you informed of any action with regard to this application.

    Sincerely,

    Alex Kelly
    Legal Assistant

[DOCUMENT LOCATOR CODE]
Enclosures: [LIST]
[DOCUMENT LOCATOR CODE]

Form 18.20. Transmittal of Filing Receipt

DeLost, Ernst, Miessner, Powell & Wilcox
Attorneys at Law
1257 Main Street, Suite 900
Los Angeles, CA 90066
(310) 555-6000

[DATE]

[NAME AND ADDRESS]

                                    ATTORNEY-CLIENT PRIVILEGE
                                    WORK PRODUCT PRIVILEGE

        Re: [NAME]
            Trademark Search for
            use on [DATE AND NAME]
            Our Docket No.

Dear [NAME]:

    As you requested, we performed a trademark search on the [SUBJECT]
mark for use on the [SUBJECT] goods. Enclosed is a copy of the search
results and our analysis follows.

    It is important to remember that no search can cover all the possi-
bilities. The United States Patent and Trademark Office files or other
files may not be complete at the time the search is made. Also, pending applications for the same or similar marks may not be available for
search. Additionally, there may be common law usages not reported in appropriate trade directories or other discoverable indices.

    Should any entity listed in the enclosures (or any other person) be-
lieve they would be damaged by your use or registration of the mark,
they could:

   •   bring suit against you in the courts for trademark infringement,
   •   file an opposition to your application, and/or
   •   file a petition for cancellation of your registration in the Unit-
        ed States Patent and Trademark Office.

Naturally, we cannot predict how a judge or board would determine the
outcome of such actions.

    As you know, trademarks are never considered alone, but always in con-
nection with the goods upon which they are utilized. Trademarks, the
mark, and the goods upon which it is used, must be considered together
in comparison with other marks and the goods upon which such other marks
are utilized. This is done to evaluate the basic concept of potential
liability—is there a likelihood of confusion? Doubts are always resolved
against the second user since trademark rights commence with first use.

    The enclosed search report is divided into four separate parts:

Form 18.21. Trademark Search Information Letter

[RECIPIENT]
[DATE]
Page 2

(1)   The listing of the materials from the United States Patent and
        Trademark Office including:

        •   issued registrations,
        •   canceled registrations,
        •   expired registrations,
        •   pending applications, and
        •   abandoned applications.

(2)   A listing of the issued trademark registrations in the vari-
        ous States.

(3)   A listing of the common law usages found from a search of ma-
        terials such as telephone books and other directories.

(4)   A printout of the materials furnished by the Dun & Bradstreet
        trademark directories.

The records of the United States Patent and Trademark Office include:

•   the issued United States trademark registrations,
•   canceled United States trademark registrations,
•   expired United States trademark registrations,
•   pending United States trademark applications,
•   abandoned United States trademark applications, and
•   intent-to-use applications awaiting filing of a statement of use

In those records we found a registration (Reference 1) for "SNACK RITE,"
Registration No. 1,520,017, registered January 10, 1989 for goods com-
prising crackers. In our opinion, this registration would be a bar to
your obtaining registration of "RIGHT SNAX" for use on food products.
Further, if the mark is still in use by the registrant, your use of
"RIGHT SNAX" could subject you to a trademark infringement action.

There were no other common law usages that would appear to be a bar
to your proposed registration.

With respect to the trade name search, we did not discover any trade
names that would be a bar to your proposed usage.

Based on the above, it is our recommendation that you do not adopt
"[*]" as a trademark for food products.

As always, if you have any questions regarding the above, please do
not hesitate to contact us.

                            Sincerely,

                            John B. Watson
                            Paralegal
[AUTHOR/TYPIST]
Enclosures: [LIST]
[DOCUMENT LOCATOR CODE]

Form 18.21. Trademark Search Information Letter *(Continued)*

DeLost, Ernst, Miessner, Powell & Wilcox
Attorneys at Law
1257 Main Street, Suite 900
Los Angeles, CA 90066
(310) 555-6000

[DATE]

Commissioner of Patents and Trademarks
Box TRADEMARKS
Washington, DC 20231

     Re: <u>Trademark Applications for [IDENTIFY MARK]</u>

Dear Sir or Madam:

  Enclosed please find three intent-to-use trademark applications to register the marks [IDENTIFY MARKS] in Class 16 for filing on behalf of [CLIENT NAME].

  The applications are accompanied with a drawing of the mark sought to be registered. Three checks, each in the amount of $[AMOUNT], payable to the Commissioner of Patents and Trademarks, are also included.

  Please direct all correspondence concerning this application to [NAME] at the above address.

                  Sincerely,

                  Alex Kelly
                  Legal Assistant
[AUTHOR/TYPIST]
Enclosures: [LIST]
[DOCUMENT LOCATOR CODE]

              Certificate of Express Mail

  Express mail mailing label number:

  Date of Deposit:

  I hereby certify that this correspondence is being deposited with the United States Postal Service "Express Mail Post Office to Addressee" service under 37 C.F.R. §1.10 on the date indicated above in an envelope addressed to: Commissioner of Patents and Trademarks, Box TRADEMARKS, Washington, DC 20231.

Date: _____   Signed: _____

Form 18.22. Transmittal of Application for Trademark

DeLost, Ernst, Miessner, Powell & Wilcox
Attorneys at Law
1257 Main Street, Suite 900
Los Angeles, CA 90066
(310) 555-6000

[DATE]

Commissioner of Patents and Trademarks
Box TRADEMARKS
Washington, DC 20231

     Re: <u>Service Mark Application for [STATE]</u>

Dear Sir or Madam:

  Enclosed please find a service mark application to register the mark
[IDENTIFY] in Class 38 for filing on behalf of [CLIENT].

  The application is accompanied by a drawing of the mark to be registered and a check in the amount of $[AMOUNT] payable to Commissioner of
Patents and Trademarks.

  Please direct all correspondence concerning this application to [NAME]
at the above address.

          Sincerely,

          Alex Kelly
          Legal Assistant

[AUTHOR/TYPIST]
Enclosures: [LIST]
[DOCUMENT LOCATOR CODE]

Form 18.23. Service Mark Application

DeLost, Ernst, Miessner, Powell & Wilcox
Attorneys at Law
1257 Main Street, Suite 900
Los Angeles, CA 90066
(310) 555-6000

[DATE]

Commissioner of Patents and Trademarks
Box ITU
Washington, DC 20231

        Re: <u>Request for Extension of Time Under 37 C.F.R. §2.89 to File</u>
            <u>a Statement of Use</u>

            Mark: [SPECIFY]
            Serial No.: [SPECIFY]
            Filing Date: [SPECIFY]
            Applicant: [SPECIFY]

Dear Sir or Madam:

   Enclosed you will find a Request for Extension of Time to file a
Statement of Use on behalf of [CLIENT NAME], pursuant to 37 C.F.R.
§2.89. This relates to the [IDENTIFY] service mark, Serial No. [NUMBER].

   Also enclosed is a check for $[AMOUNT] made payable to the Commis-
sioner of Patents and Trademarks.

   Please don't hesitate to call if you have any questions.

                        Sincerely,

                        Alex Kelly
                        Legal Assistant

[AUTHOR/TYPIST]
Enclosures: [LIST]
[DOCUMENT LOCATOR CODE]

Form 18.24. Request for Extension of Time to File Statement of Use

DeLost, Ernst, Miessner, Powell & Wilcox
Attorneys at Law
1257 Main Street, Suite 900
Los Angeles, CA 90066
(310) 555-6000

[DATE]

Commissioner of Patents and Trademarks
Attn: OATPA Data Base Maintenance Staff
Washington, DC 20231

        Re: Request for Correction to Filing Receipt
            Serial No.:
            Date of Filing:
            Owner Name:
            Mark:

Dear Sir or Madam:

  A copy of the Filing Receipt for the above-referenced trademark is
enclosed. The mark should be [IDENTIFY], not [IDENTIFY] as stated in the
Filing Receipt. Please make the correction and confirm in writing that
the mark has been corrected.

  Thank you for your assistance.

                        Sincerely,

                        Alex Kelly
                        Legal Assistant

[AUTHOR/TYPIST]
Enclosures: [LIST]
[DOCUMENT LOCATOR CODE]

Form 18.25. Request for Correction to Filing Receipt

End Notes

[1]This listing of Intellectual Property paralegal responsibilities is used by the kind permission of the National Federation of Paralegal Associations.

[2]Angela Schneeman, *Paralegals in American Law: Introduction to Paralegalism*, p. 19 (1995).

[3]Id.

[4]Id.

REFERENCE BOOKS

Good Writing Guides

Richard C. Wydick, *Plain English for Lawyers* (66 Cal L. Rev. 727, 1978).

Highly recommended! Reprints are available for $3 from: University of California Press, Journals Division, 2120 Berkeley Way, Berkeley, CA 94720. For more information, call (510) 642-4191. Orders can also be FAXed to: UC Press Journals Division (510) 642-9917.

Edit Yourself: A Manual for Everyone Who Works with Words, by Bruce Ross–Larson (1982); W. W. Norton & Co.
"In the first part of this book the author shows how to solve common problems of writing. The reader will learn how to recognize words and phrases that should be cut; how to shorten cumbersome sentences; [and] how to be consistent in spelling and punctuation .... The second part consists of more than 1,500 alphabetized recommendations for common cuts, changes, and comparisons...."

Word Perfect: A Dictionary of Current English Usage, by John O. E. Clark (1987); Henry Holt & Co.
"*Word Perfect* is one of the most basic and useful texts for the student. It is both a handy reference and an interesting and informative resource for anyone concerned with the practical uses of language. Day-to-day questions of style and grammar, problem meanings, general and technical uses, and background information about the continuing evolution of the language are presented in a clear and accessible way."

The 29 Most Common Writing Mistakes (And How to Avoid Them), by Judy Delton (1985); Writer's Digest Books.
Written primarily for professional writers, this book still contains some of the most clear-cut advice on avoiding writing problems. From Problem #9, "Don't Depend on Adjectives, Use Strong Verbs," to Problem #11 "Don't Overdo Punctuation," the author's advice is clear, well-illustrated and quite useful.

Writing with Precision: How to Write So That You Cannot Possibly Be Misunderstood, by Jefferson D. Bates (5th ed. 1990); Acropolis Books, Ltd.

Sets forth—in ten principles and seven axioms—concise, logical guidance on how to produce lean, unambiguous letters, memos, and reports. "The new edition of this book addresses communication problems of the '90s with new sections on organizing, file management, word processing and computerized writing aids."

On Writing Well: An Informal Guide to Writing Nonfiction, by William Zinsser (4th ed. 1990); Harper Perennial (div. of HarperCollins Publishers, Inc.).
Starting with a statement of Principles ("Clutter is the disease of American writing"), this book presents a series of essays on good writing. Not a "rules" book in the strictest sense, it nonetheless teaches (with an obvious love of language) the principles of "writing well."

Starting From Scratch: A Different Kind of Writers' Manual, by Rita Mae Brown (1989); Bantam Books.
Although written primarily for creative writers, this book also contains very effective advice for business writers. Particularly helpful are the chapters discussing passive voice ("dump it"), and the use of verbs ("strong verbs are hot").

Grammar and Punctuation Reference Books

The Elements of Grammar, by Margaret Shertzer (1986); MacMillan Publishing Co.
"In one easy-to-use, compact volume, *The Elements of Grammar* presents a concise, comprehensive course in the basic rules of grammar and usage, along with tips on how to implement these rules in everyday writing." Contains hundreds of examples of correct grammar, and addresses punctuation, capitalization, parts of the sentence, subject–verb agreement, and often-confused words.

The World Almanac Guide to Good Word Usage, Martin Manser & Jeffrey McQuain, eds. (1989); Avon Books.
Over 1,500 entries presented in dictionary format, the *Guide to Good Word Usage* will help you "spot the buzzwords ... and jargon that make so much of American speech and writing turgid and overblown." Covers five main areas of language: spelling, pronunciation, grammar, punctuation, and usage.

Provides clear examples of proper usage.

Dr. Grammar's Writes From Wrongs: A Supremely Authoritative Guide to the Common and Not-So-Common Rules of the English Language, by Richard Francis Trancz (1991); Vintage Books (div. of Random House).
"The answers to countless questions about English grammar, usage, mechanics, and punctuation are in this invaluable book by a prominent authority in an often thorny field. Arranged in a simple question-and-answer format."

Commas Are Our Friends, by Joe Devine (1989); Ivy Books.
Reviewers write: "This book is for those who are intimidated or perhaps bored by standard grammar manuals," and "[Those] who want a painless refresher course in grammar basics will find this [book] unique, creative and educational."

Pinckert's Practical Grammar: A Lively, Unintimidating Guide to Usage, Punctuation, and Style, by Robert C. Pinckert (1986); Writer's Digest Books.
This book "transforms the sometimes stiff, rule-ridden study of grammar, usage, punctuation, and style into a 'game' that's fun to play. . . . You'll learn . . . where to place punctuation both according to the rule books and to the melody of speech, for effective emphasis."

Grammar for Smart People, by Barry Tarshis (1992); Pocket Books (div. of Simon & Schuster).
"English is a tricky language. And, no matter how many years you've gone to school, you are probably confronted almost daily with a grammar or usage question that makes you stop and think—and maybe just sweat a bit. Here, at last, is a user-friendly guide that zeroes in on the areas that give everyone the most trouble, and does it with an advantage most grammar books lack—a light touch."

Letter and Report Writing Guidebooks

The Business Writer's Handbook, by Charles T. Brusaw, Gerald J. Alred, and Walter E. Oliu (3d ed. 1987); St Martin's Press.
"A standard guide in schools and businesses throughout the nation, the *Handbook* offers not

only comprehsnsive coverage of grammar, usage, style, and writing procedure (planning, research, outlining, idea development, etc.), but includes information on different types of letters, memoranda, proposals, reports of various kinds, minutes of meetings, job descriptions...."

Handbook of Business Letters, by L.E. Frailey (3d ed. 1989); Prentice Hall (div. of Simon & Schuster).
"This is the *original* model letter book, by one of the most highly regarded business communications experts .... Fist published over 40 years ago and now fully revised, it contains over 700 ready-to-use model letters for every business occasion."

Lifetime Encyclopedia of Letters, by Harold E. Meyer (rev. ed. 1991); Prentice Hall.
"Whether it's answering a customer's complaint, welcoming a new employee, requesting a favor, collecting past due accounts, accepting a speaking invitation (or declining one), . . . or any other situation that calls for written communication, this complete one-volume resource provides you with the precise letter that clearly expresses the proper tone and exact message you want to convey. Simply scan the index and flip to the letter that matches your needs." Contains 853 sample business and personal letters.

The McGraw-Hill Handbook of Business Letters, by Roy W. Poe (3d ed. 1994); McGraw-Hill.
"Each full-length letter comes with a brief analysis of its style, tone, and psychology. Use the letter as is, or follow the guidelines and adapt it to your specific situations. You'll even find simple ways to improve your grammar, write clearly and directly, and use action words that make your ideas come alive." Contains 199 model business letters.

Business Writing Quick & Easy, by Laura Brill (1981); AMACOM (div. of American Management Ass'n.).
"Nothing goes on record like the written word. This book shows you what makes business communication weak or strong, what your weaknesses are (and how to correct them), and what people want and don't want to see when they receive a written

communication." Illustrated with sample letters, reports, memos, and meeting summaries.

Write to the Point! Letters, Memos, and Reports That Get Results, by Rosemary T. Fruehling and N.B. Oldham (1988); McGraw-Hill.
"Offering a wealth of carefully selected and skillfully presented guidelines, *Write to the Point!* can serve either as a crash course in the essentials of good letter writing, or as a handy reference." Presents a thorough discussion of effective writing skills and several sample documents.

Letters for All Occasions, by Alfred Stuart Myers (rev. ed. 1993); HarperCollins Publishers, Inc.
"[A] comprehensive guide to social and business correspondence is completely up-to-date, with advice on faxes, electronic mail and current forms of address.... Hundreds of model letters stand as striking illustrations of the practical advice that is the mainstay of the book."

Dictionaries and Thesauruses

The American Heritage College Dictionary (3d ed. 1993); Houghton Mifflin.
"Definitions are written in straightforward, jargon-free language that conveys meaning quickly and clearly. To make looking things up even more convenient, the most common meanings of a word are listed first, where they can be found most easily.... How is *harass* pronounced? Is it acceptable to use *hopefully*? No other comparable dictionary gives you the answers so definitively and offers the depth of usage guidance. ..."

The Doubleday Roget's Thesaurus in Dictionary Form (rev. ed. 1987); Doubleday & Company.
"Not based on any other thesaurus, and omitting archaic, outdated, and trite words and phrases, the entries, selected from the Doubleday Dictionary, include slang terms, new words, and words with newly developed meanings in sync with today's word usage."

The New Roget's Thesaurus in

Dictionary Form, Norman Lewis, ed. (rev. ed. 1978); G. P. Putnam's Sons.
"Each entry contains synonyms that define the word plus a cross-reference to at least one other word. Important words are listed in noun form and include synonyms in the forms of nouns, verbs, adjectives, and prepositions. These major entries also give antonyms and cross-references."

The Oxford Dictionary of New Words, Sara Tulloch, comp. (1991); Oxford University Press.
Subtitled "A popular guide to words in the news," the *Dictionary of New Words* is "[a] language lover's guide to the origin and definition of over 2,000 words and meanings that have become popular/current in the English language in the last decade." Includes such words and phrases as *laptop, spin doctor, gentrification, cursor,* and *techno-babble.* Presents graphic icons to reflect the source or subject of each word or phrase.

The Bias Free Word Finder, a Dictionary of Nondiscriminatory Language, by Rosalie Maggio (1991); Beacon Press Books.
"*The Bias Free Word Finder* is a comprehensive guide for everyone interested in using language accurately, gracefully *and* respectfully. The book suggests thousands of specific and varied alternatives for terms that are biased against people on the basis of sex, race, age, sexual orientation, disability, ethnicity, class or religion."

The Penguin Dictionary of English Idioms, by Daphne M. Gulland and David G. Hinds–Howell (1986); Penguin Books.
"'Putting the cart before the horse,' 'letting the cat out of the bag,' and 'queering the pitch' are among the many thousands of phrases in daily use which are likely to cause confusion. *The Penguin Dictionary of English Idioms* is uniquely designed to stimulate understanding and familiarity with these idioms by explaining their meanings and origins and giving examples of typical usage."

The Dictionary of Clichés, by James Rogers (1985); Ballantine Books.
"The cliché has a bad name as an overworked and therefore

banal expression. Spoken or written by someone who is not thinking much about what he [or she] is saying or writing, it usually upholds that reputation. Among people who *do* pay attention to their phrasing, however, clichés can serve as the lubricant of language: summing up a point or a situation, easing a transition in thought, adding a seasoning of humor to a discourse."

Quotation Books

The Quotable Lawyer, David Shrager and Elizabeth Front, eds. (1986); Facts on File Publications.
"Drawing together the best and brightest commentary on all aspects of the law, *The Quotable Lawyer* presents nearly 2,600 observations from every sector of society. The quotes cover 140 topics related to the law." Includes both Subject and Author Indexes.

Words of Wisdom: More Good Advice, William Safire & Leonard Safir, eds. (1990); A Fireside Book (published by Simon & Schuster Inc.).
"The brothers Safir(e), noted for their erudition and uncommon good sense, have compiled the best aphorisms, caveats, and advice from such quotable figures as Charlie Parker to Ronald Reagan." Arranged by subject.

Style Manuals

The Elements of Style, by William Strunk, Jr. and E.B. White (3d ed. 1979); MacMillan Publishing Co.
First published in 1935, *The Elements of Style* is known for its concise presentation of writing guidelines. "Omit needless words!" is one of its most famous strictures. "This style book gives, in a brief space, the principal requirements of plain English style." It concentrates on fundamentals: the rules of usage and principles of composition most commonly violated.

Write Right!, by Janet G. Venolia (rev. cd. 1988); Ten Speed Press.
"This popular desktop guide to punctuation, grammar, and style was first published a decade ago. Now in its first major revision, *Write Right!* reflects how the language has changed since the book first appeared. It simplifies the most

important points of written English." Lists frequently misspelled and misused words.

Webster's Standard American Style Manual (1985); Merriam Webster, Inc.
Billed as "not a grammarian's academic treatise," the *American Style Manual* presents, in readily understandable fashion, the most common and acceptable ways of handling questions of writing style. Focuses on the basic elements of style: punctuation, capitalization, italicization, hyphenation, plurals, possessives, and compound words. The basic conventions, variations, and exceptions to the "rules" are clearly explained.

The Chicago Manual of Style (14th ed. 1992); The University of Chicago Press.
For over 75 years, the University of Chicago Press *Manual of Style* has been the standard reference tool for authors, editors, copywriters, and proofreaders.

The Associated Press Stylebook and Libel Manual, Norm Goldstein, ed. (rev. ed. 1992); Addison-Wesley.
"More people write for The Associated Press than for any single newspaper in the world, and the AP's style defines clear newspaper writing. The AP Stylebook is ... an essential handbook for all writers, editors and students. More than 150,000 entries clearly present the AP's rules on grammar, spelling, punctuation, and usage."

UPI Stylebook: The Authoritative Handbook for Writers, Editors & News Directors (3d ed. 1992); National Textbook Co. (div. of NTC Publishing Group).
Compiled by the writers and editors of United Press International, this handbook addresses topics such as how to avoid sexist references, how to correctly refer to the titles of diplomatic and military personnel, when to capitalize trademarks, and the proper usage of words like "jail" and "prison."

The Washington Post Deskbook on Style, Thomas W. Lippman, ed. (2d ed. 1989); McGraw-Hill.
"The *Deskbook* provides essential rules for good writing and correct usage, for abbreviations and capitalization, [and] for punctuation and spelling...."

INDEX

Accepting candidate for employment, 7.3
Accepting new client, 8.2
Acknowledgement with Outline of Fee Structure, Form 8-4
Acknowledging Documents from Another Law Firm, Form 8-2
Acknowledging Documents Received for Review, Form 8-3
Acknowledging File and Documents to the Client, Form 8-1
Additional Copyright Certificate, Form 18-5
Additional Medical Records, Request for, Form 16-10
Additional page identification, 4.17
Address, recipient's, 4.5
Address, sender's, 4.3
Administrative Duties, Importance of, 6.1
Administrative letters
  See generally Ch.6
  administrative duties, importance of, 6.1
  Appreciation, Letters of, 6.7, Form 6-5, Form 6-6
  Complaint Letters, 6.4, Form 6-2
  denying payment, 6.5
  Invitation to Meeting, Form 6-8
  Letters of
    Appreciation, 6.7, Form 6-5, Form 6-6
    Complaint Letters, 6.4, Form 6-2
    Denying Payment, 6.5, Form 6-3
    to Professional Colleagues, 6.8, Form 6-8, Form 6-7
    Requesting Payment, 6.6, Form 6-4
  locating vendors, 6.2
  Notice and Invitation to Meeting, Form 6-8
  professional colleagues, letters to, 6.8
  Requesting Payment, 6.6, Form 6-4
  Requests for Proposal (RFP), 6.3, Form 6-1
  Response to Survey Request, Form 6-7
  vendor requests for proposal (RFP), 6.3
  vendors, locating, 6.2
Advising Equipment Availability and Sale, Form 17-8
After Sale of Equipment, Form 17-9
Amendment for Alleged Use of Patent, Form 18-17
Announcement of New Employee Arrival, Form 7-9
  to All Staff, Form 7-10
Answers to Interrogatories, Obtaining, Form 8-13
Application to Record Copyright Registration, Form 18-4
Application for Trademark, Form 18-22
Appreciation, letters of, 6.7
Appreciation, notes of, 7.5
Appropriate tone, choosing, 1.6
Assignment Report, Form 5-6
Attachments or enclosures, 4.14
Attorney-Client Agreement, Letter Transmitting, Form 13-3

Attorneys, reports to, 5.4
Authorization for Release of Medical Information, Form 16-2

Basic Parts of a Letter, Form 4-1
Before writing, 1.3
Benefit Plan, Application for, Form 10-3
Billing Records, Request for, Form 16-12
Body of the letter, 4.8
Business language vs. legal language, 2.1

Candidate for employment, accepting, 7.3
Carbon copies, 4.15
Case, rejecting, 8.3
Case Status Reports, Reminder Memo, Form 5-2
Certification and Demonstrations, Form 10-9
Change of Position/Address Notification, Form 7-13
Claim of Community Property Interest, Form 13-5
Claim of Interest to Employee Benefits, Form 13-6
Clerk of the Court, Letter to, Form 8-38
Client, accepting new, 8.2
Client, Assisting with Discovery, 8.7
Client Contact Information, Obtaining, Form 8-30
Client, Letter about Scheduled Mediation, Form 8-31
Client, Letter Describing Demurrer, Form 8-5
Client Letter Re: Delinquent Account, Form 17-1
Closing Documents, Instructions to Escrow, Form 15-5
Closing phrase, 4.9
Collections and Creditors' Rights
  See generally Ch.17
  Advising Equipment Availability and Sale, Form 17-8
  After Sale of Equipment, Form 17-9
  Client Letter Re: Delinquent Account, Form 17-1
  Demand Letter, Form 17-3
  Instructions for Levy of Personal Property, Form 17-7
  Notice of Intent to Sell Repossessed Equipment, Form 17-11
  Second Client Letter Re: Delinquent Account, Form 17-2
  Setting Forth Earnings Withholding Procedures, Form 17-6
  Settlement Letter, Formal, Form 17-5
  Settlement Letter, Informal, Form 17-4
  Transmittal of Sister State Judgment, Form 17-10
Collections, Paralegal Role in, 17.1
Complaint Letters, 6.4, Form 6-2
Computer File Locator Information, 4.16
Confidentiality Agreement, Form 11-1

Confidentiality, importance of maintaining, 3.1
Confidentiality when sending facsimiles, 3.6
Confirmation Granting Extension to Respond, Form 8-11
Confirmation of Receipt of Extension to Respond, Form 8-12
Confirming Extensions of Time to Respond, 8.8
Conflict of interest and ethical walls, 3.2
Conveying complex information, using memos, 5.6
Copyright Certificate and Registration, Form 18-6
Copyright responsibilities, 18.4
Corporate Dissolution Information to Client, Form 9-9
Corporate law
  See generally Ch.9
  Dissolution Acknowledgement and Information, Form 9-9
  Filing UCC-1, Form 9-4
  Information Letter after Formation of Corporation, Form 9-6
  Information to and Request from Client, Form 9-3
  Memo Re Corporate Document Findings, Form 9-10
  Paralegal role in, 9.1
  Preincorporation Information Request to Client, Form 9-5
  Reservation of Corporate Name, Form 9-1
  Restricted Stock Letter, Form 9-8
  Setting up the Corporation, Form 9-2
  Stock Transaction Information Letter, Form 9-7
Corporation, Setting up, Form 9-2
Correspondence
  See Effective correspondence,
  with the Client re Subrogation, Form 14-2
  with Opposing Party, Form 14-3
  purposes of, 4.1
  replying to, 1.7
  See also Ch.1
Court Documents, Request for Copies, Form 13-1
Cover memo, 5.5
Cover Memo Accompanying Reports, Form 5-7
Creditors' rights and collections
  See Collections and creditors' rights
  paralegal role in, 17.1

Damage Claim Letter to Opposing Counsel, Form 16-5
Date of the letter, 4.4
Dealing with Witnesses, 8.10
Declining Representation, Letter to Potential Client, Form 16-3
Demand for Beneficiary Statements, Form 15-2
Demand Letter, Form 17-3
Demand Letter to Opposing Counsel, Form 16-4
Demand/Notification of Lawsuit, Form 14-1
Demand for Payoff of Subordinate Liens, Form 15-3

Denial of Payment Letter Form 6-3
Denying payment, letters, 6.5
Depositions, 8.9
Deposition as Exhibit, Providing to Court, Form 8-21
Deposition of Opposing Party's Expert Witness, Form 8-25
Deposition Transcript Review, Form 8-19, Form 8-20
Discovery
  assisting client to respond, 8.7
  confirming extensions of time, 8.8
  depositions, 8.9
  lack of response to, 8.6
  preparing for, 8.4
Document locator information, 4.16
Documents, searching for, 8.5, Form 8-9
During the trial, 8.12

EEOC Acknowledgment Letter, Form 10-2
EEOC Information Letter, Form 10-1
Effective correspondence
  See generally Ch.1
  appropriate tone, choosing, 1.6
  before writing, 1.3
  correspondence, replying to, 1.7
  facts, stating the, 1.5
  goals in writing, 1.2
  good communication, importance of, 1.1
  organizing your writing, 1.4
  replying to correspondence, 1.7
Employee Access to Medical Records, Form 10-8
Employee benefits and labor law
  See Labor law and employee benefits
  paralegal role in, 10.1
Employment and recruiting
  See Recruiting and employment
Employment Solicitation, Form 7-11
Employment-related correspondence, overview of, 7.1
Enclosures or attachments, 4.14
Environmental law
  See generally Ch.11
  Assignment of FOIA Request for Identification, Form 11-4
  Confidentiality Agreement, Form 11-1
  FOIA Request
    for Documents, Form 11-5
    to Federal Agency, Form 11-6
    for Specific Item, Form 11-3
    to State Agency, Form 11-7
  Public Records Act Request
    for Documents and Records, Form 11-9
    for Specific Information, Form 11-8
  Transmittal of Assessment Statements, Form 11-2
Estate planning and probate
  See generally Ch.12
  Hearing Advisement Letter, Form 12-1
  Information Letter to Client/Attorney, Form 12-3

Outline of Information, Duties and Responsibilities, Form 12-4
Signature Documents Transmittal, Form 12-2
Ethical Walls
  curing conflicts, 3.2
  Memorandum, Form 3-1
  Notice of, Form 3-2
Ethics and paralegals
  See generally Ch.3
  confidentiality
    importance of maintaining, 3.1
    when sending facsimiles, 3.6
  conflict of interest and ethical walls, 3.2
  ethical walls
    curing conflicts, 3.2
    Memorandum, Form 3-1
    Notice of, Form 3-2
  facsimiles
    confidentiality when sending, 3.6
    Transmittal Cover Sheet, Form 3-3
  paralegal, identifying as, 3.3
  signatures
    firm policies about, 3.4
    legal secretaries and, 3.5
Expert Deposition, Letter to Opposing Counsel, Form 16-7
Expert Deposition, Scheduling, Form 8-24
Execution of Patent Assignment, Form 18-11
Extension of tme, confirming, 8.8
Extension to File Statement of Use, Form 18-25

Facsimiles, confidentiality, 3.6
Facts, stating the, 1.5
Failure to Respond to Discovery, Form 8-10
Family law
  See generally Ch.13
  Attorney-Client Agreement, Letter Transmitting, Form 13-3
  Claim of Community Property Interest, Form 13-5
  Claim of Interest to Employee Benefits, Form 13-6
  Information Request Letter, Form 13-2
  Notice of Continued Health Coverage Entitlements, Form 13-9
  Notification of Attorney Unavailability, Form 13-8
  Outline of Dissolution Agreement, Form 13-7
  paralegal role in, 13.1
  Preliminary Disclosure and Asset/Debt Checklist, Form 13-4
  Request for Copies of Court Documents, Form 13-1
  Transmittal of Final Dissolution, Form 13-10
Fax Transmittal Cover Sheet, Form 3-3
Filing UCC-1, Form 9-4
Final Dissolution, Transmittal of, Form 13-10
Firm name in the signature block, 4.10

FOIA Request, Assignment of Identification Number, Form 11-4
FOIA Request for Documents, Form 11-5
FOIA Request for Specific Item, Form 11-3
FOIA Request to Federal Agency, Form 11-6
FOIA Request to State Agency, Form 11-7
Foreign Filing Patent Listing, Form 18-12
Formal and informal memos, 5.2
Formats, letters
  See Letters,structure and formats
Formation of Corporation, Information Letter, Form 9-6
  See Letter format
Forwarding Address, Request to Postmaster, Form 8-23
Freedom of Information Act Request, Form 10-7
Frequently used letters in litigation, 8.14
Full-block format, 4.21
Full-block letter, Form 4-4

Good communication, importance of, 1.1
Grammar, 2.3
  See also Language and grammar

Hearing Advisement Letter, Form 12-1
Humor, Use of, Form 5-3

Identifying initials, 4.13
Identity as paralegal, 3.3
Indication of Interest without Commitment, Form 7-5
Informal and formal memos, 5.2
Information Letter to Client/Attorney, Form 12-3
Information Re: Notice of Patent Allowance, Form 18-18
Information Request Letter, Form 13-2
Information, Requests for, 5.5
Information to and Request from Client, Form 9-3
Information Transmittal to Client, Form 14-4
Informing Client of Settlement Conference, Form 8-28
Informing Client of Trial Date, Form 8-29
Initials, Identifying, 4.13
Instructions for Levy of Personal Property, Form 17-7
Instructions for Service of Subpoena, Form 8-42
Instructions for Service of Summons and Complaint, Form 8-41
Insurance defense
  See generally Ch.14
  Corresponding with Opposing Party, Form 14-3
  Corresponding with the Client re Subrogation, Form 14-2
  Demand/Notification of Lawsuit, Form 14-1
  Information Transmittal to Client, Form 14-4

Notification of Lawsuit, Form 14-1
paralegal role in, 14.1
Request for Corporate Information, Form 14-6
Request for Execution of Verification, Form 14-5
Intellectual property
  See generally Ch.18
  Additional Copyright Certificate, Request for, Form 18-5
  Amendment for Alleged Use of Patent, Form 18-17
  Application to Record Copyright Registration, Form 18-4
  Application for Trademark Transmittal, Form 18-22
  Copyright Certificate and Registration Transmittal, Form 18-6
  copyright responsibilities, 18.4
  Execution of Patent Assignment, Form 18-11
  Extension to File Statement of Use, Form 18-25
  Foreign Filing Patent Listing, Form 18-12
  Information Re: Notice of Patent Allowance, Form 18-18
  Intent to Use Status to Client, Form 18-19
  Notice of Copyright Registration Renewal, Form 18-7
  Notice of Patent, Form 18-13
  paralegal role in, 18.1
  Patent Application Transmittal, Form 18-10
  Patent Information to Client, Transmittal, Form 18-9
  Patent Responsibilities, 18.3
  Patent, Transmittal of, Form 18-14
  Permission Granted to Reprint, Form 18-2
  Permission to Reprint, Request for, Form 18-1
  Registration Information, Form 18-16
  Registration Notification and Information, Form 18-15
  Request Extension to File Statement of Use, Form 18-24
  Service Mark Application, Form 18-23
  Special Handling of Copyright Application, Form 18-8
  Trademark Filing Receipt, Transmittal, Form 18-20
  trademark responsibilities, 18.2
  Trademark Search Information Letter, Form 18-21
  Unauthorized Use of Copyrighted Material, Form 18-3
Intent to Use Status to Client, Form 18-19
Invitation to Meeting, Form 6-8

Job market, 7.4

Labor law and employee benefits
  See generally Ch.10

Answer to Request for Information from Union, Form 10-6
Benefit Plan, Application for, Form 10-3
Certification and Demonstrations, Form 10-9
EEOC Acknowledgment Letter, Form 10-2
EEOC Information Letter, Form 10-1
Employee Access to Medical Records, Form 10-8
Freedom of Information Act Request, Form 10-7
Letter Agreement Re Binding Arbitration, Form 10-5
paralegal role in, 10.1
Termination Letter, Form 10-4
Lack of response to discovery, 8.6
Language and grammar
  See generally Ch.2
  business language vs. legal language, 2.1
  grammar, 2.3
  legal citations, 2.2
  proofreading for mistakes, 2.5
  punctuation, 2.4
Legal citations, 2.2
Legal Language, Business Language vs., 2.1
Legal secretaries, signatures by, 3.5
Letter Advising Equipment Availability and Sale, Form 17-8
Letter After Sale of Equipment, Form 17-9
Letter Agreement Re: Binding Arbitration, Form 10-5
Letter, basic parts of, 4.2
Letter, body of, 4.8
Letter, date of, 4.4
Letter format, full-block, 4.21
Letter format, modified block, 4.20
Letter format, popular block, 4.19
Letter formats, types of, 4.18
Letter Helping the Client Organize Documents, Form 8-8
Letter Inviting Future Discussion Re: Employment, Form 7-6
Letter of Advice Re: Eviction, Form 15-6, Form 15-7
Letters of appreciation, 6.7
Letter of Appreciation to Vendor, Form 6-5, Form 6-6
Letters denying payment, 6.5
Letter of Recommendation, Form 7-16
Letter Setting Forth Earnings Withholding Procedures, Form 17-6
Letter to Transmit Medical Summary, Form 16-1
Letters, structures and formats
Letters, structures and formats
  See generally Ch.4
  additional page identification, 4.17
  address
    recipient's, 4.5
    sender's, 4.3
  attachments or enclosures, 4.14
  Basic Parts of a Letter, Form 4-1
  body, 4.8

carbon copies, 4.15
closing phrase, 4.9
computer file locator information, 4.16
correspondence, purposes of, 4.1
date of the letter, 4.4
document locator information, 4.16
firm name in the signature block, 4.10
format, *See* Letter format
Full-Block Format, 4.21, Form 4-4
identifying initials, 4.13
initials, identifying, 4.13
Modified Block Format, 4.20, Form 4-3
Popular Block Format, 4.19, Form 4-2
Re: line, use of, 4.6
salutation, 4.7
signer's
    name, 4.11
    title, 4.12
    subsequent page identification, 4.17
Letters to professional colleagues, 6.8
Letters Requesting Payment, 6.6
Litigation
    See generally Ch. 8
    accepting new client, 8.2
    Acknowledgement with Outline of Fee Structure, Form 8-4
    Acknowledging Documents from Another Law Firm, Form 8-2
    Acknowledging Documents Received for Review, Form 8-3
    Acknowledging File and Documents to the Client, Form 8-1
    case, rejecting, 8.3
    Clerk of the Court, Letter to, Form 8-38
    client
        accepting new, 8.2
        assisting with discovery, 8.7
        Informing of Settlement Conference, Form 8-28
        Informing of Trial Date, Form 8-29
        Instructing Client about Discovery, Form 8-15
        Letter about Scheduled Mediation, Form 8-31
        Letter Describing Demurrer, Form 8-5
        Obtaining Answers to Interrogatories, Form 8-13
        Obtaining Contact Information Before Trial, Form 8-30
        Predeposition Meeting, Scheduling, Form 8-17
        Release Letter for Signature, Form 8-35
        Settlement Letter with Release for Signature, Form 8-34
        Transmittal Letter of Discovery, Form 8-14
    Confirmation Granting Extension to Respond, Form 8-11
    Confirmation of Receipt of Extension to Respond, Form 8-12

confirming extensions of time to respond, 8.8
Daily Trial Transcripts, Arranging for, Form 8-32
dealing with witnesses, 8.10
depositions
    Expert Deposition, Scheduling, Form 8-24
    Notice to Client, Form 8-16
    Opposing Party's Expert Witness, Form 8-25
    Predeposition Meeting, Scheduling, Form 8-17
    Providing as Exhibit, Form 8-21
    Scheduling, Form 8-18, Form 8-24
    Transcript Review, Form 8-19, Form 8-20
    use of, 8.9
discovery
    assisting client to respond, 8.7
    confirming extensions of time, 8.8
    depositions, 8.9
    Failure to Respond to Discovery, Form 8-10
    lack of response to, 8.6
    Obtaining Answers to Interrogatories, Form 8-13
    preparing for, 8.4
    Transmittal Letter of Discovery, Form 8-14
Documents, Letter Helping Client Organize, Form 8-8
Documents, Searching for, 8.5, Form 8-9
during the trial, 8.12
extensions of time, confirming, 8.8
Forwarding Address, Request to Postmaster for, Form 8-23
lack of response to discovery, 8.6
litigation, paralegal role in, 8.1
Magistrate, Letter to, Form 8-40
Notice of Deposition to Client, Form 8-16
Obtaining Client Answers to Interrogatories, Form 8-13
Obtaining Client Contact Information Before Trial, Form 8-30
Potential Client, Rejection of, Form 8-6
preparing for discovery, 8.4
preparing for trial, 8.11
Providing Deposition as Exhibit, Form 8-21
Receipt of Daily Trial Transcripts, Arranging for, Form 8-32
Rejecting a Case, 8.3, Form 8-6
Release Letter for Client's Signature, Form 8-35
Request to Postmaster for Forwarding Address, Form 8-23
Scheduling Depositions, Form 8-18
Scheduling Expert Deposition, Form 8-24
Scheduling Predeposition Meeting with Client, Form 8-17
searching for documents, 8.5
settlement, 8.13

Settlement Letter with Release for Signature, Form 8-34
Settlement Letter to Opposing Counsel, Form 8-33
Subpoena, Instructions for Service, Form 8-42
Summons and Complaint, Instructions for Service, Form 8-41
transmittal letters
    Documents to Clerk of the Court, Form 8-39
    Discovery to Client, Form 8-14
    Short form, Form 8-36
    Instructing Client about Discovery, Form 8-15
    Form Letter, Form 8-37
trial, letters used
    during, 8.12
    Memo to Attorney Before, Form 8-7
    Obtaining Contact Information Before, Form 8-30
    preparing for, 8.11
    Trial Transcripts, Arranging for, Form 8-32
witnesses
    dealing with, 8.10
    Letter to, Form 8-22
    Letter Re: On-Call Agreement, Form 8-26, Form 8-27
    Thank-You Letter After Trial, Form 8-43
Litigation, frequently used letters, 8.14
Litigation, paralegal role in, 8.1
Locating vendors, 6.2

Magistrate, Letter to, Form 8-40
Maintaining confidentiality, importance of, 3.1
Medical Information, Authorization for Release, Form 16-2
Medical Records, Employee Access to, Form 10-8
Memo of Appreciation to Department, Form 7-15
Memo content, effective presentation of, 5.3
Memo Outline, Form 5-1
Memo Re: Corporate Document Findings, Form 9-10
Memo, Use of Humor in, Form 5-3
Memos and reports
    See generally Ch.5
    Humor, Form 5-3
    information, requests for, 5.5
    content, effective presentation of, 5.3
memos
    conveying complex information, using memos, 5.6
    cover, 5.5
    Cover Memo Accompanying Reports, Form 5-7
    formal and informal, 5.2
    Humor in, Form 5-3
    Outline Form, Form 5-1
    policy 7.5
    use of, 5.1
    Project Assessment Memo, Form 5-9
    Reminder Memo for Case Status Reports, Form 5-2
Reports

Assignment Report, Form 5-6
to attorneys and managers, 5.4
Cover Memo Accompanying, Form 5-7
status report, 5.5
Status Report, Format of, Form 5-5
Work Status Report, Short Form, Form 5-4
Requests for Information, 5.5
Status Report, 5.5
Status Report, Format of, Form 5-5
Supply Request Memo, Form 5-8
Work Status Report, Short Form, Form 5-4
Modified block format, 4.20
Modified Block Letter, Form 4-3
Modify Terms of Loan, Letter to Title Company, Form 15-4
Notice of Continued Health Coverage Entitlements, Form 13-9
Notice of Copyright Registration Renewal, Form 18-7
Notice of Deposition to Client, Form 8-16
Notice of Intent to Sell Repossessed Equipment, form17-11
Notice and Invitation to Meeting, Form 6-8.
Notice of Patent, Form 18-13
Notification of Attorney Unavailability, Form 13-8
Notification of Lawsuit, Form 14-1

Offer of Employment, Tentative, Form 7-8
Organizing your writing, 1.4
Out-of-Office Policy Memo, Form 7-14
Outline of Dissolution Agreement, Form 13-7
Outline of Information, Duties and Responsibilities, Form 12-4
Overview of Employment-Related Correspondence, 7.1

Paralegal, identifying as, 3.3
Patent Application Transmittal, Form 18-10
Patent Information to Client, Form 18-9
Patent Responsibilities, 18.3
Patent, Transmittal of, Form 18-14
Permission Granted to Reprint, Form18-2
Permission to Reprint, Form 18-1
Personal injury
    See generally Ch.16
    Authorization for Release of Medical Information, Form 16-2
    Damage Claim Letter to Opposing Counsel, Form 16-5
    Declining Representation, Potential Client, Form 16-3
    Demand Letter to Opposing Counsel, Form 16-4
    Expert Deposition, Letter to Opposing Counsel, Form 16-7

Letter to Transmit Medical Summary, Form 16-1
Request for Additional Medical Records, Form 16-10
Request for Billing Records, Form 16-12
Request to Client for Additional Information, Form 16-6
Request for Copies of Medical Records, form16-9
Request for DMV Collision Reports, Form 16-14
Request for Medical Charges and Records, Form 16-8
Request for Records, History, and X-Rays, Form 16-11
Request for Records of Driver, Form 16-13
Personal injury, paralegal role in, 16.1
Policy memos and notes of appreciation to staff, 7.5
Popular block format, 4.19
Popular Block Letter, Form 4-2
Potential Client, Rejection of, Form 8-6
Preincorporation Information Request to Client, Form 9-5
Preliminary Disclosure and Asset/Debt Checklist, Form 13-4
Probate and estate planning
See Estate planning and probate
Probate, paralegal role in, 12.1
Professional colleagues, letters to, 6.8
Project Assessment Memo, Form 5-9
Proofreading, 2.5
Prospective Employees, Rejection Letters to, 7.2
Public Records Act Request for Documents and Records, Form 11-9
Public Records Act Request for Specific Information, Form 11-8
Punctuation, 2.4
Purposes of correspondence, 4.1

Re: line, 4.6
Real estate
See generally Ch.15
Closing Documents, Instructions to Escrow, Form 15-5
Demand for Beneficiary Statements, Form 15-2
Demand for Payoff of Subordinate Liens, Form 15-3
Letter of Advice Re: Eviction, Form 15-6, Form 15-7
Letter to Title Company to Modify Terms of Loan, Form 15-4
Transmittal to Client for Review and Execution, Form 15-1
Real estate, paralegal role in, 15.1
Recipient's Address, 4.5
Recruiting and Employment
See generally Ch.7
Advertised Position, Response to, Form 7-2
Announcement of New Employee Arrival, Form 7-9

Announcement of New Employee to All Staff, Form 7-10
appreciation
Memo to Department, Form 7-15
notes of, 7.5
candidate for employment, accepting, 7.3
Change of Position/Address Notification, Form 7-13
employment-related correspondence, overview of, 7.1
Employment Solicitation, Form 7-11
Indication of Interest Without Commitment, Form 7-5
job market, 7.4
Letter Inviting Future Discussion Re: Employment, Form 7-6
Letter of Recommendation, Form 7-16
memos, policy, 7.5
Offer of Employment, Tentative, Form 7-8
Out-of-Office Policy Memo, Form 7-14
overview of employment-related correspondence, 7.1
policy memos and notes of appreciation to Staff, 7.5
policy memos to staff, 7.5
prospective employees, rejection letters to, 7.2
Reference Check Letter, Form 7-7
Reference Letter, Form 7-17
Rejection Letter to Prospective Employees, 7.2, Form 7-1
Response, Unsolicited Inquiry, Form 7-3
Return of Information Letter, Form 7-4
Thank-You Letter After Interview, Form 7-12
Reference Check Letter, Form 7-7
Reference Letter, Form 7-17
Registration Information, Form 18-16
Registration Notification and Information, Form 18-15
Rejecting a case, 8.3
Rejection Letter, Long Form, Form 7-1
Rejection Letters to prospective employees, 7.2
Release Letter for Client's Signature, Form 8-35
Reminder Memo for Case Status Reports, Form 5-2
Replying to correspondence, 1.7
Reports and memos,
See Memos and reports
to attorneys and managers, 5.4
Cover Memo Accompanying, Form 5-7
status, 5.5
Request for Additional Copyright Certificate, Form 18-5
Request for Additional Medical Records, Form 16-10
Request for Copies of Court Documents, Form 13-1
Request for Copies of Medical Records, Form 16-9
Request for Corporate Information, Form 14-6

Request for DMV Collision Reports, Form 16-14
Request for Execution of Verification, Form 14-5
Request for Extension of Time to File Statement of Use, Form 18-24
Request for Information from Union, Answer to, Form 10-6
Request for Medical Charges and Records, Form 16-8
Request for Payment from Opposing Counsel, Form 6-4
Request for Permission to Reprint, Form 18-1
Request for Proposal, Form 6-1
Request for Records, History, and X-Rays, Form 16-11
Request for Records of Driver, Form 16-13
Request for Special Handling of Copyright Application, Form 18-8
Request to Client for Additional Information, Form 16-6
Request to PTO for Extension to File Statement of Use, Form 18-25
Requesting payment, letters, 6.6
Requests for information, 5.5
Requests for proposal (RFP), 6.3
Reservation of Corporate Name, Form 9-1
Response Regarding Advertised Position, Form 7-2
Response to a Survey Request, Form 6-7
Response to an Unsolicited Inquiry, Form 7-3
Restricted Stock Letter, Form 9-8
Return of Information Letter, Form 7-4

Salutation, 4.7
Scheduling Depositions, Form 8-18
Scheduling Expert Deposition, Form 8-24
Scheduling Predeposition Meeting with Client, Form 8-17
Searching for documents, 8.5
Second Client Letter Re: Delinquent Account, Form 17-2
Sender's address, 4.3
Service Mark Application, Form 18-23
Setting Forth Earnings Withholding Procedures, Form 17-6
Settlement, 8.13
Settlement letter
to Client with Release for Signature, Form 8-34
formal, Form 17-5
informal, Form 17-4
Opposing Counsel, Form 8-33
Signature block, firm name in, 4.10
Signature Documents, Transmittal of, Form 12-2
Signatures by legal secretaries, 3.5
Signatures, firm policies about, 3.4
Signer's name, 4.11
Signer's title, 4.12
Special Handling of Copyright Application, Form 18-8

Stating the facts, 1.5
Status Report Format, Form 5-5
Status reports, 5.5
Stock Transaction Information Letter, Form 9-7
Subsequent page identification, 4.17
Supervising attorneys, reports to, 5.4
Supply Request Memo, Form 5-8

Termination Letter, Form 10-4
Thank-You Letter After Interview, Form 7-12
Trademark Filing Receipt, Form 18-20
Trademark responsibilities, 18.2
Trademark Search Information Letter, Form 18-21
Transmittal of Application for Trademark, Form 18-22
Transmittal of Assessment Statements, Form 11-2
Transmittal of Copyright Certificate and Registration, Form 18-6
Transmittal of Discovery to Client, Form 8-14
Transmittal of Documents to Clerk of the Court, Form 8-39
Transmittal of Final Dissolution, Form 13-10
Transmittal Form Letter, Form 8-37
Transmittal Instructing Client about Discovery, Form 8-15
Transmittal Letter, Short Form, Form 8-36
Transmittal of Patent, Form 18-14
Transmittal of Patent Information to Client, Form 18-9
Transmittal of Sister State Judgment, Form 17-10
Transmittal of Trademark Filing Receipt, Form 18-20
Transmittal to Client for Review and Execution, Form 15-1
Trial
Memo to Attorney Before, Form 8-7
preparing for, 8.11
role during, 8.12
Transcripts, Arranging for, Form 8-32

Unauthorized Use of Copyrighted Material, Form 18-3

Vendor Requests for Proposal (RFP), 6.3
Vendors, locating, 6.2

Witness
Letter Re: On-Call Agreement, Form 8-26, Form 8-27
Letter to, Form 8-22
Thank-You Letter After Trial, Form 8-43
Witnesses, dealing with, 8.10
Work Status Report, Short Form, Form 5-4
before beginning, 1.3
goals in, 1.2
organizing, 1.4